FROM LOG CABIN TO
WHITE HOUSE

"He often stopped in his work to watch a vessel gliding over t

From L

FROM LOG-CABIN TO WHITE HOUSE

LIFE OF
JAMES A. GARFIELD
President of the United States.

BOYHOOD, YOUTH, MANHOOD
ASSASSINATION

BY
WILLIAM M. THAYER

WARD, LOCK & CO., LIMITED
LONDON AND MELBOURNE
1920

PREFACE

MANY years ago the author prepared a book for youth and young men upon the life of Abraham Lincoln, entitled THE PIONEER BOY, AND HOW HE BECAME PRESIDENT. The favourable reception of that volume carried it through thirty-six editions. After the nomination of General Garfield, the publisher suggested that a similar work at the present time, upon his life, would furnish one of the noblest examples of success for young men to imitate.

The materials for the work were furnished by General Garfield ; several of his early associates, two of whom were born in log-cabins near him ; several of his teachers and pupils ; the owner and captain of the canal-boat on which he served ; and intimate friends of his manhood —the most reliable sources of information possible. The materials forcibly suggest the similarity between the lives of President Lincoln and President Garfield.

Both of these statesmen were born in log-cabins, built by their fathers, in the wilderness, for family homes. Both were poor as mortals can well be. Both were born with talents of the highest order ; but neither enjoyed early advantages of schools and teachers. At eight years of age Lincoln lost his mother ; and when Garfield was eighteen months old he lost his father. Both worked on a farm, chopped wood, and did whatever else was needful for a livelihood, when eight years of age. Both improved every leisure moment in study and reading.

z

Both read all the books that could be borrowed for miles around ; and each was known, in his own township and time, as a boy of remarkable mental ability and promise. Both of them early displayed great tact and energy, turning a hand to any kind of labour—farming, chopping, teaming, carpentering. In his youth, Lincoln ran a flat-boat down the Ohio and Mississippi rivers to New Orleans, eighteen hundred miles, on a trading expedition ; Garfield, at about the same age, served on a boat on the Ohio and Pennsylvania Canal, driving mules and acting as steersman. Both were well known for their industry, tact, perseverance, integrity, courage, economy, thoroughness, punctuality, decision, and benevolence. Both taught school in the backwoods as soon as they knew enough to teach. Each of them studied law when pursuing another vocation for a livelihood—Lincoln a surveyor, and Garfield a teacher. Each became a member of the legislature in his native State before thirty years of age. Both served the country in war, when about the same age—Lincoln in the " Blackhawk War," and Garfield in the " War of the Rebellion." Each was the youngest member of the legislature, and the youngest officer in the army when he served. The talents and eloquence of both made them members of Congress—Lincoln at thirty-seven years of age, and Garfield at thirty-three ; each one of them being the youngest member of the House of Representatives of the time. Both of them took high rank at once as debaters and eloquent speakers, as well as stalwart opposers of slavery. Both, also, won a reputation for wit and humour and geniality, making them popular with both sides of the House. Neither of them was a candidate in the National Conventions that nominated them for the Presidency—both were compromise candidates when it became apparent that union could be secured upon no others. Their names were introduced amid the wildest enthusiasm ; thousands cheering, hats swinging, handkerchiefs waving, and the bands playing national airs. The nomination of each was hailed with demonstrations of joy throughout the country

And now, the most remarkable of all coincidences in their lives we record with sadness—both died in the Presidential office by the ASSASSIN'S SHOT History has no parallel for this amazing fact. We search in vain the annals of all countries for a kindred record. Beginning life in the obscurity of the wilderness, and ending it on the summit of renown! Their first home a log-cabin! their last, the White House! Beloved by a trusting nation, and shot by the assassin!

A more inspiring example to study and imitate cannot be found in the annals of our Republic. As a model of whatever belongs to noble traits of character, heroic achievements, and the highest success fairly won, we present him in this book.

CONTENTS

IV

TRIALS AND TRIUMPHS

V

BOY FARMER

VI

SUNDAY IN THE WOODS

VII

HIGHER UP

VIII

BOY CARPENTER

IX

BARN-BUILDING

X

A BLACK-SALTER

XI

A WOOD-CHOPPER

XV

GEAUGA SEMINARY

XVI

AFTER VACATION

XVII

KEEPING SCHOOL

FROM

LOG-CABIN TO WHITE HOUSE

I

FIRST DAY AT SCHOOL

A RUMOUR came to the log-cabin that a school would open soon at the village, one-and-a-half miles distant. It was only a rumour at first, but the rumour grew into fact in the course of a week.

"Jimmy must go, mother," said Thomas, who was nearly thirteen years old, a boy of heroic spirit and true filial and fraternal devotion.

"Yes, Jimmy must go," responded his mother, with such a smile as lights up the face of those mothers only who think what a treasure and joy there is in the little three-year-old; for Jimmy had not yet reached his fourth birthday. "I wish you could go, Tom, also," she added.

"I wish I could, too," the thoughtful lad replied; "but the potatoes would hardly be dug, and the corn would hardly be harvested, nor the winter rye be put in, if I should go The girls and Jimmy can go, and my work will get us food and clothes." The last sentence was spoken with so much interest, as if the son and brother found his highest pleasure in being able to run the little farm alone, while his sisters and precious little brother could attend school together, that his good mother could scarcely suppress her honest pride over the unselfish and noble boy. Her maternal pride came very near making a demonstration and applying some pet names to Thomas, but her excellent judgment, which usually ruled, guided her into a wiser course, and she let the occasion pass with only a few well-chosen words of approval.

"It is a good chance for Jimmy," added Thomas, after a moment had passed, in which remark his mother saw the " heap" of love he had for his little brother ; and every one else would see it now, too, could they understand the circumstances. More than one person had remarked that Thomas thought a " heap " of James.

It was a busy time in the cabin, preparing the children for school. The girls and Thomas went to school before the family removed to Orange, so that it was not a new thing to them Besides, their mother had taught them much She had made no special effort to teach James, except to tell him Bible stories, and answer his multitudinous questions in her instructive way. Still James knew nearly all his letters, and was better versed in Bible history than most children of his age at the present day. The stories of the Ark, Cain and Abel, Joseph, Ishmael, Isaac, Jacob, Absalom, Daniel, the Bethlehem Babe, and many others, were familiar to him at that time. The little fellow possessed a remarkable memory, and he was bright and sunny, the light and joy of the log-cabin It would not suffice to say that his mother thought that he was particularly a bright and talented boy ; for mothers are quite apt to think very well of their offspring. But when we add that Thomas and his sisters, and the neighbours also, regarded James as a very precocious and promising lad, the reader may safely conclude that the hero of this volume was none of your simple-minded " children of the wood "— neither a juvenile drone nor ignoramus. He was just the little fellow to make music at home or in the school-house.

"Jimmy can't walk half the way," said Thomas; "he will be tired to death before he hardly gets out of sight of home."

"I'll see to that," replied his sister, with an air of assurance that indicated her plans were all laid. "Jimmy won't be tired."

"What is going to prevent it?" inquired Thomas.

"You'll see," answered his sister, somewhat evasively, though Thomas knew by her appearance that there was real significance in what she said.

"Well, what's up now?" added Thomas, sure that some project was in her head.

"Nothing is up, except Jimmy; he will be *up*—on my back," answered the brave girl, who had resolved to spare her lively little brother's legs by carrying him to school.

"Carry Jimmy to school!" exclaimed Thomas; "you will be more tired than he will be to walk. It is a bigger load than our great-grandfather carried in the Revolutionary war. You'll get sick of that."

"It won't be the first thing I am sick of that I have done," was all the girl's reply.

We did not mean to tell this resolute maid's unpoetical name; but we desire to say something about her, and so we must tell her name. It was MEHETABEL. The name was load enough to carry to school without adding the burden of Jimmy. Mehetabel was fifteen years old, just such a strapping girl as would grow up in the woods among tall trees; but she did not merit such a name as that. It sat upon her better at fifteen than it could have done in babyhood, undoubtedly. Just think of a baby bearing the name of MEHETABEL! We have looked for its origin, and find that it belongs to the old Jewish dispensation, and ought to have been dumped into oblivion with its lumbering ceremonial. But, somehow, it slid over into the new dispensation, and after the lapse of eighteen hundred years and more it now confronts us in Ohio !

Well, the first day of school arrived, and MEHETABEL took her two burdens—her name and brother—and trudged off to school. Jimmy was mightily pleased with his new mode of conveyance, and so were the whole family , and they made a jolly morning of it in starting off the pioneer troupe, who were only forty-six years distant from the White House. The log-cabin smiled as it had not smiled since that terrible day of sorrow of which we shall soon speak. Thomas was the happiest boy in Ohio on that blessed morning, although he did not know it , and he went to work with fresh vigour and determination, splendid fellow that he was. While the children are in school, and Thomas is driving work on the farm, and the good mother is having a lonely day in the cabin, with her spinning-wheel, we will stop to tell how this family came to be in the woods of Ohio, and add some definite information about the father.

In the year 1799 Thomas Garfield was a farmer in Worcester, Otsego Country, N.Y. That year a son was born to him, to whom he gave the name of Abram. Thirty-two years afterwards, this son Abram became the father of James A. Garfield.

Before Abram was two years old, his father suddenly sickened and died, leaving his wife and several children penniless—a sorrow that was singularly repeated in the life of Abram, who died, as we shall see, when James was less than two years of age, leaving his wife and four children to battle with the hardships of life. It was not possible for Abram's mother to keep the family together, and provide for so many mouths ; so a neighbour, James Stone, took Abram into his family, and reared him as one of his own children.

When the lad was ten years old, Widow Ballou removed into the neighbourhood, from New Hampshire,

Mrs. Ballou had a daughter, Eliza, about a year younger than Abram, a very bright, promising girl. Abram and Eliza became playmates, and thought very much of each other.

Eliza was fourteen years old when her mother conceived the idea of emigrating to Ohio, which was then the " Far West," and great stories were told about its prolific soil and future wealth. Emigrants from New York, and also from the New England States, were removing thither in considerable numbers. James Ballou, her son, now a young man, saw emigrant wagons passing through New York, or starting from it, their destination being Ohio, and became more enthusiastic than his mother to go. At last she decided to remove thither, sold her little farm, packed her household goods into an emigrant wagon, and with her children started for the West. Abram was a lonely boy when Eliza left, and the two separated regretfully.

It was a long and tiresome journey of six weeks—a trip that could be accomplished now in twelve hours. The family were in the wagon, except when the wagon was stuck in the mud, and they were compelled to unload, and, with levers, lift it out. The roads were fearfully bad, without a bridge over a single river ; so they had streams to ford, swamps to wade, and quagmires to avoid, enough to test the courage and patience of the most experienced woman and the bravest girl. On the way James shot game, so that there was no lack of food. At length they reached Zanesville, Muskingum County, one of the oldest settlements in Ohio at that time ; and there they settled.

About five years later Abram Garfield took the " Ohio fever," as it was called, or else the memory of the fair-haired maiden inspired him to nobler deeds, and he, too, started for the West—a young man of twenty years, hopeful, fearless, ambitious, and smart. He found work in Newburg, near Cleveland. Cleveland was then only a small collection of log-cabins, containing about one hundred people. Newburg was newer and more isolated. But, for some reason, the young adventurer selected the latter place for his home.

It is quite evident that he not only worked, but cast about to learn something of the maiden he could not forget. For he learned, after a time, that the Ballou family were at Zanesville, whither he wended his way on a visit, as soon as possible. The family gave him a hearty greeting, especially Eliza, who had grown into a winsome damsel of almost nineteen. That Abram was glad to see her would be a tame way of stating the fact. If Eliza had constituted all the " Far West" there was at that time, Abram would have been fascinated by the country, making no account at all of New York in the comparison. Without stretching out the tale into a " long yarn," it will suffice to say, that Eliza just filled Abram's eye, and in less than two years from that time became his wife. They were married February 3, 1821, and repaired at once to his chosen home, Newburg, where a log-cabin, eighteen by twenty feet, containing but one room, awaited them. It was a very humble abode, but true love put as much happiness into it as could have been there if it had been a palace The cabin was destitute of sash or glass, though places for three windows, covered with greased paper, admitted light. Greased paper was a common substitute for glass, and was the " stained-glass " of that day. The furniture was manufactured by her noble husband, of whom she was as proud as he was of her ; and it was the latest style of that region, therefore fashionable. It consisted of several three-legged stools, a puncheon-table, a bed in one corner, constructed of poles and slabs, a frying-pan, one iron pot, two wooden plates, with knives and forks to match, and a " Dutch oven," which was simply a kettle with a rimmed cover, on which live coals were laid. Here James A. Garfield's father began life in

earnest, and here he lived nine years, during which time
three of his children were born. He tilled the soil and
also at two different times took contracts on the Ohio
and Pennsylvania Canal which was in process of construction.

The young adventurer was not satisfied, however.
His growing family demanded larger provision for the
future, so he purchased fifty acres of land, at two dollars
an acre, in Orange, Cuyahoga County, seventeen miles
from the first home of his wedded life. He selected this
locality because Amos Boynton, whose wife was sister to
Mrs Garfield, had purchased a tract there; and the
families could remove thither together. One log-cabin
was erected first, in which both families lived, thick as
" three in a bed," until another cabin could be built.
When these cabins were built, the nearest neighbour was
seven miles away. It was January, 1830, when Abram
Garfield removed to this new home in the wilderness.
His cabin was larger and more substantial than the one
he left. It was twenty by thirty feet, made of unhewn
logs, notched and laid one upon another, in what boys
call the " cob-house" style, to the height of twelve feet
or more in front, and eight feet or more on the back
side. The spaces between the logs were filled with clay
or mud, making a warm abode for winter, and a cool one
for summer.

The chimney was constructed of wood and mud,
rising from the roof like a pyramid, smallest at the top.
The roof was covered with slabs, held in place by long
weight-poles. The floor was made of logs, each split
into two parts and laid the flat side up, hewn smooth
with an axe. There was a loft above, to which the family
ascended by a sort of permanent ladder in one corner of
the cabin. The children slept upon the floor of the
loft, on straw beds. The only door of the dwelling was
made of plank; and three small windows furnished all
the light possible, though not so much as was needed.

This, briefly, was the pioneer home in which James A. Garfield was born, on the 19th day of November, 1831, and from which he went forth to his first day at school, as already described.

Abram Garfield was a tall, heavy, handsome man, capable of great endurance ; just the man to plunge into a wilderness to make a home and clear land for a farm. He possessed the strength, will, and wisdom for such an enterprise. His brain was in fair proportion to his body, large and active, making him a strong-minded man ; and, under other and more favourable circumstances, he might have made a broad and deep mark on his day and generation. But he thought of little except his family in that day of hardship and want, and so he chose a home and occupation where honour and fame were out of the question. But, with all his physical strength, the loving husband and father was not exempt from the attacks of disease. One day, in the midst of his hard toil, he heard the alarm of " Fire in the forest." Forest fires were common in summer time, and often large tracts of wood were burned over ; and sometimes pioneer cabins were destroyed, and the crops on little farms in the wilderness were injured.

" It is coming this way certainly," said Mr. Garfield, with some anxiety, after satisfying himself as to the danger. " I'm afraid it will make trouble for us. Mehetabel, run to the house with my axe, and bring me the shovel."

The girl was assisting her father. Within five minutes Mr. Garfield had the shovel, and Mrs. Garfield, and all the children, except the baby, were out to watch the fire.

" We must fight it," said Mr. Garfield, " or only ashes will be left of our home at sundown."

" I fear as much," replied Mrs. Garfield " These forest fires are terrible."

" Mehetabel, you and Thomas follow me ; " and he ran

across the house-lot to the edge of the woods to prevent the fiery demon from attacking his habitation.

Thomas and his sister followed. The fire reached the spot almost as soon as they did, and the battle with it began. It was a long and hard fight. Mr. Garfield met the enemy with all the vigour of a father contending for his children. He fully realized what their situation would be if the sun should go down upon the ruins of their home, and the thought impelled him to super-human efforts. For nearly two hours, in the burning sun of a hot July day, he fought the fire with his strong arm. Sometimes the battle seemed to turn in favour of the fiery element, and again the resolute pioneer appeared to have the advantage over it. At last, however, the fire was conquered, or rather, was prevented from devouring the little cabin and desolating the crops, though it swept on beyond the farm, whither the wind drove it.

Thoroughly heated and exhausted, Mr. Garfield sat down upon a stump to rest, and enjoy the cool, refresh-ing breeze that sprang up from the West. He did not dream that he was exposing his health by sitting, covered with perspiration, in that cool wind. But that night he was seized violently by congestion of the throat, and his stout frame writhed in pain, threatening speedy disso-lution. As early in the morning as possible, Mehetabel was posted away to Mr. Boynton's, and Thomas to a neighbour in another direction, for their assistance. There was no physician within many miles ; but one of the neighbours summoned claimed to possess some medical knowledge, and the patient was passed over into his hands, substantially, after he arrived. He applied a blister, thereby aggravating the disease, and hurrying the sick man to his grave. Mrs Garfield did all that true love and remarkable efficiency could do to save her husband, but her tender and faithful ministra-tions were fruitless ; he sank rapidly, and at last died without a struggle. His last words were, looking upon his children, and then addressing his wife:

"I have planted four saplings in these woods; I must now leave them to your care."

Oh, what a dark pall settled upon that abode! A happier family never dwelt in a palace than was found in that cabin. And now the burden of sorrow that rested upon the widowed wife and fatherless children was gauged by the greatness of bereaved affection. Little James was but eighteen months old when his father died—too young to understand the irreparable loss, or to feel the pangs of grief that well-nigh crushed other hearts. It was well that his baby-spirit could not take in the sorrow of that hour; there was anguish enough in that stricken home without adding his touching wail thereto.

The neighbours came, what few there were (only four or five families within a radius of ten miles), and sympathized and wept with the widow and fatherless ones. With their assistance the lifeless remains were enclosed in a rough box, and borne out through the low doorway, and buried in a corner of the wheat-field, near by. No sermon, no remarks, no prayers, except the silent prayers that went up for grace from aching hearts! Reader, you will never know, you never *can* know, nobody can ever know, except by the dreadful experience, what the death and burial of a loved one is in the wilderness, amid the gloom and silence of primeval forests. That bereaved widow still lives, and after the lapse of nearly fifty years she bears the marks of that great sorrow. A kind Providence that "tempers the wind to the shorn lamb" has wonderfully sustained her, and she has found her Saviour to be as "the shadow of a great rock in a weary land." Still the brow of almost eighty years is furrowed by the severity of that affliction.

An incident should be recorded here. It occurred a short time before Mr. Garfield's death; and he was reading a volume of Plutarch's " Lives," with James in his lap. The latter could speak the words, " papa," " mamma," and others. " Say Plutarch," said his father. James repeated it very distinctly. " Say it again," continued Mr. Garfield. James repeated it plainly, as before, and continued to repeat it. Looking up to his wife, Mr. Garfield remarked, with a true father's love and pride, " Eliza, this boy will be a scholar some day ! "

Winter was approaching ; and winter in the wilderness, especially when the stalwart arm upon which loved ones depend for support and defence is palsied in death, is not calculated to dispel gloom from a dwelling. Could human experience be more dreary than when a woman is left a widow, alone with her children, in a wilderness swept by wintry storms ; and that affliction intensified by extreme poverty, so that economy and careful planning are needful to keep the wolf of hunger from the door ? What a winter it was ! The snow lay deep and heavy upon the earth, burying the sacred mound in the corner of the wheat-field out of sight, and the high winds moaned through the naked forests as if wailing for the dead. The howl of wolves and the cry of panthers never sounded so terrible as they did during those long, desolate, wintry nights. The children, realizing the loneliness of their situation, now that their strong protector was dead, would lie awake at night to listen tremblingly to the howls and cries of these hungry animals, at the door of their cabin. Sometimes it seemed to them that the panthers knew that their courageous father was lying dead in the wheat-field, and so they ventured to come to the very door to moan and cry, as famishing children cry for bread Baby James, however, slept on, oblivious alike to the sorrows and perils of the hour. God was keeping him against the night of national danger, when he would listen to the yell of the wolves of plunder at the door of the republic.

That winter, alone in the almost pathless forest, with the warring elements and beasts of prey uniting to make desolation more desolate, could not have had more sad thoughts, bitter tears, hours of loneliness, and blasted hopes, crowded into it than were the natural outcome of the direful situation.

It seemed to the weary ones that spring would never return ; but it did, after a long, never-to-be-forgotten winter. And spring swept the snow and ice, and the streams ran singing again, and the dead things of the field and forest returned to life, save only the dead in the corner of the wheat-field. There was no resurrection there ; and so hope was not revived in the cabin, and a gloomy outlook made even spring-time sad. There was no money in the house, and there was a debt on the farm. Food, also, was running low ; and the widowed mother might hear her children cry for bread What could she do ? Leaving the children still at school, we will continue the story of her sufferings.

II

BEFORE SCHOOL-DAYS

IN her strait, Widow Garfield sought the advice
of neighbour Boynton, whose real kindness had
been a solace to her heart.   He said :

" No woman with four children can carry on a farm
like this alone, and support her family.   I see no possible
way out of your trouble except to sell your place and
return to your friends."

" And   leave   my   husband   in   the   wheat-field ? "
responded Mrs. Garfield   " Never ; I can't do that."

" But what else can you do ? " continued the neighbour.

Looking at the circumstances squarely, with her
accustomed good sense and courageous spirit, she
answered :

" When I have sold, paid the debts and the expense
of removal to my friends, I shall have little or nothing
left ; and that, too, without a rod of land on which to
raise corn to make a loaf "

" Your friends could help you," suggested the neighbour.

" I can never cast myself upon the charity of friends,"
Mrs. Garfield replied, with an emphasis that showed she
meant what she said.   " So long as I have my health, I
believe that my Heavenly Father will bless these two
hands so as to support my children.   My dear husband
made this home at the sacrifice of his life, and over log

in this cabin is sacred to me now.   It seems to me like a holy trust, that I must preserve as faithfully as I would guard his grave "

The heroism that came out through these words was worthy of a Revolutionary matron ; and the woman's fortitude fairly drew tears from the eyes of the neighbour.

" Then you would not sell the farm any way ? " added the neighbour, inquiringly.

" Not all of it," she replied.   " Part of it might go ; enough to pay the debt."

" I never thought of that," answered the neighbour. " Perhaps that is the way out of your trouble   Better think that over, and I will.   I'll look about, too, and see what can be done by way of selling a part of it "

The neighbour left, and Mrs. Garfield went immediately to a greater than he, where she had often been in her want and woe for counsel   On her knees in one corner of the cabin she laid her case before God, and promised to follow His guidance if He would only make duty plain.   God did make it plain as day to her.   She arose from her knees without a doubt in her heart.   She was happier than she had been any time since death darkened her home.   She felt like singing the twenty-seventh Psalm : " The Lord is my light and my salvation ; whom shall I fear ? the Lord is the strength of my life ; of whom shall I be afraid ? "

Calling Thomas, who was not quite eleven years old, but now the only male dependence on the farm, she laid the case before him as if he had been a man of thirty years, and the resolute and trusty boy replied :

" I can plough and plant, mother.   I can sow the wheat, too, and cut the wood, milk the cows, and do heaps of things for you."

" You are a small boy to do so much," responded his mother ,   " but with my help perhaps it can be done   God :   will   fatherless, I don't feel that I can move away from this place."

"We needn't," Thomas said, quickly. "I want to live here, and I will work real hard."

"Not too hard, my son, lest there be two graves instead of one in the corner of the wheat-field," answered Mrs Garfield, with much emotion. "We must finish the fence around the wheat, and that will be very hard work; but I thin. that I can split the rails, and together we can set the fence."

"And I can finish the barn, I know," added Thomas His father had partially fenced the wheat-field, and had been putting up a small barn, which was nearly completed

And so the whole subject was canvassed; and plans laid, in the full expectation of remaining on the pioneer farm. Nor did the widow have to wait long to sell a portion of her land Settlers were coming into that part of Ohio occasionally, and one of them heard, through the neighbour spoken of, that Mrs Garfield would dispose of part of her land. He lost no time in finding her humble abode, and at once bargained with her for twenty acres, paying cash for the same. With this money she paid all the debts, although it took the last dollar to remove this incumbrance

Spring was fairly upon them when the sale was effected, so that she and Thomas proceeded at once to put the little farm in order. He procured a horse of the nearest neighbour, who was generous enough to offer him the use of the animal, and prepared the ground for wheat, corn, and potatoes, and a small garden for vegetables. It was truly wonderful to witness the tact and endurance of this boy-farmer of ten years, toiling from early morning till night set in, his young heart bounding with delight over his ability to assist his widowed mother. Without any assistance, except such as his mother and sister of twelve years rendered, he did the planting and sowing in a style that assured a good harvest in the autumn.

At the same time his mother prepared the fence for the wheat-field. She found trees in the forest already felled, and she split the rails, every one of them, severe as the labour was, sometimes almost exhausting her strength, and always making a large draft upon her nerves. But the necessity was laid upon her, and she stopped not to inquire, as she did in the case of Thomas, whether there might not be another grave in the wheat-field at no distant period. Before July the house-lot, which was the small plot of cleared land sowed and planted, was fenced in, and the little farm was doing well   There was no school for Thomas and his sisters to attend, so that he had all the time there was from morning until night to labour, and wait—wait for the seed to grow. He did his work, apparently, with as much ease and efficiency as a young man of twenty would have done it.

But another trial awaited the afflicted family. Food was becoming scarce, and no money to purchase more. An examination satisfied the widow that the corn would be exhausted long before harvest unless the family were put upon a daily allowance. So, without speaking of this new trial to her children, she counted the number of weeks and days to harvest-time, and estimated the amount of corn that would be required each day. To her surprise and grief, a fair daily allowance would exhaust the bin of corn before harvest. She took in the situation at once, and, bravely and quickly as a general on the field of battle, decided she would forego supper herself that the children might have enough   For a while the devoted mother lived upon two meals a day. though working harder than she had ever worked any previous summer ; for she assisted Thomas on the farm to the extent of her strength, and even beyond her strength

A few weeks elapsed, and the doting mother discovered some mistake in her calculation, and she was startled to find that the present daily allowance of corn would consume the last ear before the new crop could be gathered. Without murmur, and with a martyr spirit, she resolved to forego dinner ; and from that time until harvest she indulged in but one meal a day. All this self-denial was practised in a manner to conceal it as much as possible from the children. They were growing and hearty, and Thomas especially needed substantial food, since he was doing almost a man's labour. Seldom was a pioneer family found in more straitened circumstances in mid-summer than was Widow Garfield's in the year 1834. Had not the spirit of a Revolutionary matron presided over the cabin, and the grace of Him who does not suffer a sparrow to fall without His notice sustained the presiding genius, the history of that family would have closed that year in the forests of Ohio.

But the harvest came, and a blessed harvest it was! The crops were abundant, and of excellent quality. Want fled at the sight of the bending sheaves and golden ears. The dear mother had come off conqueror in her long contest with the wolf of hunger, and her heart overflowed with gratitude to the Great Giver. The twenty-third Psalm had new significance in that log-cabin—" The Lord is my shepherd, I shall not want," etc.—and the grateful mother repeated it over and over, from day to day, as the real language of her soul in the hour of deliverance from distressing want. The first full meal which the abundant harvest brought was a benison to that household, and never again did hunger and starvation threaten to destroy them.

We have told the reader somewhat about the father of this family, and now that so much has been said of the mother we need to say more. We stop here to record briefly some facts of her early history.

She was a descendant of Maturin Ballou, a Huguenot of France, who was driven from that country on the revocation of the edict of Nantes. He joined the colony of Roger Williams and came to America, settling in Cumberland, R. I. There he built a church, which still stands, and is carefully preserved as a relic of the past. It is known as the " Elder Ballou Meeting-house." When it was built there were no saw-mills in the country, and no nails, and few tools to work with, so that the old " meeting-house " is a great curiosity. Its galleries and pews are hewn out of solid logs, and put together with wooden pegs. Even its floor was hewn out of logs, and fastened down with wooden pegs. Here Maturin Ballou preached the gospel while he lived, and was followed by his son, then his grandson, then his great-grandson, and so on to the tenth generation. A race of preachers sprang from this pioneer minister. In one family of the Ballous the father and four sons were clergymen ; then followed three grandsons, one great-grandson, and one great-great-grandson, all from one branch There were also many lawyers, doctors, and other public men among the Ballous, eminent for their talents and remarkable force of character. Some of them figured in the American Revolution, both as officers and privates, as heroic and efficient in war as they were renowned in peace. They were a conscientious people, and one of them, who preached in the old meeting-house about the year 1775, would not receive any salary for his services. He protested against being a " hireling." And yet he was so poor that one of his sons was forced to learn to write upon " birch-bark, in lieu of paper, and use charcoal, instead of pen and ink." This son was the celebrated Hosea Ballou, founder of Universalism in the United States. His father broke away from the Cumberland fold before Hosea was born, and removed to New Hampshire, where he settled. A
cc u f l m, mar-

ried, and became the father of Eliza Ballou, who, as we have seen, was the mother of James A. Garfield.

It is not difficult, therefore, to discover the origin of Mrs. Garfield's (mother of James) great fortitude, indomitable perseverance, tact, talents, and large executive ability. Were she otherwise, she would not fairly represent the long line of illustrious ancestors whose record is found upon two hundred years, and more, of our nation's history

In the spring of 1835, a family moved into the vicinity, which proved of great benefit to the Garfields. They had sewing to be done, and Mrs Garfield was glad of the opportunity to do it. A boy was needed, also, to plough and chop occasionally, and Thomas found it a good opportunity to earn a little money for his mother. It was additional sunshine let into the log-cabin.

It was an era when Thomas brought home the first money that he earned. A happier boy never crossed a threshold than he was when he handed the avails of his labour to his mother, saying :

" Now the shoemaker can come and make Jimmy a pair of shoes."

" Certainly," answered his mother ; " and he will be indebted to you for the first pair of shoes that he ever wore. You'll never be sorry."

" I never expect to be sorry," replied Thomas. " Jimmy ought to have had a pair a long time ago, and he would have had a pair if there had been any way for me to earn them."

" Well, you can send word to the shoemaker as soon as you please," continued his mother ; " the quicker the better."

James was three-and-a-half years old at that time, and he had not known the luxury of a pair of shoes, no, not even in the winter. To come into the possession of the first pair of shoes in the circumstances was an event of great importance. To a child in the woods, it was like the accession of a fortune to a poor man now. Be assured, reader, that Jimmy greeted the advent of the shoemaker with hearty good will when he came ; and he came very soon after the shoe question was settled, for Thomas lost no time in securing his services.

Then, in that part of the country, shoemakers did not have shops of their own, but they went from cabin to cabin, boarding with the families while they were making shoes for the members. In this case the cobbler boarded with Mrs Garfield, and his board paid part of the cost of the shoes. Shoemakers were not experts in the business at that time and in that region, so they required much more time to produce a pair of shoes ; and when they were completed, no one could say that their beauty added to their value. They answered every purpose, however, in a region where fashion was at a discount.

The acquisition of that pair of shoes elated the little possessor more than an election to Congress did less than thirty years thereafter. He was rich now, and well equipped for pioneer life He could defy the snows of winter as well as the stubbs of summer.

One thing more should be told here. Abram Garfield and his noble wife were Christians. Before removing to Orange they united with a comparatively new sect, called Disciples, though Campbellites was a name by which they were sometimes known, in honour of the founder of the sect, Alexander Campbell. Their creed was very short, plain and, good. It was as follows :

1. A belief in God the Father.

2. That Jesus is the Christ, the Son of the living God, the only Saviour.

3. That Christ is a Divine Being

4. That the Holy Spirit is the Divine agent in the conversion of sinners, and in guidance and direction.

5. That the Old and New Testament Scriptures are inspired of God

6. That there is future punishment for the wicked, and reward for the righteous.

7. That God hears and answers prayer.

8. That the Bible is the only creed.

With such decided opinions, of course their cabin home was dedicated to God, and the Bible was the counsellor and guide of their life. The voice of prayer was heard daily in the rude abode, and the children were reared under the influence of Christian instruction and living.

It has taken us so long to relate the history of this family previous to Jimmy's first day at school, that we must now hasten to meet the children, on their return as told in the next chapter.

III

GETTING ON

MRS. GARFIELD was making her spinning-wheel hum when the children came home. She was obliged to economize her time in order to clothe her family with goods of her own manufacture. The spinning-wheel and loom were just as indispensable to pioneers, at that time, as a "Dutch oven" was. The age of factories had not come, certainly not in that part of the country. In New England, even, factories were in their infancy there—small affairs.

"Oh, such a good time as we have had!" exclaimed Mehetabel, as she came rushing into the cabin with James and her sister.

"Twenty-one scholars," added her sister, under considerable excitement. "Mr. Sander's children were there, and they have twice as far to go as we have. They have to walk over three miles"

"And how did Jimmy get on at school?" inquired their mother, as soon as there was a place for her to put in a word.

"He liked it," answered Mehetabel; "he said his letters; and he asked the master how he knew that letter was R."

"Just like him," ejaculated Thomas, laughing outright. Thomas had just come in, leaving his work when he saw the children return. "The master will have enough to do to answer all his questions. What did the master tell him ? "

" He told him that he learned it was R at school, when he was about as old as he was," replied Mehetabel. And Thomas was giving Jimmy a toss in the air, by way of sport, while she was relating the facts, and Jimmy himself was making a most vigorous attempt to embellish the occurrences of the day from his imperfect vocabulary.

" How did you like your ride, Jimmy ? " inquired Thomas.

" Me like it," was the child's answer, uttered in a gleeful way.

" You liked it better than Hit did, I guess."

" I liked it well enough," responded Mehetabel.

" Wa'nt you awful tired ? "

" I wa'nt tired much "

" Did you carry him all the way ? "

" Pretty much. He walked a little of the way home. He isn't much of a load "

" Did he sit still in school ? "

" Pretty still. He left his seat once, and went over to scrape the acquaintance of another boy opposite."

" What did the master say ? "

" He took him by the hand and led him back, looking at us, and smiling ; and he told him that each boy had his own seat in school, and he must keep it."

" You are a great one, Jimmy," exclaimed Thomas, tossing the little midget into the air again. " You will make music for them in school."

" Well, children, I am glad that you like your school so well," remarked their mother, who had been listening to the prattle with maternal interest. " You must make the most of it, too, for we can't expect many school advantages in these woods. Poor opportunities are better than none."

Ohio schools were of the poorest that the most and

miserable. The teachers knew but little to begin with, and children had to travel so far to school that their attendance was limited to certain parts of the year. In many schools reading, spelling, and writing were the only branches taught. Geography and arithmetic were added to the studies in some schools. All of these branches were pursued in the school which the Garfield children attended. Teachers in the new settlements, at that time, were usually males ; it was not supposed that females could teach school well. That females make the best teachers, as a class, is a recent discovery.

The books used in the best pioneer schools of Ohio were Webster's Spelling-book, the English Reader, Pike's and Adam's Arithmetic, and Morse's (old) Geography. The Garfields possessed all of these They had, also, the Farmers' Almanack, and a copy of Davy Crockett's Almanack, which was found, at one time, in almost every cabin of the West. Reading-books were scarce then throughout the country, in comparison with the present time ; in the winds of Ohio they were not so plenty as panthers and wolves. Many of the few books found there related to exciting adventures with beasts of prey, hair-breadth escapes on perilous waters, and the daring exploits of pirates and rascals ; and they were illustrated with very poor pictures. Three or four volumes, besides the Bible and school-books, constituted the whole literary outfit of the Garfields. They had more brains than books, as the sequel will abundantly prove.

The village where the school was located was not much of a village after all. In addition to the log school-house, eighteen by twenty feet, there was a grist-mill, and a log-house, in a part of which was a store, the other part being used for a dwelling. The place is now known by the name of Chagrin Falls, and derived its singular name from the following fact. A bright Ya‧l⸳ ⸳ ⸳ ⸳ ⸳ ⸳ ⸳ ⸳ ⸳ ⸳ ⸳ ⸳ ⸳ ⸳ by the stream of water. He removed to the place in the winter time, when the stream was swollen and swift, and he erected a saw-mill. But when the summer came the stream dried up, and his hopes dried up with it. His *chagrin* was so great over his *dry* enterprise that he named the locality as above, in order to warn his Yankee relations against repeating his folly.

We cannot delay to rehearse much that transpired in school during the first term that James attended Two or three matters of special interest only can be noticed.

We have said that James was very familiar with Bible stories ; and we have intimated, too, that he was very inquisitive. His questions often created a laugh in school, both teacher and scholars enjoying their originality and pertinency very much. The fact was, James meant to understand things as he went along, and so his active brain put many inquiries over which the school was merry. They were not merry because his questions were pointless and childish ; far otherwise. They were merry because such a little fellow showed so much brightness and precocity by his inquiries. Scholars and teachers came to regard him as a sort of prodigy.

One day, at noon, an older scholar set him upon the table, saying,—

" Now, Jimmy, you be master and ask questions, and we will be scholars and answer them."

" Take 'oo seats, then," responded Jimmy, by way of consenting, his bright eyes sparkling with delight.

The pupils took their seats in glee.

" Now go ahead, Jimmy," cried out Jacob Lander. " Don't ask too hard questions "

Jimmy immediately began on his hobby—Bible questions.

" Who made the ark ? "

" Noah," answered a half-dozen voices.

" Who told him to make the ark ? "

" God," replied several.

" What for did God want he should make the ark ? "

There was a pause ; no one answered. It was one of Jacob Lander's hard questions, that James should have avoided.   After waiting in vain for an answer, he answered it himself.

" To save his self and family in."

" Save from what ? " cried out Jacob.

" From the flood," replied James

" Who was the oldest man ? " James continued.

" Methuselah," several answered.

" How old was he ? "

Nobody could tell, and so James told them.

" Who was the meekest man ? "

" Moses," was the prompt answer.

" Who had a coat of many colours ? "

" Joseph," equally prompt.

" Who was swallowed in the Red Sea ? "

Nobody replied.   He told.

And thus, for ten or fifteen minutes, this child of not quite four years interrogated the scholars around him, presenting one of the most marvellous scenes on record, whether in wilderness or city. From his earliest years his memory was very remarkable, embracing and retaining stories, facts, and whatever he heard, with unusual accuracy.   He acquired very much information in school by listening to the recitations of other and older pupils. Nothing was more common during his first term at school, than for him to repeat at home something he had learned from the recitations of older scholars. Then, too, nothing escaped his notice. His faculty of observation was ever on the alert. Language, manners, apparel, methods of work, conversation, almost everything attracted his attention ; so that he was ever surprising friends, from his childhood, by the amount of information he possessed.

He was a great imitator, too. Children differ very mu. .. ... r. ... ... is ... ... this faculty appeared to be large by inheritance. It was encouraging to behave well in his presence, it was perilous and doubly wicked to set a bad example before him. Coupled with his observation, this quality made him sharp and critical, for one of his years.

" School will keep through the winter," said Mehetabel to her mother, as she came home one day, near the close of the term. " Jacob's father is raising the money to pay the master."

" How did you learn ? I have not heard of it," answered Mrs. Garfield.

" Several of the scholars said so ; and they are all going "

" Going to have a vacation ? " inquired her mother.

" Yes ; two or three weeks ; school will begin in December for the winter "

" I am very glad indeed that you can have such an opportunity to attend school," continued her mother.

" Then I can go, can I ? "

" Yes ; you can all go except Jimmy. He cannot go so far in the winter ; and it will be too hard for you to carry him through the snow."

" Will Tom go ? "

" I hope so ; he has worked very hard that the rest of you might go, and now he should go."

Ten minutes afterwards Thomas was discussing the matter, and presenting reasons why he could not attend.

" I shall find enough to do taking care of the cows and chopping wood, even if there is no snow to shovel, which is not very likely."

" But we must let some things go undone, if possible, that you may learn when you can," suggested his mother. " In this new country you must take education when you can get it."

" I can study at home evenings and stormy days," replied Thomas.

"That is what Jimmy must do—study at home," continued Mrs. Garfield. "He has a good start now, and he can make a good reader before next summer."

The result was that Thomas did not attend the winter term, nor James. Their two sisters went, and Mrs Garfield instructed James and assisted Thomas somewhat in his studies.

Long winter evenings in the woods were favourable for study by the light of the blazing fire, that made the cabin more cheerful even than it was in the daytime Pioneers could not afford the luxury of a tallow candle or an oil lamp. Sometimes they adopted a substitute for both—the pitch-pine knot. But usually in winter pioneers depended upon the light of the fireplace. Fireplaces were very large, so as to admit logs four feet long with a quantity of smaller fuel in like proportion. When the mass of combustible material was fairly ablaze, the light and heat penetrated into every corner of the cabin ; and the heat below greatly modified the excessive cold of the loft above.

That winter was a memorable one for James He made decided progress in spelling and reading before the next summer came, with its hot days and growing crops. It was after the winter was over and gone, and the warm sunlight was bathing the forests and gladdening the earth, that James came into possession of a child's volume somehow—either it was a present or was borrowed of a neighbour—from which he derived much real pleasure. One day he spelled out and read aloud the following line :

"The rain came pattering on the roof."

"Why, mother !" he shouted, under visible excitement, "I've heard the rain do that myself"

"You have ? "

"Why, yes, I have," he continued, as if a new revelation were made to him And then he read the line

over again, with more emphasis and louder than before :
"The rain came pattering on the roof."

"Yes, mother, I've heard it just so!" and the little
fellow appeared to be struggling with a thought larger
than ever tasked his mind before It was the first time,
probably, that he had learned the actual use of words to
represent things, to describe objects and events—the
outside world on paper.

From that time James was introduced into a new
world—a world of thought. Words expressed thoughts
to him, and books contained words ; and so he went for
books with all his mind, and might, and strength.
There was nothing about the cabin equal to a book. He
preferred the "English Reader" to anything that
could be raised on the little farm. He revelled in books
—such books as he could find at that time, when there
was a dearth of books. Day after day the "English
Reader" was his companion. He would lie flat upon the
cabin floor by the hour, or sprawl himself under a tree,
on a warm summer day, with the "English Reader"
in his hand, exploring its mines of thought, mastering
its wonderful knowledge, and making himself familiar
with its inspiring contents. This was before the lad
was five years old ; and he was scarcely six years old
when he had committed to memory a great portion of
that "Reader." Other volumes, too, occupied much of
his attention, though none to such an extent as the
"English Reader." Such was his childish devotion to
books that his mother could scarcely refrain from
prophesying, even then, an intellectual career for him.
She knew not how it could be done—all the surroundings
of the family were unfriendly to such an experience—
but somehow she was made to feel that there was a
wider, grander field of action for that active, precocious
mind.

IV

TRIALS AND TRIUMPHS

'WE can have a school-house nearer to us," remarked
Mrs. Garfield to Mr. Boynton. "For the
sake of my James, I wish we could have."

" There are scarcely enough families yet to make such
a change," replied Mr. Boynton ; " some of them would
have to go as far as they do now."

" That is very true ; but more families would have a
shorter distance to go than they have now. I think
that fact is worth considering"

Mrs. Garfield was giving utterance, for the first time,
to thoughts that had been in her mind for several
months. In her own mind she had numbered the
families which might be induced to unite in erecting a
log school-house upon one corner of her farm. She
continued :

" Suppose you inquire of Mr. Collins and others, and
learn what they think about it. If eight or ten families
will unite, or even eight families, we can have a school
nearer home. I will give the land on which to build
the house ; and three days' labour by seven or eight
men will complete the building. It is not a long or
expensive job, and it is just the time to start now if the
thing is to be done."

" Perhaps it can be done," Mr Boynton answered,
thoughtfully. " The more I look at it, the less difficult
it ·· ᴵ ·ᵗ¹ ,ₒₙₛₑₜ the neₐᵧhlₒᵤᵣₑ ᵥₒᵤ mention,

and others, too. I should be as pleased as anybody to have it done." And as he spoke the last sentence he turned towards home.

Without recording the details of this new enterprise, we need only say that it was very easily accomplished; and before winter set in, a log school-house stood on the Garfield farm. Neighbours welcomed the project, especially because it would be an advantage to Widow Garfield, whom they very much respected, and to whom their warmest sympathies had always been tendered in her affliction.

"Now you can go to school by your own conveyance," said Thomas to Jimmy, one day after the school-house was finished. "You won't have to make a beast of burden of Hit any longer. You will like that, won't you?"

James assented, when his mother added.—

"Your master is coming from New Hampshire, where I was born. You will like him; and he is to board here to begin with."

Mrs. Garfield had four children, and Mr. Boynton six, to go to school—ten in all from two families.

It was through Mrs. Garfield's influence that the school-house was built; and then, it was through her influence that a schoolmaster was imported from New Hampshire. The school-house was twenty feet square, with puncheon floor, slab roof, and log benches without backs—large enough to accommodate twenty-five scholars. Teachers always "boarded round," dividing the time equally among the families; and it was considered quite an advantage to a family of children to have the "master" board with them.

By hard labour, assisted by his mother and sisters, Thomas harvested the crops in the autumn, cut and hauled wood, and did other necessary work, so that he could attend the winter term of school with his sisters and James. He had everything about the farm in fine order when December and the schoolmaster, whose name was Foster, arrived. They came together, and one was about as rough as the other. The " master ' was a young man of twenty years, uncouth in his appearance, large and unwieldy, but a sensible sort of a Yankee, who had picked up considerable knowledge without going to school or reading much   On the whole, he was full as much of a man as pioneers could expect for the small wages they were able to pay.   He was kind-hearted, of good character, and was really influenced by a strong desire to benefit his pupils.

He took up his abode at the beginning of school with Mrs. Garfield, and slept in the loft with Thomas and James.   At once his attention was drawn to James as a very precocious child.   Good terms were established between them ; and when they started off together for the school-house, on the first day of school, the teacher said to him, putting his hand kindly on his head :—

" If you learn well, my boy, you may grow up yet and be a General."

James did not know exactly what a General was, but then he concluded that a General must be some great affair, or a schoolmaster would not speak so favourably of him.   The remark fastened upon the lad's mind ; somehow he felt, all through the day, that he was beginning just then to make a General, whatever that might be.   It was not out of his mind for a minute , and he laboured somewhat upon the point, how long a time it would take to make him into a General.   However, he knew that there was one being who stood between him, and all learning, and all the future—and that being was his mother.   What he did not know, she would know.   As soon as he reached home, after school, he inquired :—

" Ma, what's a gen'ral ? "

" What's what ? " his mother answered, not comprehending his question.

" What's a gen'ral ? " James repeated, somewhat more distinctly

" Oh, I see now—a General ! " she answered ; " that is what you want to know."

" Yes , the master said I might make a gen'ral if I learn."

" That is what put it into your head, then," continued his mother, laughing " You don't know whether you would like to be one or not, I suppose , is that it ? "

" I want to know what it is," James replied.

" Well, I will tell you, my son, for your great-grand-father fought in the Revolutionary War under a General. You ought to know something about that, and something about your ancestors, too, as well as about a General "

She proceeded to tell him about his paternal ancestors : " How Edward Garfield came to this country from England, with John Winthrop, John Endicott, Francis Higginson, and many other Puritans, to escape oppression at home, settled at Watertown, Mass , which was as much of a wilderness then as Ohio was when your father removed here. The Indians were his neighbours, and he bought land of them, and lived in peace with them There he and his descendants lived, some of them removing into other towns, and many of them among the most influential citizens of that time. By-and-by, England, the mother-country, made war upon the people there, and the fight of Concord Bridge occurred, on the 19th of April, 1775. The soldiers of England wore red coats, glistening with brass buttons, and they carried guns with which to shoot down the farmers and people of Massachusetts Colony, unless they would surrender and obey the king of England. But the men would do neither They seized their guns, determined to defend themselves, and shoot the red-coats rather than continue to be subject to the king. Your great un le Abraham Garfield, was among the

soldiers at Concord Bridge   This was the beginning of
the Revolutionary War, in which our soldiers fought
bravely for their rights, and your great-grandfather,
Solomon Garfield, was one of them.   Then our soldiers
wore blue coats, trimmed with brass buttons, and they
were led by Generals who were the most distinguished
men, like General Washington.   The Generals wore
coats that shone with gold lace, and epaulets, or orna-
ments, on their shoulders, and hats like the one General
Washington wears in the almanack picture, made showy
with gold lace and a feather   Generals carried swords
instead of guns ; and they rode horseback, and led the
soldiers into battle.   I hope we shall never want any
more Generals in this country, for it is terrible to shoot
down men as they do in war.   But by study and learning you can make a man equal to a General, and be as
honoured, without killing your fellow-men.

" When the Revolutionary War was over, your great-
grandfather removed into the State of New York, where
he had a son, whom he named Thomas   Thomas grew
up to be a man, and was married, and had a son, whom
he named Abram ; and this Abram was your father.
Now, it will be easy for you to remember that Solomon
Garfield was your great-grandfather, a soldier of the
American Revolution ; that Thomas Garfield, a pioneer
of New York State, was your grandfather, and Abram,
his son, a pioneer of Ohio, was your father.   There was
no General among all your ancestors, though some of
them were equal to Generals.   If you should ever
become a General, you will be what no one of your
ancestors ever was, as far back as we can trace them—
two hundred and fifty years."

James listened to this recital with wonder.   He
scarcely knew before that he was connected with the
world outside of the Ohio wilderness.   Now he clearly
understood that his relations acted a conspicuous part
in ⸱'ʿ.ı   tʰi ᴄᴏ ɪɑtᴄⱱ, ɑɪ¹ ᴡ⸱⸱ ⱱ ⸱ᴅ ᴜⱭ ⸱⸱ᴄh con-

sequence It was a new and inspiring thought to him
His cabin home was invested with new interest and
more importance. How far his life was influenced by
this revelation of the past, we cannot say, but there is
no doubt that his active brain was stirred to nobler
thought, and his young heart stamped by indelible
impressions.

James believed in his teacher, and his teacher believed
in him. There was mutual attraction from the outset
The teacher saw that the backwoods boy was a great
man in embryo He was glad to have such a scholar
under his tuition. He was somewhat taken aback, however, by subsequent occurrences. The second day of
school he established the following rule :—

" Scholars cannot study their lessons and look about
the schoolroom therefore gazing about is strictly for-
bidden."

It was a novel rule to the pupils. It savoured of more
strictness than they had been accustomed to. It was
a very difficult rule for James to observe. He acquired
much information by his close observation. His two
eyes and two ears were more than books to him. Besides, he had never undertaken to perform the feat of
sitting bolt upright upon a log bench without a back,
and looking down upon his book with steady gaze. It
was a severe ordeal for a boy who never sat still in his
life, and who evidently was not constructed upon the
principle of sitting still. However, his heart accepted
the rule, and he meant to do the best thing that he could
with it. If he were to make a General, or something
else as good, he must do as the " master " told him to do.
As much as that was clear to him. But the first thing
he knew his eyes were *off* his book, and *on* the class
reciting.

" James ! " said the teacher pleasantly, " have you
forgotten the rule so quick ? "

" I forgot," was James's laconic reply ; and down

dashed his eyes upon his book   Not long, however. A
taking answer to a question in the class on the floor
brought up his eyes again as if by magic.

"What ! so soon forgetting the rule again, James ? "
exclaimed the teacher. "You have a very short
memory."

James looked down upon his book abashed, but he
made no reply. The fact was, he meant to mind the
rule, and do his best to please his teacher. But it was
never intended that two such eyes and two such ears
as James possessed should come under a rule like that.
The teacher was unwittingly at fault here. He did not
quite understand his pupil ; and so he insisted upon the
observance of the rule, and for two weeks continued to
correct James, hoping that he would finally bring his
eyes and ears into complete subjection. But his effort
was fruitless. James was incorrigible, when he meant
to be obedient, and he grew nervous under the discipline.
He thought so much about keeping his eyes in the pre-
scribed place that he could think very little about his
lessons , and so he became comparatively dull and
defective in his recitations

At length, just before the teacher left Mrs. Garfield's
for another boarding-place, he said to her in James's
presence .—

"I do not want to wound your feelings ; James is
such a noble boy; but then I want to tell you——"

"Say on," replied Mrs. Garfield, quite startled by the
solemn tone of the "master."

"James is not quite the boy in school that I expected."

"How so ? " interrupted Mrs Garfield, completely
taken by surprise. "You astonish me "

"I know that you will be grieved ; but I think it is
my duty to tell you." And Mrs Garfield could see that
he shrunk from telling her, and she began to think that
something awful had happened , still she repeated .—

"Say on "

" Well, it is only this : James don't sit still, and he don't learn his lessons. I fear that I shall not be able to make a scholar of him."

" Oh, James ! " his mother exclaimed, as if the teacher had put a shot through her body That was all she said ; and it was uttered in a tone of agony that went straight to the little fellow's heart, as he stood looking and listening She sent him to school that he might make a scholar, and now her hopes were dashed in a moment. No wonder that her response was an exclamation of disappointment and grief !

" I *will* be a good boy ! " ejaculated James, bursting into tears, and burying his face in his mother's lap. " I *mean* to be a good boy." And he never told more truth in a single sentence than he did in the last one. It never will do for a philosopher, however wise, to attempt to repress the centrifugal force of nature ; and that was what the teacher was trying to do.

" Perhaps he can't sit still," at length Mrs Garfield suggested , " he never was still in his life."

" I *will* sit still ! " was the boy's response, still sobbing as if his heart would burst, yet speaking before the teacher had time to reply.

" Perhaps so," answered the teacher thoughtfully, as if the grieved mother had awakened a new idea in him.

" I never knew him to fail of learning before," Mrs. Garfield continued : " never."

" I *will* learn, mother ! " the boy shouted between his sobs.

" You mean to learn, I have no doubt," answered his mother. " Some boys do worse than they intend ; perhaps that is the trouble with you."

" You dear child," said the teacher, putting his hand upon his head, touched by the lad's piteous appeals , " you and I are good friends, and I think we shall have no more trouble I will try you again. So wipe up, and let us laugh and not cry "

The teacher saw his mistake. The child's mother had opened his eyes by her wise suggestion. In his mind he resolved to let the centrifugal force alone, and adopt another policy. So the subject was dropped, and James went to school on the following day, to sit still or not, as he pleased The teacher resolved to leave him to himself, and see what the effect would be. The result was excellent. The boy did not sit still, of course he did not , but he was natural and happy, and his eyes fulfilled their function in roaming about more or less, and his ears heard what was going on in the school-house. The teacher could not make a blind and deaf boy of him, any way, and so he ceased to try. He allowed him to see and hear for himself ; and it just filled the lad with happiness. It fired his ambition, and brought out his brilliant parts, so that he became the star of the school.

It was quite a number of days before Mrs. Garfield saw the teacher again, as he went to board with another family. Then he called to cheer the mother, whom he had so thoroughly grieved. Her first question was, as he entered her house :

" How does James do now ? "

" Oh, grandly," the teacher replied, in a tone that indicated great satisfaction in being able to speak so approvingly.

" I am so glad ! " was the mother's only response ; and her heart was healed.

" He is perpetual motion in school," continued the teacher, " but he learns ; no scholar learns so fast as he."

" Then you have given up your rule ? " Mrs Garfield remarked, inquiringly.

" Yes ; I think you are right about him. Such a rule cramps him ; he can't be himself under it. I guess he tried hard to obey it."

" Children are) y alike," continued Mrs Garfield.

" James is unlike my other children in his restlessness and energy, as well as in his precociousness. I hope that he will come out all right."

" Come out all right ! " responded the teacher. " My word for it, he will make his mark in the world , you can depend on that."

" I hope so ; " and Mrs Garfield put her whole mother's heart into those last three words.

The restive nature of James was a theme of remark frequently. Thomas sometimes complained of it. He lodged with James, and the latter would toss and tumble about, often awaking Thomas by his movements, kicking off the clothes, and thereby putting himself and brother to considerable inconvenience. Often he would turn over, and feeling cold after having kicked off the bed-clothes, he would say in his sleep

" Tom, cover me up "

Thomas would pull the clothing over him, and lie down to his dreams, but only to repeat the operation again and again. It was said of James, twenty-five years after that time, when he had become a General, that one night, after a terrible battle, he laid down with other officers to sleep, and in his restlessness he kicked off his covering ; then, turning partly over, he said :

" Tom, cover me up "

An officer pulled the blanket over him, and awoke him by the act. On being told of his request in his sleep, James thought of his good brother Thomas and of the little log-house in the woods of Ohio ; and he turned over and wept, as he did in childhood, when the teacher concluded that he could not make a General of him.

At the beginning of the school the teacher had said :

" At the close of the term I shall present this Testament (holding up a pretty Testament of rather diminutive size) to the best scholar—best in study, behaviour, and all that makes a good scholar "

It was a new thing to them, and it proved quite an incentive to most of the pupils. Several tried hard for it ; but it was pretty well understood before the term was half through who would have the book. None were surprised when, at the close of the last day of school, the teacher said :

"James ! step this way."

James lost no time in obeying.

"This book," passing the Testament to him, " is yours. I think you have fairly earned it as the best scholar in school. I have no fault to find with any scholar ; but your remarkable progress entitles you to the book."

The pupils were all satisfied , James was a happy boy, and his mother wept tears of joy.

From the time that James was permitted to be himself in school, his advancement was remarkable Every teacher regarded him as a boy of uncommon talents, and every scholar was attracted to him as by magnetic influence. He read every book that he could beg or borrow ; yet he was efficient to assist Thomas on the farm at six years of age He went to school whenever there was a school ; but that was only a few weeks in a year. He improved his evenings and leisure time at home, however, and all the books at hand were read over and over, until he was perfectly familiar with their contents. His mental appetite was always craving, nor was it ever gorged by excess of food. It appeared to be capable of appropriating and digesting all that the times and locality could furnish.

About this time the Garfield and Boynton children formed a kind of club for improvement in spelling. The spelling-book became the field of their exploits They studied it enthusiastically, and drilled each other in its contents, as if they meant to master it The result was great proficiency in spelling—all of them excelling their comrades in school The drill was of great advantage to them in spelling matches, when the winter school was going ; especially to James, who became quite an enthusiast in that branch.✻ He was the best speller in school, when more than half the pupils were older than he Some of them said James could spell every word in the book correctly. Whether he could or not, in choosing sides for a spelling match, James was sure to be the first one chosen.

V

BOY FARMER

AT eight years of age, James had his daily labour
to perform as steadily as Thomas The
latter went out to work among the neighbours,
often imposing thereby quite a responsibility upon
James, who looked after the stock and farm at
home. He could chop wood, milk cows, shell
corn, cultivate vegetables, and do many other
things that a farmer must do

It was very great assistance to the family when Thomas
could earn a little money by his labour. That money
procured some indispensable articles, the absence of
which was a real privation both to mother and children.
They needed more money now than ever, because all
must have shoes, and all must have books , and there
were the teachers to pay, and occasional meetings at the
school-house now were some expense. So that the earn-
ings of Thomas just met a demand of the time, in which
every member of the household shared.

" You are eight years old, my son, and Thomas is
seventeen," said Mrs. Garfield to James. " Thomas was
not eleven years old when your father died, and he had
to take your father's place on the farm. You must be
getting ready to take Thomas's place, for he will soon
be of age, and then he will have to go out into the world
to seek his fortune, and you will have to take care of
th f .n "

"I can do that," James answered.

"Not without learning how to do it," said his mother " 'Practice makes perfect,' is an old and true proverb."

"I know that I can take care of the farm if Tom could," interrupted James, with some assurance.

"Yes, when you are as old as he," suggested his mother.

"That is what I mean—when I get to be as old as he was."

"I hope that some day you will do something better than farming," continued Mrs. Garfield

"What is there better than farming?" James asked.

"It is better for some men to teach and preach. Wouldn't you like to teach school?"

"When I am old enough, I should."

"Well, it won't be long before you are old enough. If you are qualified, you can teach school when you are as old as Thomas is now"

"When I am seventeen?" James responded with some surprise All of his teachers had been older than that, and he could scarcely see how he could do the same at seventeen.

"Yes, at seventeen or eighteen. Many young men teach school as early as that. But farming comes first in order, as we are situated."

"And it is time to get the cows now," remarked James, hurrying off for them, and terminating the conversation.

James was a self-reliant boy, just the one to take hold of farm work with tact and vigour. He scarcely knew what " *I can't* " meant It was an expression that he never used. The phrase that he had just employed in reply to his mother, " *I can do that*," was a common one with him. Once it put him into a laughable position. He was after hens' eggs in the barn, with his playmate Edwin Mapes It was just about the time he was eight years old, perhaps a little older. Edwin found a pullet's egg, rather smaller than they usually discovered.

"Isn't that cunning?" said Edwin, holding up the egg

"I can swaller that," was James's prompt answer.

"Whole?"

"Yes, whole."

"You can't do it."

"I *can* do it"

"I stump you to swaller it," continued Edwin, eager to see the experiment tried.

"Not much of a stump," responded James "Here it goes;" and into his mouth the egg went, proving larger than he anticipated, or else his throat was smaller, for it would not down at his bidding.

"No use, Jim," exclaimed Edwin, laughing outright over his failure. "The egg is small, but it won't fit your throat."

"It's going down yet," said James resolutely, and the second time the egg was thrust into his mouth.

"Shell and all, I s'pose," remarked Edwin. "S'pose it should stick in your crop, you'd be in a pretty fix."

"But it won't stick in my crop," replied James; "it's going down. I undertook to swaller it, and I'm goin' to"

The egg broke in his mouth when he almost unconsciously brought his teeth together, making a very disagreeable mush of shell and meat. It was altogether too much of a good thing, and proved rather of a nauseating dose. His stomach heaved, his face scowled, and Edwin roared; still James held to the egg, and made for the house as fast as his nimble limbs could take him, Edwin following after, to learn what next. Rushing into the house, James seized a piece of bread, thrust it into his mouth, chewed it up with the dilapidated egg, and swallowed the whole together.

"There!" he exclaimed: "It's done."

He did what he said he would, excepting only that the egg did not find its way down the throat whole, and

he felt like a conqueror. Edwin swayed to and fro
with laughter ; and, although forty years have elapsed
since that day, it is not impossible for him to get up a
laugh over it still. Mrs Garfield looked on with curious
interest, not comprehending the meaning of the affair
until an explanation followed. Then she only smiled,
and said " Foolish boy ! "

It was true what she said. He was a foolish boy to
undertake such a feat , " foolish," just as many promising boys are " foolish " at times. But the spirit of the
lad appeared through the " foolish " act. Nevertheless,
the " *I can* " element of his character rather dignified
the performance. The more we think of it, the more we
are inclined to take back our endorsement of that word
" foolish," because the act was an outcome of his self-
reliance. When William Carey, the renowned mission-
ary to India, was a boy, he possessed a daring, adventurous spirit, that expressed itself in climbing trees and
buildings, and in going where, and doing what, few boys
would do because of the peril. One day he fell from the
top of a tree, on which he perched like an owl, and broke
one of his legs. He was confined to the house, and bed,
several weeks ; but the first thing he did on his recovery
was to climb that identical tree to its very top, and
seat himself on the bough from which he had fallen, to
show that the feat was not impossible. There is no
doubt that his mother called him " a foolish boy," to
risk his limbs and life again on the tree ; but his admirers
have ever loved to rehearse the deed, as proof of the
boy's invincible, reliant spirit No one who reads of
Carey's immense labours for the heathen, his fearless-
ness in great danger, his hair-breadth escapes from death,
his tact and coolness in every emergency, can fail to see
that his " foolish " act of climbing the tree was a good
illustration of the maxim, that " The boy is father of the
man."

James was not egotistical or self confident ; these are

no part of self-reliance. Nor was he proud ; pride is no
part of self-reliance. He was not conscious of having
anything to be proud of. No boy was ever more simple-
hearted and confiding in others than was he. He did
not tell his mother that he could run the farm because
he overrated his abilities ; it was the honest expression
of what he was willing to do, and what he thought he
could do   It was the opposite of that inefficient, irreso-
lute boyhood that exclaims, " I can't," when it ought to
be ashamed to say it ; and when a decided, hearty " I
can," would prove a trumpet-call to duty, rallying all
the powers to instant action. This was one thing that
encouraged his mother to expect so much of him when
he should become a man. On one occasion, after he
began to labour on the farm, and quite a task was
before him, she said to him :

" James, half the battle is in thinking you can do a
thing. My father used to say, ' Where there's a will,
there's a way ' ; repeating a proverb that is as old as
the hills "

" What does that mean ? " interrupted James, referring to the proverb.

" It means, that he who *wills* to do anything *will* do
it. That is, the boy who relies upon himself, and deter-
mines to perform a task in spite of difficulties, will
accomplish his purpose   You can do that ? " And his
mother waited for a reply.

" I can," James answered, with emphasis.

" Depend upon yourself. Feel that you are equal to
the work in hand, and it will be easily done. ' God
helps those who help themselves,' it is said, and I
believe it. He has helped me wonderfully since your
father died. I scarcely knew which way to turn when
he died ; I scarcely saw how I could live here in the
woods ; and yet I could find no way to get out of them
and live. But just as soon as I fell back upon God and
m !,   ily We

have faied much better than I expected, and it is because I was made to feel that ' Where there's a. will, there's a way.' God will bless all our efforts to do the best we can "

" What'll He do when we won't do the best we can ? " inquired James.

" He will withhold His blessing, and that is the greatest calamity that could possibly happen to us We can do nothing well without His blessing."

" I thought God only helped people to be *good*," remarked James, who was beginning to enquire within himself whether He helped farmers.

" God helps folks to be good in eveiything—good boys, good men, good workers, good thinkers, good farmers, good teachers, good everything. And without His help we can be good in nothing."

James drank in every word, and looked very much as if he believed that he and God could run the farm successfully. His mother continued :

" If you do one thing well you will do another well, and so on to the end. You will soon learn that your own efforts are necessary to accomplish anything, and so you will form the habit of depending upon youiself—the only way to make the most of yourself."

Such was the instiuction that James received from the wisest of mothers, just when such lessons respecting self-reliance would do him the most good. It was on this line that he was started off in his boyhood, and he followed that line thereafter. He had no one to help him upward, and he had no desire to have anybody help him. Unlike boys who depend upon some rich father or uncle to give them " a good start " or upon superior advantages, he settled down upon the stubborn fact, that if anything was ever made out of him he must do it himself. Hard work was before him, and hard fare, and he expected nothing less A statesman who iose from obscurity to eminence once said " Whatever may be thought of my attainments, it must be conceded that I made as much out of the stuff put into my hands as was possible." That the germ of such an impulse must have taken root in James's heart early, is quite evident from some remarks of his to young men after he was forty years old.

" Occasion cannot make spurs, young men. If you expect to wear spurs, you must win them. If you wish to use them, you must buckle them to your own heels before you go into the fight. Any success you may achieve is not worth having unless you fight for it. Whatever you win in life you must conquer by your own efforts, and then it is yours—a part of yourself . . . Let not poverty stand as an obstacle in your way. Poverty is uncomfortable, as I can testify ; but nine times out of ten the best thing that can happen to a young man is to be tossed overboard, and compelled to sink or swim for himself. In all my acquaintance I have never known one to be drowned who was worth saving. . . . To a young man who has in himself the magnificent possibilities of life it is not fitting that he should be permanently commanded ; he should be a commander. You must not continue to be *employed* ; you must be an *employer*. You must be promoted from the ranks to a command. There is something, young man, that you can command ; go and find it, and command it. You can at least command a horse and dray, can be a generalissimo of them, and may carve out a fortune with them."

Another incident of James's early life illustrates the phase of his character in question, and, at the same time, shows his aptitude in unexpected emergencies. He was eight or ten years of age when it occurred, a pupil in school with his cousin, Henry Boynton. Sitting side by side, one day they became more roguish than usual, without intending to violate the rules of school. Sly looks and an occasional laugh satisfied the teacher, who was a sharp disciplinarian, that something unusual was going on, and he concluded that the wisest treatment would be to stop it at once.

"James and Henry!" he called out, loudly, "lay aside your books and go home, both of you"

A clap of thunder could not have startled them more They looked at each other seriously, as if the result was entirely unexpected, and delayed for a moment.

"Don't dilly-dally," exclaimed the teacher; "both of you go home immediately."

"I will go," answered James. Henry said nothing; and both passed out. James made an express of his dexterous legs, shortening the distance from the schoolhouse to home to about three or four minutes, and an equal time to return. Returning to school he entered the room, puffing like an engine, and resumed his seat.

"James! did I not tell you to go home?" shouted the teacher, never dreaming that the boy had had time to obey the mandate.

"I have been home," answered James, not in the least disconcerted He had obeyed his teacher promptly though he took very good care that his mother did not see him when he reached the cabin.

"Been home?" responded the teacher, inquiringly, surprised that the boy had been home in so short a time

"Yes, sir, I have been home," replied James; "you didn't tell me to *stay*."

"Well, you can *stay* here, now," answered the teacher, with a smile, thinking that it was the best way to dispose of so good a joke. James remained, and was very careful not to be sent home again, lest the affair might not terminate so pleasantly. Henry sulked about the school-house for a while, and then went home and stayed the remainder of the day That was the difference between the two boys. James saw the way out of the trouble at once, through the most literal obedience, and, believing he was equal to the emergency, he started promptly to fulfil the command   He was neither sulky nor rebellious, but happy as a lark, lively as a cricket, and smiling as a morning in May.   Such a little episode rather tightened the bond existing between the teacher and James.   The former discovered more of that sharp discrimination and practical wit in the affair, for which he had already learned that James was distinguished.

James was now eleven years old, and Thomas was twenty.   The district concluded to erect a frame school-house, and sold the old one to Thomas for a trifle. Thomas and James, assisted by their cousins, the Boynton boys, took it down and put it up again directly in the rear of their mother's cabin, thus providing her with an additional room, which was a great convenience. Thomas did it in anticipation of leaving home when he should attain his majority.

VI

SUNDAY IN THE WOODS

" PIONEERS need a Sabbath full as much as anybody else," was Mrs. Garfield's remark to James and her other children. "' Remember the Sabbath day to keep it holy,' is a commandment that must be kept in the woods as faithfully as elsewhere In large towns and cities people prepare for this by building houses of worship, some of them with tall and handsome spires pointing to heaven, with bells in the towers."

" What for do they want bells ? " inquired James, to whom this announcement about houses of worship and bells was a revelation. Neither James nor the other children had seen a house of worship, or heard a Sabbath bell, and their mother touched upon a theme as new and fascinating as a novel when she described Sabbath scenes in large towns.

" The bells call people to worship promptly, by ringing at the time of meeting," Mrs. Garfield replied to James's question

" Bells would not be of much use to pioneers, who live so far apart, even if they could afford to have them," she continued.

" Wouldn't they sound splendid in the forests ? " exclaimed James.

" Indeed they would," responded his mother ; " and they would be good company, too. I imagine it would not be s   ;   th   h   he

wilderness.   But pioneers ought to be thankful that
they can have preaching, under any circumstances
whatever "

" I should like to live in a big town where they have
meetin'-houses with tall spires," added James.

" Perhaps you will some day," suggested his mother
" None of us will live to see them in the town, probably "

The last remark was rather of a damper upon James's
aspirations, who scarcely expected, then, ever to find
a home elsewhere.   The foregoing conversation will
derive significance from an acquaintance with the reli·
gious privileges of the family

At the time of which we are speaking, there was no
stated preaching in the vicinity of the Garfield estate.
The sect called Disciples held occasional services in
school-houses and dwelling-houses   These occasional
services began before the death of Mr Garfield   As the
latter, with his wife, had united with that sect before
removing into the township of Orange, they were especially ready to welcome the itinerant preacher to their
log-cabin, and to the school-house   Sometimes the
meeting was at a cabin or school-house five, six, and even
eight miles away.   It was not unusual, in James's
boyhood, for pioneers to travel six and eight miles to a
religious meeting, on Sunday.   They went with ox-
teams and horse-teams, single and double, and some
men and boys walked the whole distance.   Often in
some sections the father would ride horseback to meet·
ing, with his wife on a pillion behind him, carrying her
youngest child, the older children following on foot
The meagre religious privileges were highly valued, and
there was much labour and hardship involved in availing
themselves of them.

The preachers of that day were illiterate men—good,
but uncultivated.   They were *pioneer* preachers, just
as the settlers were *pioneer* settlers.   They were well
sui·d ;··r·,·i·s, to the times and locality   rough, sincere,

earnest men, who found real satisfaction in travelling through the destitute country, usually on horseback, to do the people spiritual good. Occasionally there was a remarkable preacher among them, possessing great native ability, force of character, and singular magnetic presence. These were especially welcome, although any one of the number was received cordially. In their travels they called at all cabins, as pastors now make visits from house to house, their visits being chiefly of a religious character. They ate and lodged in cabins, wherever noon and night overtook them. The best fare that a cabin had was cheerfully set before them, and the best advice and sympathy the preacher could command were freely proffered It is not possible for us, at this day, to say how great was the influence of this pastoral work Men may read about it, and laugh over it now, but there can be no doubt that it provided a much needed and indispensable source of Christian power, influence, and enjoyment It contributed largely to make pioneer life nobler, and, in an important sense, educational.

James enjoyed no better opportunities of religious worship then we have described before he was ten years of age Occasional worship was a privilege that he highly prized, as others did. He did not readily let slip an opportunity to attend public worship. And the impressions it left upon his heart were gauged by his deep interests in such occasions

Whether there was any meeting or not, however, the weekly Sabbath was recognised in the Garfield cabin. No labour upon that day, except works of necessity, was the rule carefully observed. The Bible stood in the place of the preacher. It was both read and studied. Mrs. Garfield's rule was to read four chapters daily on week-days, and more on the Sabbath, when she formally expounded it in her sensible and thoughtful manner. The children asked questions as well as she. James was especially inquisitive about the Scriptures, and, after he learned to read, he read them much, both on the Sabbath and week-days. Bible stories that he learned from his mother's lips before he could speak plainly, became invested with new charms when he could read them at his leisure. He became so familiar with many narratives, that he knew just where in the Bible to turn to them ; and he had a multitude of questions to ask about " God's book," as his mother reverently called it

" How do you know that it is ' God's book,' mother ? " he asked.

" Because it is not like any book that man ever wrote "

" You said once that Moses, Isaiah, David, Matthew, Paul, and others wrote it," recalling his mother's explanation of different books.

" Yes, that is true, they did write it ; but they wrote as they were moved by the Holy Ghost They could not have written it without God's help. They wrote just what God told them, by His Spirit, to write "

" And that is why you call it God's book ? " James inquired.

" Yes ; He is the Author of it, although He directed men to write it, and guided them, also, in doing it."

" Are all the stories in it true stories ? "

" Yes ; every one of them "

" Is it true that Joseph had a coat of many different colours ? "

" I expect it is."

" Why didn't he have a coat of *one* colour ? Would it not be easier to make such a one ? "

" His father loved him more than he did his other children, and he made such a coat for him out of his partiality "

" Did he do right to love one of his children more than he did others ? "

" No , he did not "

" W.. |: .:l. .. .: . . .l. .

" Yes. Some good men do wrong."

" If good men do wrong, how do you know them from bad men ? "

" They don't do so many wicked things, nor so bad things, as bad men do "

" Can't good men stop doing bad things ? "

" Yes ; with God's help."

" Don't God always help them ? "

" No "

" Why don't He ? "

" Perhaps they don't deserve it."

" Can't men be good without His help ? "

" No ; and what is worse, they won't be."

" Why won't they ? "

" Because they are so wicked."

" How can they be good then ? " meaning that he could not see how a good man could be a wicked man at the same time.

In this dialogue appears the inquisitiveness of James, as well as his discrimination and thoughtfulness. Often his mother was unable to answer his boyish questions about the Bible. Their depth and point confounded her. It was here, especially, that she had unmistakable proof of his remarkable talents. It was around the old family Bible that the chief interest of the Sabbath clustered in her rude home. It was to her family what a Constitution is to the State. and what character is to the individual. Largely it made up for the absence of books, teachers, money and conveniences. It would be quite impossible to say how much unalloyed happiness it contributed to the family. Certainly its wise teachings were so indelibly impressed upon James's heart, that its contents were more familiar to him at forty years of age then they are to most Christian men so that its figures, symbols, and laconic sentences adorned his public addresses, to the admiration of listeners.

It is not strange that James and his brother and sisters

received more real valuable lessons, to assist in the formation of good habits, and to establish noble purposes, in their western cabin, than the children of many Christian families do from the constant ministrations of public worship. The absence of religious advantages was a good reason for the best improvement of the few enjoyed. The mother, too, felt additional obligations to guide, instruct, and mould the hearts of her offspring, because there was so little outside of her cabin to aid her. For these reasons, perhaps, James enjoyed better advantages to become distinguished than he would have had in the more populous and wealthy parts of the country.

When James was eight years old, the Temperance Reformation was moving on with power. The New England States presented a scene of enthusiasm without a precedent, and the interest spread into the north-eastern Ohio. Even the cabins of pioneers were reached by the wave of influence for temperance Mrs Garfield was just the woman to welcome such a reform, and to appreciate its full value. The subject was a fitting one for the Sabbath, although it was not neglected on other days. As the handmaid of religion, it challenged her best thoughts and efforts.

" Drunkenness is a terrible sin," she said, " and I was always glad your father had the same view of it that I have."

" Didn't he drink rum or whisky ? " asked James.

" Seldom ; and he got out of patience with men intoxicated. He thought they were very weak men by nature "

" Why don't men stop drinking it, when it is hurting them ? " James inquired.

" It is difficult to say why they don't. Some think they can't do it."

" Can't stop ! " James exclaimed, with surprise.

" It is said that they can't stop that they form

such a terrible appetite that they can't control it."

" I would," responded James, with characteristic firmness

" Better never begin to use intoxicating liquors ; that is the only safe course. It is easier not to begin to go wrong, than it is to turn back and do better after beginning."

" What do men drink liquor for ? "

" It would be difficult to tell what some of them drink it for, I think. Most men drink it because they like it, I suppose."

" Does it taste good ? "

" I suppose it does to those who like it."

" I should like to taste of some just to see what it tastes like," added James.

" I rather you would never know how it tastes, my son. If you never taste it, you can never become a drunkard, that is certain. ' Look not thou upon the wine when it is red, when it giveth his colour in the cup, when it moveth itself aright. At the last it biteth like a serpent, and stingeth like an adder.' Nothing could be truer than that "

" What is there in rum that makes it hurt people so ? " continued James

" There is alcohol in it, and it is that which makes drunkards. It don't hurt anyone to drink milk or water, does it ? "

" Of course it don't."

" Well, there's the difference between these wholesome drinks and intoxicating liquors ; there is no alcohol in the milk and water "

" What for do they put alcohol into them if it hurts people ? "

Mrs. Garfield explained the last question as best she could, assuring him that the alcohol was not put in, but was developed in the drink by an artificial process and that men wanted to produce the alcohol in order to make money.

In this way the great reformatory idea of that day found a lodgement in the Garfield cabin. James did not obtain a very definite idea of the enormous evil of intemperance, living where he had no opportunity to observe it ; but his idea was distinct enough to cause him to abhor the cause of the woe. His mother gave him facts enough respecting the curse of intemperance, that had come under her own observation, to show him that intemperance was a terrible evil, and his young heart was fully resolved to avoid the way to it.

Another lesson that made Sunday in the woods a memorable day to James, although it was prominent on other days also, was loyalty to the country. Mrs. Garfield's memory was full of facts respecting the sacrifices and sufferings of her ancestors to defend and preserve American Independence , and many an hour, as we have already intimated, was whiled away in recitals of their heroic deeds.

There is no doubt that James formed an exalted idea of what we call LOYALTY from these stories that were so inspiring and marvellous to the young. It is often the case that indirect methods fasten upon the young mind so tenaciously that they outlast many lessons that have been imparted with the utmost care and hopefulness. It is certain that James derived an impulse from some source, in regard to loyalty, that contributed to make this virtue one of the most prominent elements of his character in manhood. Although his mother did not formally imitate the example of the father of Hannibal, who led his son to the altar of his divinity at eight years of age, and made him swear eternal hate to the enemies of Rome, yet she did what was tantamount to that, and what secured as effectually the devotion of her son to the defence of his country.

"Never be afraid to do what is right," Mrs Garfield remarked "The biggest coward in the world is the man who is afraid to do right."

"I shouldn't think men would be afraid to do right," remarked James.

"I shouldn't think *boys* would be afraid to do right," responded his mother, perceiving that James scarcely thought there was an opportunity for this sort of bravery in boyhood. "Boys don't dare to do right sometimes."

"When?" inquired James, as if he questioned the truth of the latter statement.

"When they don't dare to obey their mothers or teachers because their companions don't want they should," answered his mother, intending to remind him of certain facts in his own boyish life

"I thought you meant when I got to be a man," said James, with a look denoting that he was *hit*

"I meant when a boy, as well. If you don't begin to stand up for the right when you are young, you never will when you are old. 'The boy is father of the man,' is a proverb true as it is old. Then a cowardly boy is as contemptible as a cowardly man Obey your mother and teacher, though all your companions laugh at you."

"I do," answered James.

"Yes, I think you do, generally: and I speak of it now, that you may give even more attention to it in the future than in the past, and grow more and more fearless to oppose wrong when you grow older When you become a man you will meet with many more, and greater temptations, than you have now, and unless you have more decision and courage, you will not be equal to the circumstances."

"Daniel's bravery got him into the den of lions," suggested James.

"Very true; and it was better for him to be in a den of lions with God on his side, than a friend of the king with God against him. I you are like Daniel in moral

courage, I shall be satisfied.   The lions could not devour
him so long as God was his friend ; and God is always
the friend of those who stand by the right."

James never had other than royal lessons upon moral
courage and kindred qualities.   These things, which lie
at the very foundation of stability of character and
personal excellence, were ingrained into his early life.
The Sabbath furnished a favourable opportunity for
special efforts in this direction, though every day in the
week bore witness in the same line.

We must not close this chapter without reference to
one fact connected with the Garfield family that is
worthy of particular attention.   It was their " coat-of-
arms."   A coat-of-arms formerly was a " habit worn by
knights over their armour.   It was a short-sleeved coat
or tunic, reaching to the waist, and embroidered with
their armorial ensigns and various devices."   The Garfield coat-of-arms consisted of a shield, with a gold
ground, three horizontal crimson bars crossing it in one
corner, over it a helmet with raised visor, together with
a heart, and above the whole an arm wielding a sword,
on which was inscribed the motto, *In cruce vinco*—
" THROUGH FAITH I CONQUER "

What we wish to say about this coat-of-arms relates
to the motto.   It tells of a courage that was born of
faith in God, such as was found in the Ohio cabin, and
without which the sorrows and hardships that invested
its early history would have proved too much for flesh
and blood.   It is a grand spirit to brood over a human
habitation, beneath whose roof childhood buds and
blossoms into true life.   It appropriates the Sabbath,
Bible, and every other hallowed power that is accessible,
to the " life that now is," because of another " life that
is to come."   It was this spirit that James nursed from
his mother's breast, and inhaled from the domestic
atmosphere that wrapped his boyhood, to arouse heroic
qualities, and bend them to victorious work.

When James was about ten years old, his uncle, Amos Boynton, organized a congregation in the school-house, and took charge of it himself, when no minister was on the ground Mr. Boynton was a man of excellent abilities, and a very devoted Christian man He was more familiar with the Bible than any man in the township, and could repeat large portions of it. A copy of the Scriptures was his constant companion. He carried it with him into the field. If he stopped to rest himself, or his cattle, the brief time was spent in reading the Book of books. His familiarity with the Bible qualified him to conduct Sabbath services in the log school-house ; and they were of great moral and spiritual advantage to the people. To James they were of as much real value as to any one.

At that time religious controversy ran high in northern Ohio. The Disciples were a new sect, and all other sects denounced them , while they, in turn, expressed themselves freely concerning the errors and follies of their opponents. James often heard discussions at home upon these controverted religious questions, in which his mother engaged with others. It was not unusual for preachers to refer to them in their sermons ; and always, when preachers stayed at his mother's house, as they often did, these questions were discussed, and they made a deep impression upon the active mind of James. So bright a boy as he could scarcely fail to see that vast importance attached to subjects in which the ministers and his mother were so much interested. These controversies lent more or less importance to Sunday in the woods.

Among the topics discussed was Baptism, the Disciples being immersionists. The extent to which James's mind was impressed by these discussions is learned from the following fact Considerable political excitement prevailed in that part of Ohio in the " Harrison Campaign " The neighbours were all for Harrison -Whigs

—and James had heard his mother say that his father was a Whig, and a great admirer of Henry Clay, and voted for him when he was a candidate for President. One day some neighbours were discussing some politics in James's presence, when one of them asked him, in a sportive way, " Jimmy, what are you, Democrat or Whig ? "

" I'm Whig ; but I'm not *baptized*," answered James.

The subject of Baptism was so thoroughly impressed upon his mind, and the subject of Whigism also, that the little fellow supposed he could not be a properly constructed Whig until he was baptized.

VII

HIGHER UP

" HALLO, Jim ! now you'll have to be a farmer in earnest, for I am going to Michigan," said Thomas, as he returned from Cleveland. " Got a place out there."

" Where ? " inquired James, not understanding where it was that his brother was going.

" To Michigan," repeated Thomas " It is more of a wilderness than Orange is."

" I know that," answered James. " What you goin' to do out there ? "

" Clearin'," replied Thomas ; " twelve dollars a month."

" You don't get so much as that, do you ? " said James, to whom that amount of monthly wages seemed enormous.

" Yes, twelve dollars a month. It's hard work, early and late. Mother shall have a frame-house now."

" Good ! " was James's answer of evident satisfaction.

At this time James was twelve years old and Thomas was twenty-one—a period that had been much discussed in the family, in anticipation of its arrival. There was a definite understanding between Thomas and his mother that the former should leave home at twenty-one and James should run the farm It was important that Thomas should be earning something abroad now that he had attained to his majority, and James was old enough to attend to affairs at home Thomas went to

Cleveland for the purpose of obtaining work, without any definite idea of what that work would be. Emigration to Michigan was increasing, and there was considerable excitement over the resources of that State, so that labour was in considerable demand for that section   The first opportunity that opened to Thomas he accepted without hesitation, and it was, as already announced, clearing land for a farmer in Michigan, at twelve dollars a month.

Thomas passed into the house with James, to make known the result of his errand to Cleveland.

" I hope it will prove all for the best," remarked Mrs Garfield, after hearing the report. " It's farther away than I expected."

" Yes, it is some distance ; but that is of little conse-quence, after all   It's good pay "

" How far is it ? " asked James, who was intensely interested in the contemplated change.

" I don't know exactly," answered his mother , " it's farther than I wish it was."

" Will you live in a log-house, Tom ? " James con-tinued.

" Yes ; a cabin not half so large and good as this."

" How long shall you be gone ? "

" Six months certain , perhaps longer."

" And you will have to take Tom's place on the farm," said Mrs. Garfield, addressing James. " That will be taking a step higher."

" I can do it," responded James, " though I am sorry Tom is goin'."

" We shall miss him sadly," remarked Mrs. Garfield. " It will be more lonesome than ever when he is gone ; but we must make the best of it."

" It will be best all round, I'm thinking," said Thomas, " if it is the way for you to have a frame-house, mother. I mean that shall come about."

" That will be nice, won't it, mother ? " exclaimed James who was thoroughly prepared to appreciate a real house, after twelve years' occupancy of a cabin.

"Yes, it will be nice indeed; almost too nice to prove a reality," replied his mother.

"It will prove a reality," remarked Thomas, with decision

Thomas had spent much time, during the last five years, in cutting and preparing lumber for a new house, hoping the time would come when his mother could command money enough to employ a carpenter to erect it. He had prepared sufficient lumber for the house when he became twenty-one years of age; but there was no money to pay a carpenter to put it up. Now Thomas saw the way clear for erecting the house after awhile, and the prospect fired his ambition. He was willing to go to Michigan for that object alone; indeed, he rejoiced to go, if by so doing a frame-house could be secured.

Thomas was busy in preparing to leave, and James was equally busy in attending to lessons that Thomas gave him about the work to be done on the farm The ground was to be ploughed, the wheat sowed, the corn and potatoes planted, with all the etceteras usually belonging to the season's labour. Thomas had his directions to give concerning all these things, that his little brother might the more successfully perform the farmwork. However, his time at home was limited, as his engagement required him to be in Michigan at an early date, and soon he was gone.

It was almost like making another grave in the corner of the wheat-field to part with Thomas. He had been the mainstay of the family since the death of his father, and his mother had leaned upon him as mothers will upon a noble son; and now to miss his face and voice, and miss his counsels and labours, created a void in the home circle that brought tears to the eyes of all. It was a trying hour for James, to whom Thomas was both brotherly and fatherly. The most tender and loving

F

confidence existed between the two. Thomas was proud of his gifted little brother, and James had perfect confidence in his efficient big brother. It was not strange, therefore, that James felt the absence of Thomas deeply, and deplored the necessity that compelled him to leave home. Nevertheless, he went to work upon the farm with a will. He knew how to labour, because he had laboured much with Thomas for four years, and was often called the "boy-farmer"; but now he was a farmer in a more important sense, and must rely upon his own judgment, plans and efficiency to a great extent. He was much higher up than before in the matter of care and responsibility.

Here as well as anywhere, we may describe the scenery about the Garfield estate, for that may have had an important influence upon the life and character of James. He was the sort of boy who delights in beauty and grandeur, to whom a river, mountain, or wild forest was more attractive than they often are to older heads. A person reared in the locality describes the scenery as follows :—

"Orange township is situated in the south-eastern portion of Cuyahoga County, fifteen miles from Cleveland. It is now, and always has been, strictly a farming town. There is no village within its limits.

"Its surface is irregular and hilly, presenting some of the finest rural scenery to be found in this part of Ohio. On the north-east flows the Chagrin River, from which the land gradually rises towards the south-west for a distance of three miles. Looking east from this range of hills, a grand view is obtained. The valley of the Chagrin, with its simple beauty, and the country for twenty miles beyond, are distinctly visible. All combine to form a picture that is strong, charming, and impressive. It was to a spot south of this chain of hills that the parents of General Garfield came, in 1830."

We should have said that, at this time, "the Western

land speculation " was running high. People grew wild over the prospect of coining money out of the wild lands of Ohio, Michigan, Indiana, and Illinois. Men at the East bought thousands of acres of land in the West that they never saw, and did not positively know that such land existed. Hundreds and thousands of people sold houses and land in New England and in the Middle States, and removed thither, to make their fortunes. Perhaps Thomas cherished a secret hope that somehow he should become a rich man in the woods of Michigan. It is certain that the opportunity to labour in that State came to him through the " Western land mania." We will leave him there, felling trees and clearing land for the Michigan farmer, while we look after James at home.

" Well, your farmer-boy is making things lively," remarked a neighbour who called upon Mrs. Garfield. " He is handy as any one of us with his tools."

" And works as hard, I guess," responded Mrs. Garfield.

" That is so ; all of us work hard enough," rejoined the neighbour.

" Pioneer life is beset with hardships," continued Mrs. Garfield ; " though its poverty is not so hard to be borne as poverty in a large town or city."

" Do you really think so ? "

" Certainly I do."

" What makes you think so ? "

" Why, don't you see that there are no rich around us to be compared with ? We are not continually being reminded of our extreme poverty by the presence of those who can have all that money can buy."

" You think there is some satisfaction in all being poor together ? " interrupted the neighbour jocosely.

" Yes ; that is about it. ' Misery loves company,' and I suppose that is true of poverty."

" Well, we are all poor enough, if that is all," continued the neighbour ; " and on your theory we ought to be tolerabl. happy "

"We are, I think, as happy as the human race averages, and perhaps a little more than that. God averages human experiences well, after all our fault-finding."

"There must be some satisfaction in thinking so ; but I can't exactly accept that view. Pioneers have more than their full share of hardships and trials, in my opinion," replied the neighbour, just as James came in from the cornfield. Turning to him, by way of cordial salutation, he added :

"What do you think about it, James ? "

"Think about what ? "

"Whether pioneers have more hardships than other people ? "

"I don't know much about it," answered James. "If I knew what hardships other people have, I could tell something about it ; but I don't "

James never spoke a truer word. He was born and reared in the forest. He had never seen even a village, much less a large town or city. He had seen but one or two frame-houses at that time ; and these had just been erected in the vicinity. How could he understand that others enjoyed more than he did ? He was a happy boy He had his home, though it was a cabin He had his mother and brother and sisters, and they were just as dear to him as home and brothers and sisters are to those who dwell in palaces Perhaps they were more so : we incline to the belief that they were He had a mother : and if any mother was ever worth more to a child than his was he did not know it, nor could he be made to believe any such thing. So he was a contented boy. What other people, more highly blest, called hardships, he accepted as a matter of course. He scarcely knew that it was not as good as others enjoyed. Why should he not be a rollicking, wideawake, happy boy ? Hard work challenged his best endeavours now that his brother was gone ; but hard work is not necessarily hardshi   Some rich men work more hours in a day to keep heir money, than the poor man does to keep soul and body together. And often it is more annoying labour, straining the nerves, banishing sleep, fretting the disposition, and keeping up a continual fever of anxiety.

James did not call hard work hardship ; he never thought of such a thing. He was never happier than he was during that season of severe toil after his brother left home. He had greater responsibility, but responsibility is not hardship. He felt more manly and competent ; and he was both, now that the care of the farm and his mother rested on his shoulders. A close observer could see the honest pride of a noble heart cropping out through his manly bearing. Call it hardship to run the farm ! He never dreamed of it , it was his delight. The language of singing expressed his daily experience far better than complainings. Under his homely jacket nestled a spirit that had not learned discontent. No ! Neighbour Mapes put his question to the wrong party, when he said .

" What do you think about it, James ? "

James was not the passenger to awake. Break the slumbers of somebody who is happy only when he is asleep. James was happiest when he was awake, as mortals everywhere should be. And he never was more wide awake than he was on the farm during that season of excessive labour.

" Goin' to exchange work with Mr. Lamper," said James one day to his mother.

" How so ? " inquired his mother.

" He wants an extra hand once in a while, and so do I ; and then I want his oxen sometimes."

" You have seen him ? "

" Yes ; and have made the bargain."

" A good arrangement, I guess," added his mother. " Then, his head is older than yours, and he can show you some things about farming that you don't know "

" And ' Two heads are better than one, if one is a

sheep's head,' 1 have heard you say a good many times,"
added James, in his lively way.

"If they are *pioneer* heads, it is so," rejoined his mother,
whose opinion of pioneer life was more favourable than
that of neighbour Mapes. " Pioneer life requires all the
wisdom that can be got together to make life in the
woods successful."

This reference to " life in the woods " was partly in a
vein of pleasantry ; for now the designation was scarcely
appropriate. Nearly fourteen years had elapsed since
Mrs. Garfield moved into that township, and great
changes had been wrought in that time. Many settlers
had moved into the township, and the unbroken forests
had yielded to the pioneer's axe, and well-conducted
farms dotted the landscape. Neighbours were near and
many now, as compared with the distance and number
of them ten years before. The pioneer stage had really
passed, and it was not " life in the woods " that James
was living. There were a saw-mill and an ashery in the
vicinity ; also a carpenter was added to the population of
the town. All this brought a change that James,
young as he was, could but notice.

The plan of exchanging work was one that James
originated, and it proved of great value to him during
the season. It lightened his labour when " Two heads
were better than one," and gave him the use of oxen
when no other aid could be half so valuable. Then Mr.
Lamper was glad to exchange labour with a boy who
was equal to a man in his efficiency. James could turn
his hand to any sort of work upon the farm, and had
physical strength to endure almost any strain. His
honest pride of character assisted him, too, more
than ever in his work, as any sharp observer could see.

We cannot dwell upon the labours of that eventful
season, except to add, that the farm did for James what a
teacher did for some other boys. The celebrated engineer,
and inventor of the locomotive engine, George Stephen-

son, said that he studied mechanics with his engine
instead of a professor Indeed, the engine was his professor, and taught him daily the most important lessons.
He was eighteen years of age, and was running the
engine in a colliery. On Saturday afternoons, when the
workmen were released from their labour, and were
spending their time in rum-shops, or attending dog-
fights, George took his engine to pieces, and cleaned
and studied it He could neither read nor write, but
he could understand and appropriate the silent lessons
of his engine ; and these made him the renowned inventor of the locomotive. Well might he call the engine his
teacher.

James might have called the farm his teacher. It
taught him many excellent lessons. He extracted the
most valuable knowledge from its soil. He evoked inspiring thoughts from its labour. His manhood developed under its rigid discipline. His mind enlarged
its mental grasp. The season spent in the log school-
house could not have pushed him higher up than did
his experience on the farm. It was positive proof that
work is discipline as much as study, and that it can
do for boys often more than study to qualify them for
the stern duties of life James was more of a man at
the close of that season than he was at the beginning
of it.

He had little time to read during those months ; and
yet he never valued reading more. He was never more
hungry for knowledge than he was during that period of
constant labour. He thought much of going to school ;
and often the thought would force itself upon his mind,
how can I get an education ? Not that he formed any
definite plan concerning it, or even considered that such
a thing was possible ; but the vague thought would sometimes arise. And then his mother frequently dropped
remarks which showed the strong desire of her heart,
that James might, at some future time, she knew not how

or when, become a scholar. That such a boy should spend his time in tilling the earth appeared to her like wasting pearls.

" James, I hope that you will not always have to work on a farm." How often she remarked thus !

" What would you do if I shouldn't ? " was James's thoughtful reply.

" I hardly know. ' It is not in man that walketh to direct his steps,' and I am glad of it. There is my hope, that some day you can get an education."

" I should like to, if it is best."

" I know it will be best, if you can do it. You can never know too much."

" I guess that is so," replied James half humorously " I couldn't ever know too much to work on a farm. There is more to learn about it than I could learn in many years "

" That is true, no doubt ; but I have a strong desire that you should become a scholar , and sometimes the desire is so strong that I feel as if I could not be denied "

" I don't feel so."

" Wouldn't you like to study, and become a scholar ? "

" Why, yes, I should like nothing better ; but how can I do it ? "

" I don't know, and that is what troubles me, though I ought not to be troubled. I know that God will open the way, if it is best, and I ought to leave it there ; but somehow I can't help having anxiety about it."

" Well, I can't be at present," added James, as if perfectly satisfied with his situation.

Thus James was led on, and his mother too, not knowing whither Providence was guiding them. James was going up higher all the while, although it scarcely seemed so to his doting mother. The Lord was laying a deeper foundation than could have been laid if she had had her own way. " Man deviseth his own way, but the Lord directeth his steps."

VIII

BOY CARPENTER

" TOM is coming ! " was the shout Mrs. Garfield heard as she caught sight of James
bounding across the garden. " Tom is coming ! " louder
yet. One would have thought the boy had suddenly
lost his reason, judging by his antics.

Sure enough ! Looking from the cabin door she saw
Thomas approaching, and James had already reached
him in his pleasurable excitement. If James was glad
to get hold of Thomas's hand, Thomas was equally
rejoiced to get hold of James's. The greeting was
mutual and hearty. The big brother and little brother
made for the house, hand-in-hand, their tongues running
glibly all the while.

" Are we goin' to have a frame-house now ? " asked
James, almost the first thing.

" Yes, we'll have a frame-house now, and let the hens
keep house in the cabin," replied Thomas.

" It's just about good enough for them," remarked
James in response. " It will make a good hen-house "

" Rather better accomodations than they have had,"
Thomas added ; " and will compare well with our
quarters when the house is done."

By this time mother and son stood face to face, James
shouting :

" Goin' to have the frame-house now, mother ! "

Mrs. Garfield found that she was a good deal like

James, and when she saw that her Thomas was certainly coming, she forgot everything else, and hastened to meet him—not as wildly as James, but very much as all fond mothers will do when they have not seen their good sons for seven months. She went across the house-lot at double-quick, and soon had hold of the big boy as firmly as he had hold of her. It was a glad meeting. Mothers and sons who dwell in palaces scarcely know what a luxury it was. Why, it more than paid for the long separation. The meeting paid principal and interest in full The family were united again—girls, boys, and mother—one girl rather big now, twenty-three years old ; and Thomas almost twenty-two, just the age of his father when the latter was married. Happy family !

They were hardly seated in the cabin, when Thomas flung a handful of gold into his mother's lap, saying :

" Now you can have a frame-house ; " and the noble young man seemed to be perfectly satisfied, now that he was able to give his mother a better home. " We'll go about it at once."

" My ! what a lot ! " was James's exclamation when he saw the shining gold ; and he proceeded to examine the treasure in his mother's lap.

" How much is there, Tom ? " he asked.

" Seventy-five dollars, just."

" And you earned it all ? "

" Every cent of it."

James read aloud the inscriptions on the new, bright coin, while he handled it in amazement that his own brother could make such a " pile." Things had not been conducted on a gold basis in that cabin, so that it was a new spectacle that suddenly broke upon James's delighted vision. He had not seen *gold* coin before, nor had he dreamed that such an article should come out of the Michigan woods. It is not strange, therefore, that the backwoods boy was considerably elated over the sight. What a mint was to him later, that seventy-five dollars in gold was to him then.

"Why don't you say something, mother?" exclaimed James, no doubt expecting that his mother would be as gushing as himself over the gold. The fact was, she could not have said anything if she had tried. What mother could in the circumstances? That great boy, as old as his father was when she became his bride, coming home with such proof of his filial love! Thinking of his mother more than he did of himself! Happy only in helping her! Who wonders that she sat mute as a marble statue? There was no language for such an occasion. All the Noah Websters in the world could not provide words for such a moment. A mother's heart, at such a time, defies expression. At least, it was so with mother Garfield's heart. It could have taken that strapping on to itself, and folded him like a baby again, and covsred him over with kisses, which would have been onlyea figure of speech, but language was out of the question. James saw the point as soon as her tears dropped upon the gold coin. He could not exactly understand it, though, for *he* felt like hurrahing instead of crying, and he knew that his mother was glad that she could have a frame-house, for he had often heard her express a wish of that kind. So he could not quite understand it. Readers! it was because he was like all the rest of the boys and girls—they do not understand the mystery of a mother's love.

The excitement of the hour passed, however, and the equilibrium of feeling and daily duties was restored.

"I'm off again, mother, as soon as I get you into the new house," said Thomas "There's plenty of work in Michigan, and I must be doing it."

"Well, you must manage to suit yourself. I suppose that Mr. Treat can be had any time to put the house up." Mr. Treat was the carpenter.

" I will find out.   I can work with him, and we'll make a quick job of it."

" I'll work, too," said James.   " I can carry boards, drive nails, and do other things."

" You can draw the sand, too, Jimmy," replied Thomas.

" Sand !   What do you do with sand ? " exclaimed James, forgetting that mortar was necessary.   It was excusable, however, since he was familiar only with mud, that made the log-house tight.

" To make mortar with, of course ; we must have mortar for plastering," Thomas answered.   " I can get lime, bricks, nails, and windows at Cleveland."

" And you'll take me along with you, I s'pose," suggested James.

" Yes ; I can chuck you in most anywhere.   Perhaps I shall need your help "

James had not been to Cleveland at that time.   It was but a small place, of about a thousand inhabitants, though growing rapidly.

" How long will you be gone to Cleveland ? " inquired James.

" One day only ; can't spare any more time.   A long day, perhaps."

" When shall you go ? "

" Just as soon as I have engaged Mr. Treat."

Mr Treat was seen and engaged at once, and Thomas and James made the trip to Cleveland for windows, nails, etc.   Bricks were obtained subsequently, without going to Cleveland.

A few days only elapsed before the carpenter and Thomas were at work on the new house.   James, too, was not a mere spectator   He was far more interested in the erection of the house than he would have been in a circus.   It was an era in his life.   All the spare moments he could snatch from the farm-work and care of the stock, he devoted to the new house.   He had drawn the sand before the carpenter began to frame the building

"Here, Jimmy, I see you want to help," said Mr. Treat "Just take this chisel and mallet, and put this mortise through as you have seen me do the others. I guess you can do it."

"Yes, I can do that," James answered, elated with the idea of being able to render assistance ; and with mallet and chisel the mortise was hurried through.

"Give us another," exclaimed James, proud of his achievement.

"What !" responded Mr. Treat, "got that done so quick ?"

"Yes, all done ; look at it," answered James.

"And well done, too," said Mr. Treat, examining the mortise. "Pretty good for a boy."

"Can I do another ?" continued James.

"Yes, a dozen if you want to ;" and the carpenter started him on another mortise, and after that another, and another, until he completed the sixth.

"You must try your hand at planing now," said Mr. Treat. "A small boy to shove a plane, but I guess you can do it. Here" (arranging a board on his bench), "try this, and see how you make it."

At that time planing machines were unknown,—at least, in that part of the country ; all the planing was done by hand In the newly-settled townships, like Orange, also, less planing was done ; more rough boards were used. The frame-houses were of rude construction, having no particular style or comeliness—just a comfortable place to live in, more comfortable and pleasant than log-cabins. Many of them could boast only of a single room below—parlour, sitting-room, kitchen, and wash-room, all in one—the second storey remaining unfinished, and used for lodging, being divided into apartments by curtains. It was very little labour and small expense to erect such a dwelling. Others were somewhat more elaborate, having two and even three rooms below, with sleeping-rooms finished above. The Garfield house contained three rooms below, and two above unfinished. Hence, seventy-five dollars was ample to buy nails, bricks, lime, and other necessary articles, and to pay the carpenter in addition.

James went on with the planing very readily, for he had watched both Mr. Treat and Thomas in this part of the work until he comprehended the " knack," as the carpenter called it. As we have already said, his sharp observation was equal to a teacher, and it made him master of many things that he never could have known without this faculty. Captain Samuel Brown, a bridge-builder, lived on the banks of the Tweed, across which he desired to build a bridge. While he was studying the subject, he chanced to walk in his garden early one fine morning, when his attention was arrested by a spider's web across his path. A careful examination of the web suggested to him the idea of a suspension-bridge, constructed by the use of iron ropes or chains, as the spider had built his light bridge. No indifferent gazer would take the hint of a suspension-brdge from the web of a spider, but sharp, discriminating observation took the hint.

James's keen observation enabled him to build many suspension-bridges over impassable places in his boyhood and youth, and, in comparison with some of them, his success with carpenter's tools is scarcely worth mentioning.

" I like this," said James, as he turned over the well-planed board to the carpenter; " it's fun l"

" You will not find much *fun* in it when you have kept at it all day," replied the carpenter. " It takes elbow-grease to do this work well."

" Elbow-grease ! " repeated James ; " what's elbow-grease ? "

" J . . . . Jimmy,"

the carpenter replied. " Can't do much at planing without putting sweat into it."

" Sweat alone won't run a plane," rejoined James,
intimating to the carpenter that brains were needed as
much as work.

" That is so," replied Mr. Treat ; " but you understand
what I mean. The most skilful workman will find hard
labour in this business , and to do it well, he must be
willing to sweat."

" If sweat is proof of doing it well, then the board is
well planed, Mr. Treat, for I sweat enough," James added.

" You have done it well ; I couldn't have done it
better myself," replied Mr. Treat. " You was born to be
a carpenter, I guess."

" I'd like to be one," interrupted James, " if I could be
a good one."

" Well, you would make a good one, my boy, judging
from the work you have done. Perhaps you will be
a boss-carpenter before you are twenty-one. Who
knows ? "

" I couldn't be that without a chance," remarked
James, intimating that a chance was scarcely possible
for a boy in his circumstances.

" Of course not ; but where there's a will there's a
way "

" That's what mother says."

" And that is what overcomes difficulties," continued
Mr. Treat. " But there are more boards " (pointing to
a pile on the ground) " if you want to do more of this
sort of work."

Another board was laid on the bench, and James continued to drive the plane for an hour or more. He
was general errand-boy when he was about the building,
so that he could not use plane or chisel long without
interruption It was " Go here," and " go there " ;
" Get this," and " get that " ; to all of which demands
he cheerfully responded

The raising of the house was a grand affair to James. It was the first house-raising he ever attended, and it was a great novelty   He was sent to notify the neighbours of the event on a given day, and to solicit their assistance.   The neighbours were thoroughly glad that Mrs. Garfield was going to have a new house, and many were their praises of the son who thus provided for his worthy mother.   They were promptly on hand at the time, and the frame went up without mistake or accident And now came another treat for James   He had had his eye upon a keg of nails for some days, anticipating the highest kind of pleasure from driving them   It was sport for him to drive nails, as it is for boys generally, and he expected to have his fill of the fun.

"Now, Jimmy, you can try your hand at driving nails," said Mr. Treat, addressing the boy-carpenter. "That is pretty work, and won't require so much elbow-grease."

"I have a particular liking for driving nails," replied James ; "where shall I begin ? "

. "Right here, where I have put in these two   Lay them just as I have laid these, and it will be right.   See if you can ' hit the nail on the head ' , some boys never can do it, and so they grow up to be men, and live and die, without ever ' hitting the nail on the head.' " Mr Treat cast a knowing look at James as he said it, and a smile played over his face, as if curious to see how his figurative expression was taken.

"I can hit that sort of a nail on the head, if I can't any other," answered James, with a smile, understanding the drift of his figure of speech   And hastily he let drive his hammer at a nail, and missed it the first time, much to his chagrin.

"Missed the first blow ! " exclaimed the carpenter, with a shout of laughter.   "You didn't do that as well as you did the planing and mortising   How is that ? "

"Only a blunder," James replied, with evident mortification.

"Well, see if you can strike again without blundering," responded Mr. Treat, laughing. "There's a 'knack' in driving nails as well as in planing boards. Just get the 'knack' of the thing, and it will go."

"Here goes the 'knack,' then," exclaimed James, as his hammer struck the nail squarely on the head. "The 'knack' it is, every time! Nails are made to drive, and I will drive them." And his hammer flew with unerring aim, as nail after nail was driven in with a will that signified determination and force of character. Missing the first blow just set him on his taps, resolved that a steady aim and square hit should attend every blow that followed. He learned the lesson of carefulness and brave endeavour from his failure, so that he became more expert in the use of the hammer than he would have been otherwise. Such is the case with all boys who win; a failure arouses their latent skill and energy, and they bid defiance to failures thereafter. In his youth, Curran, who became the famous Irish orator, broke down on his first attempt to speak in a debating society. He was a stammerer, and when he rose in his place his stuttering speech was worse than ever. He floundered at first, stammered out something nobody could understand, and then stood speechless. His companions roared with laughter. One said, in a low voice, "Orator Mum!" Another peal of laughter followed this new title; and it aroused the invincible spirit of the boy.

"You may laugh now," he shouted finally, "but I will conquer this stammering tongue, and some day you will listen and commend." All of which came to pass exactly as prophesied. The gist of the matter was in him, and the mortifying failure served to bring it out.

"Nothing like being plucky," remarked Mr. Treat, when he witnessed James's success in driving nails. "Pluck wins when luck loses."

" Mother says there is no such thing as *luck*," responded James.

" Your mother is about right according to my notion," answered Mr. Treat. " Boys that depend on luck for a livelihood go pretty hungry sometimes. I'd rather a boy of mine would have a single ounce of pluck than a whole pound of luck. Luck is like an old United States bank bill, of very uncertain value ; but pluck is good as gold all the time."

" Well," said James jocosely, " you must admit that my first blow was a very *unlucky* one."

" Unlucky ! the deuce it was ! " exclaimed Mr. Treat. " It was just what you said it was, ' a blunder,' and a blunder is neither lucky nor unlucky. But you have made amends, so go ahead with your nailing."

And James did go ahead, spending every moment possible in labour upon the new house, and acquiring facility in the use of tools that served him a good turn many years thereafter. To the last day's labour upon the house James rendered all the assistance he could, happy only in the thought that he could make himself useful. Nor was this the best part of the discipline. James received a kind of education when the house was building that proved of great advantage to him through life. Before the house was completed, he conceived the idea of making the carpenter's trade a source of profit. It was on his mind day after day, the last thing he thought of before falling asleep at night, and the first thing when he awoke in the morning. He divulged his purpose to no one, but pondered it for several months in his own heart. The family had removed into the new house, and Thomas had returned to Michigan, and James was manager of the farm-work.

" Mother," he said one day, when he could not keep his purpose a secret any longer, " I have a plan to earn some money "

' What is it ? "

" To work at the carpenter's trade."

" I'm afraid that plan won't work."

" Why ? "

" You have enough to do on the farm now, and you can't do both."

" I only meant to work at it when I had no work on the farm to do—a job now and then."

" It will be difficult to find such jobs."

" Perhaps it will, but I can *try*, and you believe in *trying*."

James emphasized the words *try* and *trying*, because his mother often made the remark to her children, " There is nothing like *trying*."

" Yes, I believe in *trying* always, and you may *try* as hard as you please to find a job."

" I'm going to Mr Treat ; perhaps he may have a job at planing or something of the kind. I want to earn some money for you as well as Thomas. I will go to Michigan when I am as old as he is."

" One son in Michigan is enough, I think. Besides, I hope the day will come when you can be more useful than you can be in chopping wood or planing boards."

" I don't know what there is better than such work, to help you."

" There is somebody else in the world to help besides me," replied his mother earnestly ; " and I don't want you to feel that you are always to be bound to this little township and farm."

" I don't expect to be bound to it always," retorted James, " but I am bound to get a job at carpenterin' this very day, if I can ; and I am going over to see Mr. Treat."

Within less than an hour James entered the carpenter-shop.

" Halloo, Jimmy ! that you ? How's your mother ? " exclai: .l M⸱ Tr⸱ ⸱ ⸱. ⸱   ⸱⸱   ⸱⸱⸱   ⸱ ⸱ ⸱ ⸱ was wont to d ⸱.

" She is well."

" Not much farming to do just now I suppose ? " continued Mr T inquiringly.

" No, not very much , and I came over to see you about some work "

" Ah, that's what brought you here ! I see now ; what sort of work do you want to do ? "

" Your kind of work, of course,—carpenterin'."

" All right, Jimmy ! Glad to see there are no lazy bones in you I hate lazy boys above all things, and I know that you don't belong to that class."

" I hope not," answered James , " I thought I might as well be earning a little something for mother, now Tom's gone, and so I came to see if you could give me a job."

" That's noble, to help your mother Boys who stick to their mothers don't often make a failure, especially boys with such a mother as you have. You can't think too much of your mother. Them's the boys I like to give a job to."

" Can you give me a job ? " James interrupted, evidently thinking that Mr Treat was making a pretty long story over the affair.

" Yes, my boy, I can, and I am right glad to do it, too There is a pile of boards that I want planed, and I know that you can plane them well. I haven't forgot how you worked on the house."

" How much will you pay me ? "

" One cent a board ; and that will be pretty good pay "

" When do you want them done ? "

" Just as soon as you can ; the quicker the better "

" I will come to-morrow and begin."

" All right, sonny ; begin to-morrow, and end when you please."

" You wouldn't like to have me keep the job on hand a month would you ? " replied James pleasantly, thinking about the words, "at I your lease."

" You won't do that, Jimmy. I know that you will put it through just as soon as possible, and that will suit. When I said ' end it as you please,' I knew that you would please to end it as soon as you could. Your money is ready as soon as the job is done."

" I'll be on hand to-morrow, just as soon as I've done my chores," remarked James, and left.

It was a proud moment for James, and exultation beamed in his eye when he reached home, and reported his good fortune to his mother.

" It will be the first money I ever earned," said James.

" And you are pretty young to earn it," replied his mother " I'm glad you have the job. I hardly thought you would find one."

" *Trying* brought it," responded James, with a very suggestive expression on his face

" I guess Mr Treat made the job on purpose for you , he is a great friend of yours," added Mrs. Garfield. " I know he would be glad to help you to all the jobs possible. When are you goin' to begin it ? "

" To-morrow, early as I can."

" Well, be careful not to overwork Two hours a day is as much as you ought to work at planing ; three hours at most."

" I shall work *six* hours to-morrow certainly," replied James " I should laugh to see myself work two hours, and then cry, baby,' and come home , and I guess Mr. Treat would laugh, too."

" I think Mr. Treat will agree with me exactly, that boys must not overwork ; and you are so ambitious, James, that you will overwork before you know it, unless somebody warns you." Mrs. Garfield expressed just the opinion that every thoughtful parent would express. James had more energy and ambition than he had discretion, so that he was blind to the value of his mother's counsel.

"If you see me coming home to-morrow in two hours, or three, you may know that I've lost an arm or finished the job," remarked James, very suggestively. And here the conversation closed.

James went to his job the next day with more determination than ever, much as he had shown of this admirable quality before. If his mother looked into his eye, or observed his compressed lips, as he went out of the door, she must have been satisfied that three hours' planing would not satisfy his ambitious desires on that day. Mr. Treat gave him cordial words of welcome, in his jovial way, assuring him that the " Early bird catches the worm," at the same time handing him a jack-plane James stripped off his jacket and vest, leaving only his shirt and jean trousers to encumber him He was barefooted, of course, as the luxury of shoes could not be afforded, except in the winter. He was scarcely tall enough to work handily at the bench, but he seemed to straighten himself up one or two inches taller than usual for the occasion. He went to work like a man. Every board was twelve feet long ; and by the time he had planed ten of them his mind was fully made up to what nobody knew except himself. They found out, however, at night. All through the day the plane was shoved rapidly, and great beads of sweat stood upon the boy's brow. but no tired look invested his countenance for a moment. Before the sun went down he exclaimed, laying aside the plane :

" One hundred boards, Mr. Treat, done ! count them, and see."

" Not a hundred, my boy ; you don't mean that, do you ? "

" Count them, and see ; a hundred boards according to my count."

" A great day's work, if that is the case," said Mr. Treat, as he proceeded to count the boards

" One hundred and one, and this one, com

pleting the count. " Too much for a boy of your age and size to do in one day. I wouldn't advise you to do more than half that another day."

" I'm not much tired," said James.

" That is not the thing, my boy ; thirty years from now you may feel tired from this day's labour more than you do now."

" If it takes as long as that to get tired, then the tired part is far off," responded James, not appreciating the wise remark of his employer.

" Well, now comes the best part of your day's work, the pay," remarked Mr. Treat. " Let us see, one hundred boards takes one hundred cents to pay for them—that is just one dollar ! A great day's work for a boy-carpenter ! Now you count, and I'll count." And he proceeded to count out one hundred cents, making quite a little pile of coin when the dollar, all in cents, was ready for James's pocket.

Reader. We might as well stop here as to proceed further with the history of that day's labour. It would be quite impossible to describe James's feelings to you, as he pocketed the one hundred cents and started for home. That old jacket never covered just such a breast as it did then. If we could only turn that bosom inside out, and have a full view of the boy's heart, we should learn what no writer can ever describe. It was a man's heart in a boy's breast. There was not room for it under the jacket. It swelled with inexpressible emotions, as ground-swells sometimes lift the ocean higher than usual. " *One hundred cents, all in one day !* " The more he thought of it on his way home, the prouder grew the occasion. " Seventy-five days like that would yield him as much as Thomas brought from Michigan ! " The thought was too great for belief. That would not be half so long as Thomas was gone, and away from home, too And so he thought and pondered, and pondered and thought, on his way home, his boyhood putting on manhood in more than one respect. He was " Great Heart," bare-footed and in jean trousers.

Whether James intended to ape Thomas or not, we cannot say ; but on reaching home, he unloaded the coppers into his mother's lap, saying :

" Yours, mother."

" All that, James ? "

" One hundred cents," was James's reply.

" What ! earned a dollar to-day ? "

" Yes ; I planed a hundred boards "

By this time Mrs Garfield became as dumb as she was over the seventy-five dollars that Thomas brought her There was some trouble in her throat, and the power of speech left her. She could not tell what she thought, nor how she felt. If her eldest son had made her cry with kindness, the youngest one was doing the best he could to imitate his example. The little son could be handled as the big one could not be, and so the dear, good mother folded him to her breast as the only way to tell her love when the tongue was voiceless.

IX

BARN-BUILDING

JAMES'S job at Treat's carpenter-shop introduced him into further business in that line. The winter school, however, intervened, and James attended it without the loss of a single day. The day after the school closed, Mr. Treat called.

" I'm after James," said he to Mrs. Garfield. " I have a barn to build for Mr. Boynton, and can give him a job before his farm-work begins."

" That will suit him," replied Mrs Garfield. " I think he likes that kind of work better than farming."

Just then James made his appearance.

" Young man, I'm after you," said Mr. Treat to him.

" For what ? " asked James.

" Another job of work."

" Planing boards ? "

" No. Better than that."

" What ? "

" Building a barn for Mr. Boynton."

" I'd like that," said James ; " I want to learn to build a barn myself."

" You can, easily. That's not much of a job."

" When do you want me ? "

" Right off—to-morrow, if you can."

" To-morrow it is, then."

" With other work I have in the shop I can keep you at it until farming begins."

" That will just suit me Shall I work by the day ? "

"Yes, by the day, if you will. I'll give you not less than forty cents a day, nor more than fifty, according as you get along with it."

"I'll be satisfied with that, and will be on hand to-morrow morning," James answered, as Mr. Treat was leaving.

"'Nothing like trying,' mother," said James, after the carpenter was gone, repeating her old, familiar saw. "I shouldn't have got this job if I hadn't tried for one last fall."

"Very likely not," replied his mother; "and you would not have had this if you had not done the first one so well. Nothing like doing things well, always remember that."

"It's almost equal to *trying*, isn't it?" added James, roguishly.

"Perhaps it is more than equal to it. They who do their work well are the ones who get work. People don't want botchers about."

"What are botchers? Blunderers?"

"Those who don't do their work well—they are botchers. Your father used to say, 'What's worth doing at all, is worth doing well,' and he was about right. Another thing he used to say was, 'If you know a thing, know it certainly.'"

"I don't see how a person can really know anything without knowing it certainly," remarked James. "If I know anything, I know it."

"Sometimes you know a lesson better than you do at other times, do you not?" answered his mother.

"That may be; but if I don't know a lesson certainly, I don't know much about it," replied James "I should be ashamed not to know a lesson certainly."

"I hope you always will be," remarked his mother; "and, what is more, I hope you will always be ashamed not to do your work thoroughly."

"I mean to learn how to frame a barn" said James.

" I should think you might learn that easily enough,"
responded Mrs. Garfield. " It's true I don't know much
about it, but it doesn't appear to me to be very difficult
to learn to frame a barn."

" I know that I can learn how," added James.

" Mr. Treat will give you a good chance to learn how,
I think, if you tell him what you want."

" I shall do that." And James did do it. As soon as
he commenced work the next day, he made known his
wishes.

" Mr. Treat, I want to learn how to frame a barn," he
said. " Can't I learn ? "

" Most too much of a youngster for that business,"
answered Mr. Treat ; " but you can have the chance
Just keep your eyes open to see how the work is laid
out, and it is easy enough."

" Well, I can do that ; my eyes are usually open in
the daytime," said James, naively.

" And you must see with your brain as well as with
your eyes, if you would learn," added Mr. Treat. " You
see how that is, don't you ? "

" I see."

" You must have a little idea of the plan to begin
with, though ; " and Mr. Treat proceeded to exhibit his
plan to the boy, explaining it to him as well as he could.
James took in the principal idea in the outset, and proceeded to assist in framing the building with increased
intelligence. An examination of the plan showed him
that it was more necessary for his " brains to see " the
why and wherefore than he had supposed. But Mr.
Treat was deeply interested in teaching the boy, and so
kept him at work directly under his eye. He directed
his attention both to the plan and the frame, that he
might learn the real use of the former to the carpenter.

" Can't do anything without a plan," remarked Mr.
Treat one day to James.

" How is it about milking ? " asked James, facetiously.

" It is true in milking, my boy. By *plan* I mean *system*, and you can't milk without system   About such a time, morning and night, you milk the cows, and that systematic way enables you to accomplish other work more successfully   Then, too, the cows give more milk by milking them systematically."

" I didn't know that," said James, surprised that cows would give more milk by systematic milking.

" It is true, whether you knew it or not," remarked Mr. Treat. " Even the Lord would make a failure in running this world without system.   The fact is, Jimmy, you have to run your farm on God's plan, or it won't run at all.   If you should plant two kernels of corn where God means that only one should grow, you would have your labour for your pains.   You can raise no corn in that way.   You could raise a plenty of stalks, but mighty little corn.   Hens would starve to death in such a corn-field.   If you should sow two bushels of wheat where there should be only one bushel on the Lord's plan, your biscuit would be pretty small next winter."

James laughed at this eccentric way of putting things, and, at the same time, he received some very valuable ideas from the sensible carpenter, who continued very much in the same vein :—

" ' A place for everything, and everything in its place,' is an old adage, and just as true as Genesis   The men who obey this rule are the men who succeed ; and the men who never mind it are the ones who go to smash. I've seen that over and over.   There's no use a-trying to run things on the line of disorder and confusion ; they'll get upset, sure.   No man can amount to much in this world except on system.   Remember that, Jimmy, and you will come out all right."

" You mean a time to study, and a time to work, and a time to play ? " inquired James.

" That's it ; only I should cut the time to play pretty slo ,' r jied Mr. Treat. " Not much time to play in

Ohio, when we have all that we can do to make the ends meet. 'All work and no play makes Jack a dull boy,' they say, and I guess 'tis true. But, look here, have we got this right ? " (springing up to examine his work). " I have been so busy talking that I didn't stop to think what I was about. All talking and careless work will make a botch of it."

The work was found all right and in a good state of progress. And now in silence the labour went on for an hour or two, James minding his P's and Q's, and the carpenter keeping an eye on his plan and his work.

We must state the upshot of this barn-building in a word, as space is dwindling away. The barn was completed according to the contract, and without a break from the start. Perhaps James could not have framed a barn without assistance when the building was completed, but he learned a great deal about the carpenter's trade while he worked upon it. Evening after evening he studied over it alone. He drew a plan of his own, and studied it hour after hour, in order to learn how to frame a barn. With the same persistent efforts that he mastered a problem in arithmetic, he studied his plan of framing a building , and although he did not become master of the art, he, nevertheless, approximated to it. When the barn was completed, Mr. Treat paid James fifty cents a day, amounting to nearly twenty dollars, saying

" You've earned it, every cent of it, James."

During the previous winter James made great progress in his studies, by improving the long evenings. He had learned about all he could learn in the district school, although he continued to go in the winter time. In some things he was more advanced than his teacher, and often put questions which the teacher could not answer. He mastered Adams's Arithmetic during the winter. Lying flat on the floor, that the light of the fire might shine on his book, he studied arithmetic every evening for weeks, until he had learned all there was to learn in it, and he was really more competent to teach that science than the man who presided over the district school. The scholars said that James actually performed a problem one day that had proved too much for their teacher, much to the mortification of the latter.

"I think the answer in the book must be wrong," remarked the teacher, after an ineffectual attempt to solve the problem for a class. "You may try it, Henry, and when you are through, bring me the slate."

Henry Boynton was good in arithmetic, but he could not bring an answer like that in the book, though it differed from the teacher's answer.

"I can't do it," said Henry. "My answer is not like that in the book."

"Bring your slate to me," said the teacher

Henry carried his slate to the teacher, who examined his work without pointing out an error, but adding .

"The answer in the book must be wrong."

Here James interrupted by saying :

"I did it once."

"And did you get the same answer as the book ? "

"Yes, sir, I think so "

"Let me see you do it, and then bring your slate to me."

James went to work in his earnest way, and solved the problem very readily.

"I've done it," said James, carrying his slate to the teacher.

The latter closely examined his solution of the problem, and found it to be correct, agreeing exactly with the textbook.

"It is true, James, you have performed it," said the teacher, with evident mortification, which the larger scholars enjoyed. It was fun for them to have James beat the master. They had an exalted opinion of James's ability . . . . boy who was a match for the master was a prodigy in their view. They looked up to him with a kind of reverence, though he was their companion.

We must not forget to mention one book that he read during that winter, " Robinson Crusoe." We know not how it came into his hands, but he obtained it in some way, and read it twice through. Flat on his face before the blazing fire, he read the volume hour after hour, and wondered over it. He was very fond of reading about adventures ; but this book surpassed anything of the kind he had ever read.

" I wish this book belonged to me," he said to his mother one day.

" If you read it much more, its contents will belong to you," his mother replied.

" I wish I *owned* it, then," added James.

" I wish you did, too," responded his mother. " What is there about it that interests you so much, my son ? "

" It's splendid," was James's answer. " I never read such an interesting book. I could read it ten times over, and not get tired of it   I wonder if there are any more books like it."

" I suppose there are, if we knew where to find them," Mrs. Garfield answered.

" I'd be willing to *hunt* one while for them," said James

The impression made by that book upon his mind was never effaced   It not only sharpened his appetite yet more for reading, if that were possible, but it set him to inquiring more than ever concerning books which he had never seen.

Some time after this, his cousin, William Boynton, came into possession of a copy of Josephus, and he shared the pleasure of reading it with James. They read it, by the hour together, and they read it separately, too, over and over. When the winter school opened, the boys asked the teacher for the privilege of reading it in the class, for their reading lesson ; and the privilege was granted. All winter they read it in school, in addition to the hours they read it out of school. When James was through with that volume, and ready to take up another, he could repeat pages of it.

The following summer two incidents occurred that illustrate the character of James at that time. The first was a proposition from a companion, whose name we do not know, but whom we will call David, to visit a mutual acquaintance in a distant part of the township, on the Sabbath.

" Not on Sunday," said James.

" Why ? "

" Because it is not right."

" If you and I do nothing worse than that, Jim, we shall be pretty good fellers."

" We should not be any better certainly, for doing that."

" Nor any worse, in my opinion," rejoined David.

" My mother would not consent to it," continued James.

" I don't know whether mine would, and I don't care ; I shan't ask her," said David.

" I never should go anywhere against my mother's advice," continued James. " I know what she thinks of the Sabbath, and I respect her feelings I shan't go on Sunday."

" And you can't go on any other day, because you have so much to do," added David ; " so we must give up going at all, for all that I see."

" Rather than go on a Sunday, I shall not go at all," was James's emphatic reply. " But it is not certain that we can never go on another day. Wait and see."

" I guess it will be *wait*," answered David, sarcastically, " and keep waiting, and take it out in waiting."

" Well, I shall wait a good while before I shall go on Sunday " added James. " If I had no scruples of my own about it, I could take no comfort, feeling that I went against mother's wishes."

This emphatic refusal ended the matter. It was a fair illustration of the frank and open way that James had of doing things. There was no artifice about him, no double-dealing or deceitfulness. He would not consent to wrong-doing, even to please his best friend He never resorted to subterfuges to excuse himself when tempted to do wrong He spoke right out plainly and bluntly, as if it were the only way to speak. Not that he seemed to have a higher standard of morality than others, but it was his nature to be frank and honest with every one, and he wanted others to be so towards him Companions always knew just where to find him at all times. They knew that he could not be counted upon for questionable practices at all. He was full of life, and enjoyed a good time as much as any boy in town, ready for a frolic at all suitable times, social, witty, and sharp ; but he could not be persuaded or cajoled into wrong-doing. He showed his colours at once.

The other incident illustrates his kindness to animals. The old cat and James were particular friends, and appeared to understand each other perfectly He was in the garden with James one day, in whose society he seemed to find real pleasure. The same boy we have spoken of, David, came along, and observing the cat, began pelting him with stones, frightening puss so that he fled to the house. David might as well have pelted James with stones. Stone his cat, and he was stoned.

"That's outrageous ! " exclaimed James.

" Only a cat," answered David.

" Only *cruelty*, that will stone a cat," responded James.

" I didn't think it was your cat."

" It don't make any difference whose cat it is ; a cat is a cat."

"And a rat is a rat," added David, designing to mak fun of the affair.

"I can't bear to see an animal abused," continued James.

"I didn't hit him," pleaded David.

"No thanks to you; you meant to hit him. You frightened him half out of his wits."

"He hasn't any wits to be frightened out of," retorted David. "Nothing but a cat."

"And so you might abuse any animal in the world, and say, ' Nothing but a dog ' , ' Nothing but a horse ' ; ' Nothing but an ox.' I wouldn't abuse any creature so."

"I don't think you would, Jim. You are too tender-hearted for that. A mouse could play on your chin safely if he only knew you."

"He wouldn't play on yours, Dave, if he knew *you*, that's certain. It would be the most dangerous place he could find."

"Well, Jim, ask pardon of your cat for me, will you ? I'm sorry that I offended his majesty. I'll befriend cats for ever now." And David went on his way, leaving James to his reflections.

This was another good trait of James's kindness to animals. He was as kind to them as he was to human beings. He could see no reason for abusing any creature, however insignificant. Abuse was cruelty, in his view.

Still another incident may be rehearsed here as well as any place. James was a boy of spirit, though he was neither pugnacious nor malicious. He wanted to see the rights of the smallest boy respected, and he would contend for it if necessary. In school there was a fatherless boy, like himself, and no big brother to take his part. Some of the larger boys were in the habit of teasing him, and James declared that it should stop. James was older than the boy, though not as old as the boys who teased him

"It's too bad," exclaimed James; "and if you tease him any more, you tease me."

"Tease you it is, then," answered one of the boys, with a motion and remark indicating the attempt.

"Just as you like," continued James. "You can operate on me; but you shan't on that little fellow, unless you are stronger than I am. Take boys of your size, or none."

"You are mightily taken with that little chap," said another boy. "*I* don't see anything so very interesting about him."

"Well, I do, he hain't got any father nor big brother, and I'll stand in the place of both to him in this school."

"Daddy Jim and Brother Jim it is then," exclaimed a large boy, aiming to make all the fun of it possible.

"Yes: anything you please, so long as you don't run on him," answered James pleasantly. "I can stand it as long as you can."

And thus he shamed the teasing of the little fellow out of the larger boys, exhibiting both courage and principle in the defence of the helpless lad. Taking advantage of the weak, poor, and friendless, appealed to his higher and better nature.

November came, and the harvesting was done. The carpenter came also, saying:

"Another barn, James. Want another job?"

"Yes, aching for one," James replied.

"All ready for you: can you begin right off?"

"To-morrow, if you want."

"You are a minute-man, I see"

"I s'pose I am, though I don't know what that is."

"Men, in the Revolution, who stood ready to defend their country at a moment's warning were minute-men."

"Then I'm a minute-man; I'm ready any minute for building a barn."

"I want to put this one through in a hurry."

"Whose is it?"

" Bernard's, yonder "

" Oh, over there ? "

It was further for James to travel than the other barn was ; but it was all the same to him.

" It's goin' to be a larger barn."

" Much larger ? "

" No , just enough to call it larger, that's all. See you to-morrow morning." And Mr Treat hastened back, adding, as he turned to go : " Same pay as before."

The details must be omitted. The building of this barn provided James with additional facilities for learning how to frame a building ; and he improved the opportunity. In many things he was able to go ahead without depending upon his employer, the progress which he made in building the first barn being of great service to him in building the second.

" Not a word of fault to find with you, James," remarked his employer, when the barn was completed. " Work comes easy to you, and you earn your money "

" I mean to know how to frame a barn yet," answered James.

" Then you don't think you can quite do it yet ? "

" Hardly," said James.

" Pluck and brains will accomplish it, and you have both," added Mr. Treat, intending to pay his young *employé* a fine compliment.

" I'll give you another chance at it one of these days," Mr. Treat added. " I owe you fifteen dollars, just " And he counted out the money, and passed it to the happy boy.

" There ! the highest price I said, fifty cents a day ; and I'm well satisfied, too," Mr. Treat continued

James had just passed his thirteenth birthday, and he was developing rapidly into a stalwart boy for one of his age. The winter school opened, and he attended as usual although he had about all there was in the textbooks at his tongue's end. He could repeat a good part of his reading-book, and perform the problems in arithmetic with his eyes shut, yet it was excellent discipline to go over them again.

That winter he found somewhere another volume to read that greatly interested him. It was next to " Robinson Crusoe " in his estimation. The book was " Alonzo and Melissa," well suited to fascinate a boy like him. Once reading did not satisfy him. There were two books now that towered above all the books he ever read, and he wondered if there were any more like them—if so, where ? On the whole it was a profitable winter to him ; and he began to feel that he could do better for his mother than to run her little farm. Just before the close of school, he said to his mother :

" I've been thinking that I can do better for you than to stay on the farm. I could get twelve dollars a month to go out to work "

" Perhaps so," was all his mother said.

" You could keep a cow, hire a man to plant what is necessary, and take care of it ; and it wouldn't cost a quarter as much as I can earn," James continued

" And it would be four times as hard for you," responded Mrs. Garfield. " It's better for a boy like you to go to school while he can, and not labour all the time. Boys should not work too hard."

" I knew what you'd say ; I've learned that by heart," replied James. " But I was never hurt by work yet, and I never expect to be "

" Nevertheless, you may be," responded his mother.

" A feller may as well be earning something when he can , there's need enough of it in this part of the world," added James.

" In this part of the world ! " repeated his mother ; " you don't seem to have so high an opinion of this part of the country as you might. What's the trouble with it ? "

"No trouble as I know, only a feller has a better chance in some other places."

"Better chance for what ? " asked his mother.

"To get a living, or make a man, or most anything," answered James.

"There's a better chance to get an education in some other places, I admit ; and I hope you will enjoy it some day," continued Mrs. Garfield

James knew much about the world now. All that Morse's Geography could teach him about his own and other countries he knew thoroughly. He had picked up much information, too, about New England and the State of New York ; and he understood very well that the opportunities for a boy to earn money, study, and to rise in the world, were greater in many other parts of the country. It was easy to discover the aspirations of a noble spirit in the boy. He was beginning to feel cramped and confined on the little farm. His soul was outgrowing its sphere of childhood, and was waiting to plume its wings for higher flights The young eagle was getting ready to leave the nest, and soar.

His mother did not look with favour upon the boy's suggestions. James must be content to live upon the farm for a while. Providence would open the way out into the broad world at the right time. "Wait for Providence."

So James suppressed ambitious desires, and contented himself to remain at home, running the farm, working out by the day for the farmers, as opportunity offered, as well as working at barn-building. Before he was fifteen years old, Mr. Treat gave him an opportunity to work on three more barns and one shed, so that he did learn how to frame a barn, and was really a better carpenter at fifteen years of age than some of the carpenters in that region who claimed to have learned the trade. Being able to turn his hand to any kind of labour, he found ⋯ ⋯ ⋯ ⋯ ⋯ for play.

James was as fond of sports as any other boy; and his genial nature, ready wit, and gentlemanly bearing united to make him popular with pleasure-seekers. Without him they had dull times. His presence added a charm to the social circle.

As already intimated, he had grown into a large, strong boy; as Mr. Treat sometimes said, "as strong as an ox." He could lift as much as the strongest man in the vicinity, although he was not agile. He was too large and heavy to be an expert at jumping or running; but his practical wisdom was as manifest in sports as it was in works. He was such after he had passed his fourteenth birthday—more advanced and efficient than most youths of that day at eighteen.

We shall close this chapter with a single incident, that occurred in the winter after James's fourteenth birthday.

"Jim, will you go to Cleveland with me to-morrow?" inquired Edwin Mapes of James, as he called at Mrs. Garfield's in the evening. "I'm goin' for father to-morrow."

"I don't know; perhaps I will," replied James, in a hesitating manner, as if it were doubtful.

"Don't know? Who does know if you don't? Come, go; I want company," pleaded Edwin.

"You'll have a cold ride," suggested James.

"Not very cold if *you* go," responded Edwin. "You and I can keep warm anywhere in Ohio. Say yes, and I'll be off."

"Be off! what's your hurry? Sit down, and I will tell you in the course of half an hour," responded James, teasingly.

Edwin took a seat, whereupon James added:

"Yes, I'll go, and be glad to; start as early as you please."

"I shan't start very early; no particular need of it. Goin' ov... and back without stopping long,' added Edwin.

On the following day the two boys drove to Cleveland together. Mr. Mapes's horse was a capital roadster, and Edwin understood well how to drive him, and James could ride as fast as Edwin could drive, without raising a serious objection. So their trip was quick, and devoid of monotony.

On their return, a rough, bloated fellow rode up behind them, and shouted with a volley of oaths .

" Out the way, boys, I'm in a hurry ! " and suiting his motions to the word, he turned out to drive by them.

" No, you don't," shouted Edwin, as he drew the reins tight, and gave his horse a cut with the whip , and almost side by side the two teams flew along the road for a half-mile, the whisky-soaked traveller pouring out oaths at the boys with every blow of his whip.

" Come on," shouted Edwin to the fellow, at the same time beckoning with his hand to him when he had left him ten or fifteen rods in the rear. " Come on ! Come on ! "

They were too far in advance to hear his voice, but they could see the fellow's very expressive gesticulations with his fist. James enjoyed the victory hugely, and shook his sides with laughter.

" He told us to get out of the way, and we have," was about all the remark that James made during the contest.

They drove on at a very good pace three or four miles, when they came up to a little country inn, with which both of them were familiar.

" Let's go in and warm," proposed James ; " my feet are cold as ice."

" Agreed," answered Edwin ; and turned the horse into the shed. In less than five minutes they were standing before the landlord's fire. In less than five minutes more the enraged man who tried to run by them drove up and entered.

" I've a good will to thrash you boys," he shouted at the top of his voice.

The boys were very much surprised to see him in such a passion.

" What you going to thrash us for ? " answered Edwin.

" Thrash you for, you insulting scamps ? I'll let you know," and he shook his fist in the liveliest manner, at the same time belching forth a volley of oaths, that we omit, since they did not embellish his language, though they contributed some force to it.

" Why didn't you let me go by, you young rascals ? " he continued.

" You had plenty of room to pass ; as much room as we had, and the same right to the road," replied James coolly.

" But I couldn't," the fellow bellowed, " you good-for-nothing brats ! "

" That's not our fault," returned James. " Better blame your horse."

The latter sentence had a ring of sarcasm in it, especially as the boys laughed when it was spoken , and the brutal man stormed again, and swore he would thrash them.

" Better thrash *me* first," said James, straightening himself up to his full height, and appearing more like a strong man than a boy of fourteen years. The bully looked at him for a moment, as if querying whether his antagonist was not a man after all.

" Why take you first ? " he said, apparently somewhat cowed.

" Because you will never want to thrash him afterwards," answered James, in the most thundering voice he could roll out. The bully turned upon his heels jumped into his carriage, and drove on.

James and Edwin were soon on their way home, their conversation being upon the unusual experience of the last hour.

" I was glad that you scared him so," remarked Edwin. " He was a regular coward."

" I knew he was a coward when we were talking with him," James replied. " If I hadn't, I should have kept still. I don't like to get into trouble with anybody."

" I thought you was terribly courageous, for you," remarked Edwin. " You roared at him like thunder. Your big voice is enough to frighten any *coward*."

" I hope that it will never frighten anybody else," was the only reply that James made.

James was in no sense a bully. Nor was he given to brag. There was no boy in Orange township more gentlemanly and considerate than he ; none more averse to pugilistic contests. At the same time he would stand up for his rights and the rights of others. He would defend his companions, too, with great courage, if they were in the right. If they were in the wrong, he would not defend them at all ; and would frankly state his reason. These facts sufficiently explain his encounter with the bully at the hotel.

X

A BLACK-SALTER

THE following colloquy will explain a matter that must not be omitted

"I have come again for James," said Mr. Smith, entering Mrs. Garfield's cottage. "Can't get along without him when we weed the peppermint"

"Well, James will be glad to help you if he can, but he is pretty busy now on the farm," answered Mrs Garfield.

"Perhaps he can squeeze out two or three days now, and that will help me through," continued Mr. Smith. "I shall have twenty boys in the gang."

"I should think that was enough without James," remarked Mrs Garfield.

"It's altogether too many if I *don't* have him," replied Mr. Smith "You see, the boys do as well again when James leads them. Somehow he has wonderful influence over them"

"I didn't know that," remarked Mrs. Garfield.

"Well, it's true ; and if you should see him leading off, and interesting them by stories, anecdotes, and fun, you'd be surprised. He is a fast worker, and all the boys put in and work as hard as they can to keep up, that they may hear his stories. The boys think the world of him."

"I'm glad to hear such good things of him," remarked Mrs. Garfield. "I'm willing that he should help you if he can."

"I shouldn't mind paying him something extra if he

will come," Mr Smith continued. " I can afford to do that. Each boy does more work, and where there's twenty of them, it's considerable in my pocket."

" Well, you can find James,—he is somewhere on the farm ; and I'm willing he should go if you can fix it with him," said Mrs. Garfield.

Mr. Smith went in search of James, and found him hard at work in the field. Making known his errand James could not see how it was possible for him to go, at least for a week. But Mr. Smith soon removed his objections, and arranged for him to come the next day.

This Mr. Smith was a farmer, and his land, on the Chagrin Flats, was adapted to the cultivation of peppermint, which he raised for the market in large quantities It was necessary to keep it thoroughly weeded, and for this purpose he employed a gang of boys at different times in the season. James had served him more than once in that work, and the shrewd farmer had noticed that the gang would try to keep up with James, so as to hear his stories and interesting conversation. James was a capital story-teller, and all that he ever read or studied was in his head. His remarkable memory served him a good purpose in company, whether in the field of peppermint or elsewhere. He could recall almost any anecdote that he had ever heard, and could relate whatever he had learned about his own or other countries from Morse's Geography. Add to this his jovial nature, his conversational powers, and his singular tact, and we can readily understand how he could " lead the gang."

So James became general of the peppermint brigade for a few days, to accommodate Mr. Smith and again his precocity and large acquisitions of knowledge enabled him to lead them to victory over the weeds. The weeds melted away before their triumphant march, as the rebels disappeared before the Ohio Forty-second Regiment, sixteen years afterwards

We said that James assisted Mr Trent to build a shed,

in addition to the several barns. The shed was the last building on which he worked for Mr. Treat, and it was about ten miles from home, near Cleveland. It was an addition to quite a large pot-ashery, the largest in all that region. A pot-ashery was an establishment containing vats for leeching ashes, and large kettles for boiling the lye, reducing it to potash, which, in its crude state, was called " black-salts " The manufacturer of the article was called a " black-salter." The farmers in the region, when they cleared land, drew the logs and branches of trees together into huge piles, and burned them, for the ashes they could collect therefrom, and which they sold to the black-salters.

The black-salter for whom Mr. Treat built the shed took a great fancy to James It was rather singular that he did , for he was a rough, uncultivated man himself. Yet the politeness, tact, and brightness of James captivated the old man. Before the shed was completed, he resolved that he would have that uncommon boy in his employ, if possible. One day he took James aside, and said to him :

" How'd yer like to come and work for me ? "

James was just fifteen years old at the time The question was unexpected to James, and he hesitated.

" I want jist sich a hand as yer are in my business," the salter, whose name was Barton, continued. " I reckon yer can figger 'nough for me "

" I don't know about it," finally James replied : " it is something I have not thought about. When do you want me ? "

" Jist as soon as yer can ; yer can't come ter quick."

" I couldn't agree to come until I have seen my mother about it, anyway," continued James " Perhaps she will object."

" That's the sorter boy I s'posed yer was, to mind yer mother. I like yer all the better for that."

" How long will you want me ? "

" Jist as long as yer'll stay , as long as yer live, maybe."

" How much will you pay me ? "

" I'll give yer fourteen dollars a month, and that's two dollars extra pay." By this Barton meant that he would pay him two dollars a month more than he was wont to pay. The offer was proof that he was amazingly pleased with James

" I will consult my mother about it as soon as I go home, and let you know," said James. He would not go home until the shed was completed He boarded with Barton. But the shed was almost finished : two days more would complete it.

" How shall I know yer'll come ? " said Barton, when the shed was done, and James was about returning home.

" If mother is willing I should engage, I will come next Monday. If you don't see me next Monday, you may know that I shall not come."

" That's business," Barton replied " Tell yer mother I kin do the right thing by yer."

It was a rare offer to a boy fifteen years old—fourteen dollars a month. James regarded it in that light. And then, it was constant work as long as he pleased to continue ; that was a great consideration. One hundred and sixty-eight dollars a year ! The thought of so much pay elated him very much.

" I have a chance to go right to work, mother, and work as many months as I please, at fourteen dollars a month," said James, as soon as he reached home

" Where ? " inquired his mother, with an air of surprise

" For Mr. Barton, the black-salter "

" I don't think it is the right sort of business for you, James," replied his mother.

" It's the right sort of pay though," James answered. " But why is it not a good business for me, mother ? "

" Because a rough class of men carry on the business, and you will be exposed to many evils " his mother said.

"Exposed to evils enough anywhere," remarked James. "But I don't propose to attend to the evils, but to my work."

"I have no doubt of that, my son. Your intentions are good enough ; but you may be enticed away, for all that."

"I must be pretty weak, if that's the case."

"We are all weaker than we think we are. 'Let him that thinketh he standeth take heed lest he fall.' We all have reason to adopt that advice."

"Then you won't give your consent for me to go ?" James said, inquiringly.

"I don't say that."

"What do you say, then ?"

"I say that you had better consider the matter well before you take so important a step."

"Can't think of it a great while, for I have promised to begin work for him next Monday, if I begin at all."

"As soon as that ?"

"Yes ; and it looks to me as if the time had come for me to give up the farm, that I may earn more for you."

"What did Mr. Treat say about it ?"

"He said nothing about it, because he knew nothing about it. I didn't tell him about it."

"I suppose you must go out into the world some time, and perhaps now is the time."

"You told me, once, to wait for Providence to open the door," continued James ; "and if Providence didn't open this door, then I shall never know when Providence does open the door."

The truth was, Mrs. Garfield half thought that Providence would not open the door of a black-salter's establishment to her son ; but she did not say so. She smiled at James's application of her teachings about Providence, and remarked :

"Perhaps Providence did open this door. If you go to Mr. Barton's, and resist all temptations to evil, and maintain your good character, that will be proof that Providence opened this door. The proof of it depends on yourself."

"Then you give your consent?" said James.

"Yes, I give my consent, and hope it will turn out for the best."

Barton was a happy man on the following Monday, when James presented himself at his door, with all his worldly possessions tied up in a pocket-handkerchief.

"Yer've come," he said. "Yer kin put your duds in yer sleeping-room;" and he showed him where he would lodge, and then proceeded to the manufactory for work.

The establishment was a nasty place, and the business, or much of it, was dirty. Shovelling ashes, attending to the boilers, and disposing of the black-salts, was not an inviting business. However, James did not have the dirtiest part of the work to do, unless it was occasionally. He kept the books, waited on men who delivered ashes at the establishment, paying their bills, and he waited on customers also, acting as salesman. He did other things when necessary, always improving his time, and looking after the establishment, as if he were Barton's son. He was the first one at the ashery in the morning, and the last one to leave at night. Barton soon learned to trust him with implicit confidence, and a father could not have been kinder to the boy than he was.

One day a man brought a load of ashes, saying, "There are twenty-five bushels." James had not been at the establishment long before he resolved to measure all ashes purchased as they were unloaded. Mr. Barton usually took them for the number of bushels claimed. James directed the men in the ashery to measure the load in question as it was unloaded, and he kept tally. There were scarcely more than twenty-two bushels.

"Only twenty-two bushels, sir," said James, to the owner.

"There were twenty-five bushels according to my measure," said the man.

"And twenty-two according to mine," replied James. "I will pay you for twenty-two bushels—no more."

"I think you made a mistake," remarked the man.

"If there was any mistake, I think you made it," retorted James. "Three heads are better than one, and three of us attended to the measuring. Shall I pay you for twenty-two bushels?"

"Yes, pay away," the man answered, sulkily.

Barton came in just then, when James told him what had happened, and afterwards he told him further, that there was a great deal of cheating practised upon him, and it was quite time for his interests to be looked after more closely. All this served to increase Barton's confidence in James.

The men with whom James had to do about the establishment were about as his mother had supposed— a rough, wicked class. But James had nothing to do with them except in the business, and they made no impression upon him as to weakening his principles. Most of them were terribly profane, and one day James interrupted one of them, saying:

"Jake, what makes you swear so? You are awful. What good does it do you?"

"I s'pose it gits some of yer bad stuff out of me," was Jake's prompt reply.

"If that is the case, all the bad stuff ought to have been out of you long ago; you have sworn enough to empty yourself."

"Nary bisness of yers, any way," the swearer answered.

"I should think that the more bad stuff you let out, the more there was left, Jake," continued James. "I don't want you should empty any more of it about me."

"What is't to yer, anyway?" answered the godless fellow, disp'a·d at 1 ·i ·'e.

I

" It is a very bad habit, Jake, as you know," answered James. " It does you no good, and it is very unpleasant to many persons who hear you."

" Stop your ears, then," said Jake, angrily.

" There is no use being mad over it, Jake. I don't like to hear your profanity; and now suppose you just please me a little, and not spill any more of the stuff near me."

Jake laughed, and turned to his work. He could not be very angry with James, for he thought too much of him. In this frank and honest way James dealt with the men. There was no danger that he would be enticed away by that class of men. Another danger, however, met him in the house, and for a time it was an unsettled question whether Providence or Satan opened that door. If his good mother had been cognizant of what was going on, she would have discovered ample reason for her apprehensions

A book-loving boy like James would not be long in a strange place without finding all the books there were, so books were among the first things that attracted his attention in Barton's house. There were " The Pirate's Own Book," Jack Halyard," Lives of Eminent Criminals," " The Buccaneers of the Caribbean Seas," plundering a Spanish galleon; and perhaps some others of the same character. The adventure and marvellous exploits contained in these volumes were suited to fire his imagination and to inflame his heart. He was thus introduced to a new experience altogether, more perilous to him than a regiment of coarse, brutal men. He made books his most intimate companions, and trusted them with entire confidence. He could read deceitful and designing men around him, and bluff them off; but he took the volumes that he read directly to his heart, and. communed with them, as friend communes with fri

ing was

devoured, causing Mr Barton to remark to others of the
" great scholar " in his employ. Barton himself did not
understand but that the volumes in his house were as
safe for a boy to read as the Bible ; nor did he care
much. His daughter had purchased these books from
time to time, and read them, too, and why should he,
ignorant man that he was, appreciate the tendency of
such reading ? His daughter was a young woman
grown, possessing considerable native ability, but little
culture, though she was the belle of the town. She
wrote poetry occasionally for a paper that had been
started in Cleveland, a circumstance that gave her some
notoriety among the people

" I see you like reading," she said to James one evening, when he was wrapt over one of these novels.

" There's nothing I like better. I never read books
like these before," he answered.

" They are very interesting books, I think," she added.

" You've read them, have you ? "

" Yes ; I bought them, and I have read them all more
than once."

" I think I shall read them more than once. I'm glad
I came here to live These long evenings would be dull
for me without books "

" You'd have to go to Damon's with the men, evenings, if you had no books," the young woman suggested.
Damon's was the store where the post-office was kept ;
and there the male portion of the population were wont
to congregate in the evening to talk politics, nonsense,
and lewdness, according to circumstances. It was
a motley crowd, whose appearance would have terrified
Mrs. Garfield, could she have seen them ; and yet her
James was in worse company, for him, every evening
poring over those fascinating and corrupting books. He
did not know his danger, and so his danger was greater.
To the young woman's suggestion James replied :

" I wouldn't go there '

" Why ? " she asked.

" I don't like that sort of company."

" It's not very attractive, I think," she conceded.

" My mother would be frightened to see me in such company."

If James had only known, he might have said, with equal truth, perhaps, that his mother would be frightened to see him in the company of such books But he had no thoughts in that direction. He had become infatuated over these mute, yet loquacious, companions.

When the family retired at night, James would take his light and book and go to his room, but not to bed. Twelve o'clock often found him reading, almost oblivious to the cold that pinched his flesh and made him shiver. But his young blood seemed to be warmed by the excitement and enthusiasm begotten by his reading

One night he retired, excited and wakeful As he lay musing, he said, within himself :

" I will see some of the world yet. I shan't always follow this business."

Then he turned over to invite sleep, but was still wakeful.

" A black-salter ! " he continued   " It is not the sort of work for me. Can't see much of the world, tied down here "

He turned over again, restless and nervous ; but sleep was chary.

" I should like to be a sailor, and see more of the world ; go to other countries, and see the great cities ; it's splendid," his mind said ; and he was not sleepy at all.

" What's the use of staying at home always, and seeing nothing, when the great world is open ? I mean to try it some time "

And so he went on discussing the matter within himself, and reasoning away many of the staid and valuable ideas that had him nubia a

" I wonder what mother will say to it ? Women are always afraid, and want to keep their boys at home all the time. I s'pose she will make a terrible fuss about it; but I mean to see more of the world, somehow "

Sleep finally came to his relief, and he dreamed of ships bearing him over the ocean to other lands, where fairy-like cities delighted his vision ; and other enrapturing scenes, that exist only in dreams, made him thrice happy. It was quite evident now that Satan was opening the door of the future wide, instead of that Providence whose watch and care his good mother had invoked.

He continued a faithful labourer to Mr Barton, attending to the details of the business with promptness, and securing his love and confidence Barton watched him with pride, and once he said to him ·

" Yer kin read, yer kin write, and yer are death on figgers ; so stay with me, keep my 'counts, and tend to the saltery. I'll find yer, and glad to give yer the fourteen dollars a month. "

" I want to be a sailor," replied James.

" A sailor ! " exclaimed Barton, in amazement. " Yer don't mean it ! There's too much of yer for that business. What's put that idee into your head ? "

" I want to see more of the world than I can see in Ohio," answered James. " It will be dull business to make black-salts all my days."

" We'el, yer will never go to sea if yer take my advice. Stay here, and some day yer'll have a saltery of yer own."

" I don't want one," replied James. " I'd rather have something else."

" My word for it," continued Barton ; " yer are too good a boy to spile on the seas. Stay with me, and some day yer'll have a saltery as big as our'n."

" I wouldn't spend my life in this business for a dozen salteries as big as this," replied James.

Barton was exceedingly afraid that he should lose his

excellent *employé*, and so he endeavoured to make his position as agreeable as possible. His praise, too, was not stinted at all.

"Yer are a cute boy, good at readin', good at figgers, good at work, good at everything," he would say ; "stay with me, and I'll do we'el by yer."

James continued through the winter, until April opened, when the following incident terminated his career as a salter.

Barton's daughter had a beau, and he came to see her one night when James was working over some difficult problems in arithmetic. There was but one room below in the farm-house, and that was a very large one, so the young couple occupied a distant corner, James and the "old folks" sitting near the fire-place. James took in the situation well for a boy of his years, and designed to retire as soon as the girl's father and mother did ; but he became so absorbed in his arithmetic that he did not notice they had left the room, until the impatient girl startled him by the remark :

"I should think it was time for *hired servants* to be abed "

James's anger was aroused. He looked at her fiercely for a moment, but said nothing. Then he took his candle and started for his room, his very tread on the floor showing that the invincible spirit within him was thoroughly stirred. The coast was now clear for the matrimonial aspirants, though at quite a loss to the establishment, as the sequel will show.

James could not sleep. The sarcastic girl had knocked sleep out of him.

"*Hired Servant !*" he repeated to himself, over and over. "And that's all I am in this concern—'a hired servant.' I'll not be a 'servant' long, let them know." And he tried to compose himself, and forget his trouble by going to sleep, but in vain.

'Hired servant!' The words kept bidding.

He kept repeating it, in spite of himself, and the more he repeated it, the more his feelings were harrowed.

"'Hired servant!' I can rise above that, I know, and I *will*. I'll not stay in this place another day, let what will happen. I'll leave to-morrow. The trollope shall see whether I'm a '*hired servant*' or not. *I'll hire* servants yet."

The fact was, that unexpected appellation proved to James just what the kick in the stomach which the schoolmate gave to Newton did. The kick made a scholar out of Newton; the girl's remark aroused latent aspirations in James's heart to be somebody Years afterwards, when James had become a man, and was battling with the stern realities of life, he said, "That girl's cutting remark proved a great blessing to me. I was too much annoyed by it to sleep that night; I lay awake under the rafters of that old farm-house, and vowed, again and again, that I *would* be somebody; that the time should come when the girl would not call me a '*hired servant.*'"

The bad books, however, very nearly turned the aspirations awakened into the way to ruin instead of honour.

James arose early in the morning, dressed himself, and tied up his few possessions in a bundle, and presented himself to Mr Barton for settlement.

"I'm going to leave to-day," he said.

If he had fired off a pistol at his employer the latter would not have been more astounded.

"Goin' ter leave!" he exclaimed.

"Yes; I'm done working at this business."

"Hi, Jim, yer can't mean it."

"I do mean it," answered James; and he adhered to his purpose against the entreaties and good promises of his employer, and that, too, without saying a word to him about the "hired servant." The upshot was that Mr. Barton paid him off, and James was at home before noon.

XI

A WOOD-CHOPPER

" HOME for good ! " said James to his mother, on entering the house. " Got enough of saltering."

" I am glad to see you, James ; but what's the matter now ? " his mother replied.

" Matter enough. I've come home to stay."

" I'm glad of that."

" I can be somebody if I try, instead of ' a hired servant,' " continued James, speaking the last two words contemptuously.

" What now ? Have you had any trouble with Mr. Barton ? "

" None at all ; he is one of the kindest men in the world I shouldn't want to work for a better man."

" What, then, is to pay ? " urged the mother, earnestly.

James rehearsed to her the experience of the previous evening, and his determination to quit the business, together with Mr. Barton's disappointment at his leaving, and his entreaties for him to stay. Mrs. Garfield listened attentively to the recital, which closed by his saying :

" There are fifty-six dollars for you, mother."

" You are indeed thoughtful of your mother, and the money will add many comforts to our home," replied Mrs. Garfield ; " but did you not act rather hastily ? "

" Hastily or not, I've acted, and that is the end of it," replied James " I didn't exactly want to give up the job ., ~ · · . : · . ., ., · tort I h iv. "

" I should think much of Mr. Barton's kindness and his disappointment," suggested his mother.

" And minded nothing about the insulting girl, I s'pose ? "

" I shouldn't care for her. I don't suppose she meant any evil by her remark. Besides, it is not dishonourable to be a hired servant, especially if you are a good one," added his mother.

" That is not the thing, mother. I don't think it is dishonourable to be a ' hired servant ' It was the girl's insulting way of saying it, and it stirred me up to want to be somebody in the world, and I mean to be."

" I hope it will all turn out for the best, my son ; and I believe that Providence will overrule it for good."

" I must look out for another job, now," remarked James.

" And not stay at home ? "

" No , I can earn more for you away "

" Well, as you think best," said his mother. " I dare say you will have plenty of chances "

" I would like to go to sea, mother," added James, hesitatingly.

If he had struck his mother in her face she would not have been more shocked.

" Why, James ! " she exclaimed

" I've been thinking about it," James continued.

" Thinking about it, James ! What has got into you ? You shock me."

" I don't wish to go against your will, mother." James added.

" You will go against my will if you ever go to sea, James. Be a salter, or anything else, rather than a sailor.

" Why mother ? "

" You certainly can never be ' somebody,' as you say, by going to sea."

" I can be a commander of a vessel, perhaps, and some day I may own one who know "

"Who knows what you wouldn't be, James, if you should become a sailor? Say no more about such a step, if you want to make your mother happy."

The subject was dropped there, and James proceeded to look about the farm. For several days he busied himself in putting things in order, awaiting work elsewhere. At length he heard that his uncle, living at Newburg, near Cleveland, wanted to hire wood-choppers. His uncle was clearing a large tract of forest near the line of Independence township. After conferring with his mother, and seeking the advice of his uncle, Amos Boynton, he decided to go to Newburg. His mother was quite willing that he should go there, because his sister Mehetabel had married, and was living there, and James could board with her. Three days after James presented himself at his uncle's door in Newburg, making known his errand.

"Glad to see you, James," was his uncle's cordial welcome. "How you grow! almost a man now! Yes, I've work enough to be done at chopping, if men will only do it."

"I like to chop," interrupted James.

"A great many don't," replied his uncle; "and chopping wood is pretty hard work—about as hard as any work there is"

"I don't think so," remarked James. "I don't get so tired chopping as I have been sometimes planing boards."

"Well, let's see," continued his uncle; "how much of a job at chopping can you undertake? It's coming warm weather, and you don't want to chop wood when it is too hot, do you?"

"Perhaps not; I can chop two months, sure"

"Suppose you take a job of one hundred cords to cut, James, how will that do?"

"I will agree to that. How much will you pay me a cord?"

"I will give you fifty cents a cord for one hundred

cords ; and the fifty dollars shall be ready for you as soon
as the work is done. How long will you be cutting it ? "

" Fifty days," James quickly answered.

" A little longer than that, I reckon, unless you are a
mighty smart chopper," suggested his uncle. " There's a
great difference in men, and boys too, in chopping wood."

" I shall cut two cords a day, right along," said James.
" I can do it easily."

" That's pretty good chopping—better than the average by considerable," replied his uncle ; " and you are
larger and stronger than the average of choppers, I guess."

The bargain was clinched, and James passed on to
his sister's, who gave him a warm greeting, and agreed to
board him. So James was once more settled, and ready
to proceed to business. The next morning he appeared in
the *rôle* of a wood-chopper ; not a new occupation to him.

It was unfortunate for James that his work was in full
view of Lake Erie, in whose blue bosom he could see
plenty of craft sailing, at any time. The location seemed
to conspire with the bad books at Barton's to fan his
desire for a seafaring life into a flame. In the circumstances, it was not strange that James did not forget the
books he had read. He often stopped in his work to
watch a vessel gliding over the waves like a swan, and
sometimes he would seat himself upon a log to count the
sails appearing in the distance. It was a rare spectacle
to him, and his heart bounded with delight. He
cherished the secret thought that, some day, he would be
sailing over that very lake.

There were several choppers near him, one of them a
German. He was a clever man, and spoke very broken
English James thought he was a slow chopper, and
noticed that his axe did not fly briskly. At the end of
a week, however, he found that the German had cut and
corded two cords a day—just the amount he himself had
cut.

" I don't understand it," he said to his sister, on

going home "I strike two blows to the German's one and yet he has cut as many cords as I have."

"Perhaps he strikes heavier blows," suggested his sister.

"I doubt it," replied James ; "but I will find out the reason."

James was on the alert to find out the reason of the German's success. Nor was he left long in the dark. Lake Erie had no attractions for the Teutonic chopper, and so he kept steadily at his work, from morning until night, while James frequently stopped to watch the sails in the distance. The German did not strike blows so rapidly as James, nor were his blows more telling, but he was steadily at work from morning until night. James comprehended the whole, and it was a good lesson to him He took his first lesson of application and perseverance of the German wood-chopper, and reduced it to practice at once. It rather cooled his fiery ardour for the sea. He confessed to his sister that he wasted some time in watching sails on the lake. At the same time, he owned that he had a longing for the sea.

"You surprise me, James," his sister said. "I never thought that of you. You can't be in earnest, can you ? "

"I never was more in earnest in my life," answered James, coolly. "The height of my ambition is to command a ship."

"Captain Garfield ! That is the title you want to earn, is it ? " remarked his sister. "I hope you'll never get it."

"You know that was the title of one of our great ancestors, *Captain* Benjamin Garfield," suggested James.

"But he didn't get his title on a ship, by any means ; he got it in the Revolutionary war," retorted his sister. "Anything but a sailor."

"I might be something worse than that," added James.

"Not unless you become a *mean man* " quickly answered i the

"You had rather I would get the title by shooting men in war, than bringing goods from foreign ports, had you?" said James, in a sarcastic manner.

"I rather you would be a wood-chopper all your days than to be a sailor," was his sister's prompt reply. "I think mother would say the same. You have too much talent to throw away on the deck of a ship."

James received no encouragement from any quarter to become a sailor; and his aspirations in that direction became somewhat modified. He thought less of a sea-faring life for a time, and devoted himself to wood-chopping with commendable industry. Two cords a day were cut and piled with ease. He could have cut two cords and a half each day without lengthening his days inordinately. But he had fixed the limit when he began, and James was not the boy to change his purpose.

His sister owned a few books, and his uncle more; and, between them both, James was quite well provided with reading. A newspaper, that his uncle took, occupied his attention till each number was read through. Nor were the books objectionable, like those at Barton's They were healthy and profitable volumes for such a reader as James, who preferred a book to the society of the young men of the town, who might gather at any rendezvous. His reading, too, appeared to offset his growing desire for the sea. Engrossing his attention in the subject-matter of the books, excluded, in a measure, at least for the time, his hankering for a ship. His evenings were wholly given up to reading, some of them extending considerably beyond bed-time. The temptation to lengthen his evenings for reading he could not resist so readily as he could the temptation to lengthen the days for chopping.

James chopped the hundred cords of wood in fifty days, and received his pay, according to the contract. On paying him, his uncle said:

"I hope you will not always be a wood-chopper, James,

although it is a necessary and honourable business But you are competent to do something of more consequence. The way may open for you to get an education yet : how would you like that ? "

"I should like it," answered James, although he would have said, "I want to go to sea," if he had really dared to risk it. But he had good reason to suppose that his uncle would resolutely rebuke any such expression. So he desisted. Nor did he tell a falsehood by saying that he would like to acquire an education, for his taste was strong in that direction ; but he could discover no way into that field of clover

Bidding his uncle and sister good-bye, James returned home, and presented his mother with the balance of the fifty dollars, after paying for his board. His mother was rejoiced to see her boy, wondering all the while if his desire for a seafaring life survived. She thought it not best, however, to open a subject that was so unpleasant to her, for fear it might prove agreeable to him. Nothing was said about the sea

It was the last week in June, and James would like a job for the summer. His uncle Amos told him of a farmer, five or six miles away, who wanted to hire a man through haying and harvesting, for about four months. James went immediately to see him, bargained to work for him from July to November, four months, and accordingly took up his abode with the man on the first day of July.

A stout, muscular fellow like James was supposed to be an efficient hand in the hay-field. His employer liked his appearance, and expected much of him. Nor was he disappointed. His strength enabled him to swing a scythe and pitch hay with power, though he was a boy in age. Then he possessed a boy's pride in his strength, and delighted to astonish his employer by an exhibition of it. Boy-like, he found great pleasure i i· · ·   . · · i .   · ,i.· · · · ·.·   · ·.h).,eı ·in· t·he mowing field, sometimes cutting his corners. His power of endurance was remarkable ; and he never appeared to tire, or " play out," as the boys say.

James found no books here, or none worth mentioning. The people cared little about reading, though they were people of character. But farming was their business, and they worked early and late. When the day's work was done, they went to bed, and, at four o'clock in the morning, they were up and ready for another day's work. Thus it was through the whole busy season of the year. James kept abreast of them. " If I can't do what other folks can, I'll quit," he said to himself more than once.

Nothing unusual occurred during the four months, excepting only two incidents, which we will narrate.

James was digging potatoes in October, and putting them into a cellar. On going to the house with a load one day, he found a neighbour discussing the subject of baptism with his employer's daughter.

" Sprinkling is baptism," James heard him say. " Immersion is no more. A drop of water is as good as a fountain."

" Sprinkling is not baptism, according to Alexander Campbell," replied the young woman ; " and I don't see how it can be "

" I said, according to the Bible. I don't care a fig for Alexander Campbell," the neighbour rejoined.

" That makes your position harder to support," interrupted James, with the design of affording relief to the farmer's daughter, whom he very much respected

" What do you know about it ? " exclaimed the neighbour, somewhat annoyed at the boy's interruption " You know more about potatoes than the Scripters, according to my idee."

" You can't prove that sprinkling is baptism from the Bible," added James.

" That's all you know about it " retorted the man.

" See here," continued James, thinking he would sur-

prise the disputant by his familiarity with the Scriptures ; " how do you get along with this ? " And he
proceeded to quote from Hebrews : " Let us draw near
with a true heart, in full assurance of faith, having our
hearts sprinkled from an evil conscience."

" There, you see it says ' sprinkled,' " interrupted
the neighbour, quite elated.

" But hold on ! " replied James ; " wait and hear the
rest of it. You are in too big a hurry " And James
repeated the remainder of the text · " And our bodies
washed with pure water." He laid stress on the word
" washed," adding :

" Now tell me, if you can, how you can *wash* your
body in a drop of water."

Without waiting for a reply, he hurried away to the
potato-patch.

The other incident relates to his desire to go to sea.
He concluded to sound his employer one day, and he said :

" What do you think about my goin' to sea ? "

" Goin' to *see* what ? " answered the farmer

" To ship, and be a sailor," answered James.

"Likely story that you would undertake that business."

" I'm thinking of it."

" I guess you'll take it out in thinking."

" Honest though, I'm not joking. I want to com
mand a ship "

" Well, if you was my boy," retorted the farmer, " I
should *command* you to *shut up*. It's the last place for
you to go. Better dig potatoes all your days."

" I will shut up," repeated James, quite amused at the
farmer's decided way of opposing a seafaring life He
did not mention the subject again

James completed his four months' labour with the
farmer, for which he received twelve dollars a month—
forty eight dollars in all—with the farmer's laconic
endorsement :

" You've 1 - , L '

XII

A CANAL BOY

JAMES was restive and dissatisfied when he returned
home. His mother saw that he was uneasy, and
she feared that he was thinking about the sea. Nor
was she mistaken in her apprehensions, although she
remained silent on the subject. Thus matters continued
through the winter, James attending school and looking after the place. In the spring he worked at odd
jobs in the town, until the farm demanded his attention.
It was evident, however, that his heart was not in his
work. His thoughts were on the sea. At last he seemed
to reach a point where he could restrain his desires no
longer. It was about the first of July. He said to his
mother :

" Mother, you don't know how I long for the sea.
Why cannot I look after a place on a ship ? "

" Where do you want to ship to, James ? " his mother
replied.

This answer was unexpected. James anticipated a
direct refusal, but the answer indicated a change of
feeling in his mother, he thought ; and it encouraged
him to proceed. There was really no change in his
mother's feelings, but she was a sagacious woman, and
there was a change in her tactics.

" I'm not particular where ; I want to see something
of the world," was James's answer.

" It's rather queer for a boy of your ability not to

know where he wants to go," said his mother. " If I wanted to go somewhere, I would find out *where* in the first place. You don't care whether you go to Europe, Asia, or Africa ! "

" Not exactly that," replied James , " I would like to cross the Atlantic."

" And be sick enough of it before you got half across," remarked Mrs. Garfield. " Boys don't know what they want "

" *I* know what *I* want," retorted James , " and that is what I am trying to tell you. I want to try life on the ocean. If I don't like it, I'll give it up "

" That's not so easy. You get out to the Mediterranean, or to China, and it will not be very easy to give it up and come home. You will wish that you had taken your mother's advice." His mother said this with much feeling.

" I shall never know till I try," James continued. " But I will never go to sea, or anywhere else, unless you consent."

" Suppose you try a trip in a schooner on Lake Erie first, and see how you like it," suggested his mother. " Perhaps you won't like it. You will not be far from home then."

" Are you willing that I should do that ? " inquired James, brightening up at the prospect.

" I much rather you would do that than to cross the Atlantic, and I would give my consent to that," his mother answered, with reluctance.

" It is settled then," replied James. " I shall start for Lake Erie as soon as I can get ready."

Mrs. Garfield's tactics prevailed. She had given much thought to the subject, and had reluctantly concluded that, if worse came to worse, she would compromise with the boy, and allow him to ship on Lake Erie. She feared that his desire to become a sailor would pr · · . .··." `le .. .l 'b.i. l.· v...i·l ·ν· .i ually go to sea, any way. Perhaps, by allowing him to try life on shipboard, in a smaller way, and so near home as the familiar lake, would result in his abandoning the idea of a "life on the ocean wave" altogether.

James prepared for his departure as soon as possible; and taking what money was necessary, with his inevitable bundle, he returned his mother's kiss, but not her tears, and started for Cleveland, where he expected to ship. He walked the whole distance, seventeen miles and was in sight of the tempting sails at twelve o'clock, noon.

He proceeded directly to the wharf, and boarded the first schooner he found.

"Chance for another hand on board?" he inquired of one of the crew.

The sailor addressed answered, "The captain will soon come up from the hold."

So James waited, expecting soon to stand in the presence of a stout, gentlemanly, noble-looking man, just such a captain as he had read of in books. He did not wait long before the sailor whom he had addressed remarked ·

"The captain is coming."

James heard a tremendous noise below, as if there was trouble of some kind; and then he heard a human voice belching out most horrible oaths at somebody, or something, as if the captain of the infernal regions was approaching. He scarcely knew what to make of it. But, while he stood wondering, the captain appeared—a drunken, beastly, angry fellow—a whisky-barrel on legs, his mouth its bung-hole, pouring out the vilest stuff possible. James had seen some hard customers before, but if the pit could send up a more horrible sample of humanity from its "hold," he did not wish to meet him. James looked at the creature a moment, and the disgusting creature looked at him, when he ventured to approach him, saying, in a gentlemanly way:

" Captain ? "

" Yes ; what in h—— do you want ? "

" Do you want to hire another hand for your schooner ? "

" What if I do, you green land-lubber ? " exclaimed the captain, with another torrent of oaths. " Get off this schooner in double-quick, or I'll throw you into the dock, you impudent son of a——"

James attempted to excuse himself in a polite way, but the infuriated wretch only cursed and raved the more, swinging his fists in the most threatening manner.

" Get out, I say, or I'll be the death of you. S'pose I'd hire such a lubber and greenhorn to run my schooner ! " And the blackest oaths continued to roll out of his mouth.

The last sound of that terrible voice that lingered on James's ear, as he hurried from the craft, was that of profanity. Such a repulse he never dreamed of. He scarcely thought such a scene possible anywhere. He had read of sailors and captains, but he had never read of such a captain as that. He began to think that books are not always reliable. It was the first time he had ever stopped to think that men are not always what they are represented to be in books. The experience was a damper to his seafaring propensity. In this respect, it was a good thing for the boy. As it turned out, the drunken captain prevented him from becoming a sailor. It was a rather rough way of being turned aside from a purpose, but the roughest usage sometimes leads to the best results.

James sat down on a pile of wood to muse on the ways of the world, and to eat a lunch which he had put into his pocket on leaving home. He could not understand the philosophy of such a course as the captain pursued. He did nothing to provoke him. " He," he thought, " was provoked before I saw him ; for I heard his fearful oaths." He concluded, finally, that he did appear rather green and rough to the captain, for his clothes were countrified and worn; and perhaps he did not know exactly how to present himself to a sea captain, salter, wood-chopper, and farmer, as he was. The more he pondered, the more he found an excuse for the captain, and the less disposed he was to relinquish his purpose to be a sailor.

He ceased to muse, and walked along the wharf, perhaps not exactly satisfied what to do next. He was soon startled, however, by a voice:

"Jim! Jim!"

James turned about; the voice came from a canalboat.

"Halloo, Jim! How came you here?"

It was Amos Letcher, his cousin, who called to him from the canal boat.

"You here, Amos?" exclaimed James; and he was on board the boat in a hurry, shaking hands with his old friend and relative.

"How came you here?" inquired Amos. "The last I knew of you, you was chopping wood."

"I came over to see if I could find a chance to ship on the Lake," replied James.

"What luck?"

"Not much, yet."

"Seen anybody?"

Finally James rehearsed his experience on the schooner, to which Amos listened with a kind of comical interest.

"Hot reception," remarked Amos, after listening to the recital. "Some of the captains are hard customers, I tell you."

"Hard!" repeated James; "that is no name for that fellow. I s'pose he is human; he looks like a man, but he is more of a demon."

"You wouldn't like to ship with such a brute, would you?" Amos inquired.

"No; I'd rather chop wood."

"How would you like a canal boat?"

"I don't know; would it help me to get a place on a ship?"

"It might, some."

"Another hand wanted on this boat?" James asked.

"Yes, we want another driver."

"Where's the captain?"

"I am captain."

"You captain, Amos?" replied James, with much surprise

"Yes, I am captain; and I should be right glad to hire you"

"Driver! that is, I drive the horses?" asked James, inquiringly.

"That is just it; not so hard as chopping wood."

"Where do you go to?"

"To Pittsburg."

"What do you carry?"

"Copper ore."

"I think I will engage, Captain Letcher," continued James, repeating the title of his cousin, to see how it sounded. "How much will you pay me?"

"Twelve dollars a month; that is what we pay drivers"

"I'll take the position, Captain Letcher, and do the best I can."

"And I shan't ask you to do better than that," said Amos, as facetiously as James had repeated his title

"We start to-morrow morning," added the captain. "You will not lose much time."

"So much the better," answered James, thinking himself quite fortunate, on the whole.

The canal at that time was a great thoroughfare between Lake Erie and the Ohio River. Copper mining wa   .   and the ore was brought down to Cleveland in schooners, and from thence was taken to Pittsburg by canal. The name of the canal boat commanded by Captain Letcher was "Evening Star," and its capacity was seventy tons It was manned with two steersmen, two drivers, a bowman, and a cook, besides the captain—seven men in all. The bowman's business was to make the locks ready, and to stop the boat as it entered the lock, by throwing the bowline, that was attached to the bow of the boat, around the snubbing post. The drivers were furnished with two mules each, which were driven one before the other, one driver with his mules serving a given number of hours, then giving place to the other, and going on board with his mules

Boatmen, as a class, were rough fellows then. "Profane, coarse, vulgar, whisky-drinkers," describes them exactly. Rum and tobacco were among their necessaries of life, about as much so as bread or meat. They cared nothing for morals and religion, and often made them the butt of ridicule. The best fellow was the one who could drink the most whisky and sing the worst songs Of course, such fellows were no company for James. The contrast between him and one of his class was very marked. It was a new and hard school for him.

At sunrise on the following morning, James took his turn at mule-driving, the captain starting him off well by some instructions The boat was to pass through the first lock before James hitched on This done, and James stepped directly into the rank of mule-driver. It was going to sea on a small scale, and so there was some fascination about it And yet he was on the towpath instead of the water, except when he tumbled in. Within an hour James heard the captain: "Hi, Jim! Boat comin' Steady"

James knew it as well as the captain, and designed to pass the boat with signal success. But somehow, he

could scarcely tell how, the two drivers got their lines
tangled, interrupting the progress of the mules. The
lines were soon separated, but the impetus of Captain
Letcher's boat, in the delay, pushed it up square with
the horses, when the steersmen called out:

"Hurrah, Jim, whip up that team, or your line will
ketch on the bridge!" There was a waste-way just
ahead.

"Ay!" James answered, as he whipped the mules
into a trot.

"Steady, steady!" called the captain, fearing that
James was rushing into trouble by too much speed.
The caution was too late, however   Just as the team
reached the middle of the bridge the lines tightened,
and jerked driver and mules into the canal.

"Quick! help!" shouted the captain, and every
man ran to their rescue.

"Hold on, Jim!" cried the bowman, meaning that
James should understand deliverance was at hand.
James was holding on as well as he could with two
stupid mules to manage in the water. For some minutes it was difficult to tell how the affair would terminate, for there was serious danger that mules and
driver would go to the bottom together. But it had
always been James's good fortune to come to the top.
So he did here; and he was soon astride the leading
mule, urging him out of the difficulty. A few minutes
only elapsed before all were rescued, with no injury
except a good ducking.

During the process of rescuing the unfortunate victims of the accident, there was no jesting or light remarks, but one serious, earnest effort to save the mules
and to rescue James. But no sooner were the sufferers
safe on the tow-path, than a general laughter and merry
time over the mishap ensued.

"Yer a good Baptist now, Jim," exclaimed one of the
steersmen terminating his exp   in to him

"Yer see how we 'nitiate greenhorns into canal bisness," said another of the men.

"I kind o' thought yer was a gonner at first," added a third.

Finally, the captain said, jocosely, "Jim, what was you doin' down there in the canal?"

"Takin' my mornin' bath," answered James. "Refreshin'."

"Washin' the mules, I reckon'd," chimed in one of the men.

"All ready, now!" shouted the captain; "Jim has washed himself and is now ready to proceed to bisness. All aboard!" And they were off in a jiffy.

The bantering did not cease with that day. Many a hearty laugh was enjoyed over it for several days, and James was the subject of many jocose remarks all of which served to keep the crew in good humour.

James enjoyed it as well as the rest of them.

At "Eleven Mile Lock," the captain ordered a change of teams. James went on board with his mules, and the other driver took the tow path with his fresh mules.

"Goin' to take the mules into yer bunk with yer, as yer did in a-swimmin'?" remarked one of the hands.

"Put up your team, Jim, and then come on deck," said the captain addressing James; "I want to see you."

James took good care of his mules, and went on deck.

"Jim, I hear there is some come-out to you, and if you have no objections, I would like to make up my own mind in regard to it. It is a long ways to Pancake Lock, and this will be a good time; so I should like to ask you a few questions"

"Proceed," answered James; "but be sure and not ask too hard ones."

"You see, I've kept school some in the backwoods of Steuben County, Indiana," added the captain.

"Schoolmaster and Captain," repeated James.

"Honour enough for one family. What did you teach?"

"Redin', writin', spellin', g'ograpthy 'rithmetic, and grammar."

"Go ahead, then," continued James, "and examine me in these branches, I'll answer the best I know."

The captain proceeded with his questions, first in arithmetic, then in geography and grammar, and James answered every question promptly.

"You are a trump, Jim; I've heard a good deal about your talents, and I wanted to see whether it was so, or not. You'll not shame your relations; I'll own ye for cousin," remarked the captain, discontinuing his questions.

"Now, s'pose I put a few questions to you," said James, "it's a poor rule that won't work both ways."

"As many as you choose," answered the captain.

The captain could not answer the first question that James put, nor the second, nor third; nor, indeed, any of them. James had studied all the branches named far more thoroughly than the captain, so that "hard questions" were at his command He intended to confound the captain, and he did.

"If you'll let me alone, I'll let you alone," remarked the captain, after several ineffectual attempts to answer James's questions

The captain did not know so much as he thought he did Because he had taught school in Indiana, and studied arithmetic, grammar, and geography, he thought he was superior even to James, of whom he had heard large stories. A few years ago he spoke of the matter to a friend, and said: "I was just green enough in those days to think that I knew it all. You see, I had been teacher for three years in the backwoods of Steuben County, Indiana" That over-estimate of himself put him into an awkward position before James. At the close of the interview the captain said seriously:

"Jim, you've got too good a head on you to be a wood-chopper or a canal-driver."

"Do you really think so?" asked James.

"Yes, I do, honest."

"What would you have me do?"

"Teach school. Go to school one or two terms, and then you will be qualified to teach a common school; and after that you can make anything you have a mind to out of yourself."

"That is more easily said than done," answered James. "What do you think of my goin' to sea?"

"I don't think much of it, to tell you the truth, Jim. It's a terrible hard, rough life, and it's a pity to throw away your talents on the deck of a ship. Never do any such thing, Jim. That's my advice."

"But I don't intend to *serve* all my days, if I become a sailor," said James; "I intend to *command*."

"Command or serve, it will be all the same to you, Jim. You will be greater than the business, any way, and that's unfortunate for any one. It won't help the matter any to be called Captain Garfield."

"You don't know what a longing I have for life on the ocean," added James. "For ever so long I have been thinking of the matter, but mother never gave her consent till lately, and then, only to ship on Lake Erie."

"There's where your mother is right She knows your abilities, and wants you should follow what your abilities fit you to become. I shouldn't think she would ever consent to such a wild project as your goin' to sea. To be a sailor, when you might be a teacher, governor, is the most foolish thing in the world."

"Now, captain," replied James, as if doubting his sincerity, "do you really think that my talents promise any such results as that?"

"Certainly I do, I shouldn't say it if I didn't think so. I would go to school in the autumn, and teach school next winter, if I were in your place. You'll earn money enough this summer, nearly, to pay your way."

The conversation ceased ; but James's thoughts ran on. He began to wonder whether he was such a fool as would appear from the captain's remarks. It was quite evident that Captain Letcher had set him to thinking in the right direction. If he did possess talents for some high position, he was a fool, surely, to throw them away for nothing. He began to see it in that light. What his cousin had said tallied very well with what several other people had told him, and be began to think that all of them could not be wrong "In the mouth of two or three witnesses, every word shall be established."

XIII

TRIUMPHS ON THE TOW-PATH

THE boat was nearing the twenty-one locks of Akron.

"Make the first lock ready," cried the captain to his bowman. It was ten o'clock at night.

"Ay!" answered the bowman, promptly.

As the bowman approached the lock, a voice came through the darkness from the bowman of another boat:

"Don't turn this lock; our boat is just around the bend, ready to enter."

"I *will* turn it; we got here first," answered the bowman of the "Evening Star," with an oath that seemed blacker in the absence of the sun.

"You won't turn it unless you are stronger than we are," shouted bowman number one, adding sufficient profanity to match the vocabulary of the other.

A fight was imminent, as all hands on board saw, and they rallied for the fracas. Such scenes were common on the canal. The boat whose bowman reached the lock first was entitled to enter first; but when two bowmen reached the lock about the same time a dispute was about sure to arise, the result of which was a hand-to-hand fight between the two crews. The boat's crew that came to the top of the pile won the lock. Captains were usually powerless to prevent these contests, however well disposed they might be.

Captain Letcher's bowman commenced turning the gate just as the two boats came up so near that their head-lights shed the brightness of day on the exciting scene.

" Say, bowman, called Captain Letcher, motioning with his hand for attention. His bowman looked up in response.

" Was you here first ? " Evidently the captain questioned his right to the lock.

" It's hard to tell," replied the bowman ; " but we're goin' to have the lock, anyhow , " and the ring of his voice showed determination and fight

" All right ; just as you say," answered the captain, supposing that no interference of his could prevent an encounter.

The men stood panting for the fray like war-horses. They seemed to be in just the right mood for a contest. It was a new scene to James, and he stood wondering, with the loud oaths bandied falling on his ear. After having restrained himself as long as he could, he tapped the captain on the shoulder saying :

" See here, captain, does that lock belong to us ? "

" I really suppose, according to law, it does not ; but we'll have it, anyhow," was the captain's reply.

" No, we will not," answered James, with a good deal of determination.

" Why not ? " asked the captain, very much surprised at the boy's interference.

" Because it does not belong to us "

" That's so," the captain replied, seeing at once that James was right.

Probably the captain had never stopped to think whether the custom of fighting for a lock was right or not. But the suggestion of James seemed to act as inspiration on him, and he called out to his bowman :

" Hold on ! hold on, boys ! "

The men looked up in surprise as if wondering what

had happened   One minute more, and some hard knocks
would have been given.

"Hold on !" repeated the captain, in the loudest
tone of authority that he could command. "LET
THEM HAVE THE LOCK."

The order was obeyed ; the free fight was prevented ;
the other boat entered the lock , "peace reigned in
Warsaw." James commanded the situation. His
principles prevailed.

The boat was all night getting through the twenty-one
locks, but at sunrise was on Lake Summit, moving forward under as bright a day-dawning as ever silvered the
waters   The mules were moving on a slow trot, under
the crack of the driver's whip, and everything was hopeful. Breakfast was called. George Lee, the steersman,
came out and sat down to the table, and the first word
he spoke was :

"Jim, what's the matter with ye ? "

"Nothing ; I never felt better in my life," replied
James

"What did you give up the lock for, last
night ? "

"Because it didn't belong to us "

"Jim," continued Lee, in a tone of bitterness, accompanied with his usual profanity, "yer are a coward ;
yer ain't fit to be a boatman.   Yer may do to chop wood
or milk cows, but a man or a boy isn't fit for a boat who
won't fight for his rights."

James only smiled at his fellow-boatman, and went on
with his breakfast, making no reply. The captain
heard the remarks, and admired the more the courage,
coolness, and principle of his boy-driver. He saw that
there was a magnanimous soul under that dirty shirt,
and he enjoyed the evidence of its reign.

The boat reached Beaver and a steamer was about to
tow her up to Pittsburg, when the following incident
occurred, just as the captain describes it .

James was standing on deck, with the setting-pole against his shoulders, and several feet away stood Murphy, one of the boat-hands, a big, burly fellow of thirty-five, when the steamboat threw the line, and, owing to a sudden lurch of the boat, it whirled over the boy's shoulders, and flew in the direction of the boatman.

"Look out, Murphy!" shouted James; but the rope had anticipated him, and knocked Murphy's hat off into the river.

"It was an accident, Murphy," exclaimed James, by way of excuse. "I'm very sorry."

"I'll make yer sorry," bellowed Murphy, thoroughly mad, and, like a reckless bull, he plunged at James with his head down, thinking to knock him over, perhaps, into the water, where his hat had gone; but James stepped nimbly aside and dealt him a heavy blow behind the ear tumbling him to the bottom of the boat among the copper ore. Thinking to bring hostilities to a sudden close, he leaped upon Murphy, and held him down.

"Pound the fool, Jim," cried the captain. But James had him fast in his grip, so that the fellow could not harm him, and he refused to strike. He only said:

"I have him, now."

"If he hain't no more sense 'n to get mad at accidents giv it ter him. Why don't yer strike?"

"Because he's down and in my power," answered the noble boy. He never would have it said that he struck a man save in self-defence; and it is not self-defence to strike a man when he can be restrained without striking.

"Got enough, Murphy? You can get up when you have," said James to his conquered antagonist.

"Yis, 'nuff," answered Murphy. James rose and allowed his assailant to rise also; then, extending his hand, in the magnanimous spirit of a victor, he said·

"Murphy give us your hand"

And they shook hands, and were fast friends thereafter. From that time James moved among the crew not as a greenhorn and coward, but as a boy-man—a boy in age, but a man in action ; a boy in physical appearance, but a man in convictions and generous spirit.

Among the boatmen was one Harry Brown, a good-hearted, rough, dissipated fellow, who had a strong liking for James, and would do almost anything for him. Harry was impetuous, and whisky often increased his impetuosity, so that he was frequently in trouble.

" Look here, Harry, it's a little rough for you to be in rows so often ; let whisky alone, and you'll not be in trouble half so much, "said James to him, in a kind way. If any one else on board had said that, Harry would have resented it, and told him to " mind his own business."   But he pleasantly said to James :

" That's so, Jim ; I'd giv' a pile to be like yer."

" You can be, if you are a mind to," replied James. "Whisky is the last stuff I should think of drinking, Harry ; sooner drink the dirty water in this canal."

" Yer are a trump, Jim."

" I'm just what I am," replied James, " and you don't begin to be what you might be, Harry. Your generous soul could make sunshine all about you, only break your bottle."

This compliment tickled Harry in the right place, and he concluded that James was rehearsing more truth than poetry. James saw that he held the key to the rough boatman's heart, and he proceeded :

" I don't see why boatmen can't be as decent as other people, but they are not   They are about the hardest set I ever saw—drinking, swearing, bragging, fighting. Isn't it so, Harry ? "

" Yer about right, Jim," Harry answered, with a comical shrug of his shoulders.

" If I was captain of a boat I would have a new order of things or fling up the commission," James continued

" I ll bet yer, Jim ; we'd all behave well to please yer," interrupted Harry, acquiescing in the supposition.

" Well now, Harry, don't you think yourself that it would be a great improvement, on canal boats, to give whisky a wide berth ? "

" True as preachin', Jim."

" And yet you continue to make yourself a disgrace to your sex, and are in hot water half your time. Isn't it so, Harry ? "

Harry shook his sides over James's plainness of speech, and admitted that the boy was right.

" I hate this beastly way of living," continued James, " and I don't see why a fellow should act like a brute, when he is a man. I don't believe that you respect yourself, Harry."

" Right again ! " shouted Harry. " Yer see, if I did 'spect myself, I shouldn't do as I do. That's the trouble —I have no 'spect for myself." And the poor, weak fellow never spoke a plainer truth in his life. Proper self-respect will lead such devotees of vice to reform, and be men.

" Yer see, Jim," added Harry, " I couldn't be like yer if I tried."

" That's bosh ! " replied James. " Just as if a man can't be decent when he tries ! You can't make that go, Harry. Throw whisky and tobacco overboard, as Murphy's hat went, and the thing is done."

" So you'd take all a feller's comforts away, Jim, t'backer and all," interposed Harry.

" Yes ; and this awful profanity that I hear also," retorted James. " I would make a clean sweep of the whole thing. What good does it all do ? "

" What good ! humph ! " exclaimed Harry. " Yer are not fool 'nough to think we 'spect to do good in this way ! " And Harry laughed again heartily, admitting the truth of James's position, without proposing to defend himself.

"What *do* you do it for, then ? "

"Do it *for !* don't do it for nothin', Jim," responded Harry. "Nary good or evil we are after."

"You're a bigger fool than I thought you were," added James. "Making a brute of yourself for *nothing* If that isn't being a fool, then I don't know what a fool is."

Harry laughed more loudly than ever, as he turned away, accepting the advice of James in the same spirit in which it was tendered. That he was not at all offended is evident from the fact that he was heard to say to Murphy afterwards :

"Jim is a great feller. I've an orful itchin' to see what sort of a man he'll make. The way he rakes me down on whisky, t'backer, and swearing, is a caution ; and he don t say a word that ain't true ; that's the trouble And he says it in sich a way, that yer knows he means it. Jist think, Murphy ; a boy on this old canal as don't drink rum or smoke, or chew, or fight—would yer believe it, if yer didn't see it ? "

Murphy acknowledged that it was an anomaly on the Ohio and Pennsylvania Canal, and hinted that he should like to know where the " feller " came from.

" I like him, though, Murphy," Harry continued. " I allers liked a man to show his colours I like to know where a feller is, if he be agin me. And Jim is so cute ; he'll beat the whole crowd on us tellin' stories, only they are not nasty, like the rest on us tell. Isn't he a deep one ? He knows more'n all the crew put together, and two or three more boatloads added, into the bargain."

James had fairly established himself in the respect and confidence, not only of the sober and intelligent captain, but of the drunken, ignorant crew, as well. On the whole, they were proud of him. Said the steersman to ". ' -   f   th   b   t, " We've got a feller in the crew ju   t   ee.

Nary drinks whisky, smokes, chews, swears, or fights—
d'ye believe it, old feller ? " and he slapped the bowman
on the back as he said it.

"Where'd he cum from ? " the bowman inquired.

"That's what we'd like ter know, yer see ; where he
cum from, and how he happen'd to cum," responded
the steersman. "But he's a jolly good fellow, strong as
a lion, could lick any on us if he's a mind to ; and he's a
pealer for work, too ; ain't afraid to dirty hisself ; and
buckles right down to bisness, he does, jist like any on
us. I never seed just such a boy."

That the captain was won by the amount and quality
of James's work, as well as by the reliability of his character, is evident from the fact that he promoted him to
bowman at the end of his first trip. We mistrust that,
in addition to the captain's confidence in his ability for
the position, he exercised military tactics in the appointment, and concluded that it would put an end to brutal
fights for the possession of locks.

By the confession of captain and crew, most of whom
are still alive, James was a successful peace-maker on
the canal boat, and his influence elevated the rough
boatmen to some extent. He did it, too, without making
an enemy, but real friends of all. His forte lay in that
direction.

The testimony of the captain is, that James did everything thoroughly as well as promptly ; that he was as
conscientious as he was resolute, declining to partici-
pate in any project that he considered wrong ; that he
possessed remarkable tact in his business as well as in
dealing with men ; and that he was a model boy in
every respect—" not talkative, but very intelligent ;
and when drawn into conversation, he surprised us by
the depth of his knowledge on the topics of the day."

On the canal boat James had no books to read ; and
this was a serious privation. Occasionally, the captain
had an opportunity to purchase new papers, and these

James read through and through. The captain thinks, however, that the absence of reading matter was fully made up to him by the opportunity and demand for the exercise of his *observation*. He studied men and business, and asked a multitude of questions. Patrick Henry once said that he owed his success to " studying men more than books." Garfield studied men more than books, and the captain aided him materially by answering his questions Perhaps it was an advantage for him, in the circumstances, to be where no books could be had for love or money.

James appeared to possess a singular affinity for the water He fell into the water fourteen times during the two or three months he served on the canal boat. It was not because he was so clumsy that he could not keep right side up, nor because he did not understand the business ; rather, we think, it arose from his thorough devotion to his work. He gave more attention to the labour in hand than he did to his own safety. He was one who never thought of himself when he was serving another. He thought only of what he had in hand to do. His application was intense and his perseverance royal.

The last time he fell into the water he came near losing his life. It was on one very rainy night, when he was called up to take his turn at the bow. The boat was just leaving one of those long reaches of slack-water which abound in the Ohio and Pennsylvania Canal. James was awaked out of a very sound sleep, and he responded with his eyes half open, scarcely comprehending as yet the situation, and took his stand upon the platform below the bow-deck He began to uncoil a rope to steady the boat through a lock it was approaching. The rope caught somehow on the edge of the deck, and resisted several pulls that he made to extricate it. At length yielded but in the effort sent him headlong over the bow into the water. It was a very dark night, and he went down into the water, which was blacker than the night.   In the meanwhile the boat was sweeping on, and no mortal knew of his mishap, and not a helping hand was near.   Death seemed inevitable.   Fortunately his hand seized the rope in the darkness,—by accident, men will say, but by providential guidance really,— and he drew himself, hand over hand upon deck.   He saw that he had been saved as by a miracle.   The rope would have been of no service to him, only it caught in a crevice on the edge of the deck and held fast   He stood there dripping in his wet clothes, his thoughts running thus :

"What saved me that time ?   It must have been God, I could not have saved myself.   Just a kink in the rope catching in that crevice saved me, nothing else. That was almost miraculous and God does miraculous things.   He thinks my life is worth saving, and I ought not to throw it away on a seafaring life, and I won't. I will renounce all such ideas, and get an education."

During the time that he was thus reflecting he was trying to throw the rope so that it would catch in the crevice.   Again and again he coiled the rope and threw it ; but it would neither kink or catch.   Repeated trials satisfied him that supernatural causes put the kinked rope into his hand, and saved his life.

That accident made a very deep impression upon his mind.   His thoughts more than ever turned to his home and praying mother.   He knew that every day his dear mother remembered him at the Throne of Grace. He had no more doubt of it than he had of his existence. "Was it her prayers ?"   He could not evade the inquiry.   He thought of all her anxieties and wise counsels, and her undying love.   "Such a mother !"   The thought would force itself uppermost in spite of himself.   He felt that he ought to be a good obedient son.   He had not been careful enough of his mother's feelings ; he would be in future. He would quit the canal boat for ever.

It was but a few weeks after the last immersion before James was quite severely attacked by ague, a disease that prevailed somewhat in that region. It prostrated him to such a degree that he was unfitted for labour ; and this offered a favourable opportunity for him to carry out the resolution of that night of disaster.

" I must go home, captain," said James.

" It's a wise conclusion, Jim. You are too unwell for work, and there's no place like home for sick folks. I don't want to part with you, and the men will be sorry to have you go ; but I think you'd better go "

" I regret to leave your service, captain, for I've enjoyed it ; but I've been thinking of your advice, and I guess I shall put it in practice."

" You can't do a wiser thing, Jim ; and I wouldn't lose a day about it. As soon as you are able, I'd go to studying, if I was in your place."

The captain settled with James, paying him at the rate of twelve dollars a month while he was driver, and eighteen dollars a month while he was bowman ; and James started for home.

James was never so melancholy in his life as he was on the way home The ague had taken his strength away, and made him almost as limp as a child. Then, he was thinking more of his duties and his good mother. He had not written to her in his absence, between two and three months, and he rather rebuked himself for the neglect. " True," he thought, " I have been on the wing all of the time, and there has been little opportunity for writing ; " and so he partially excused himself for the neglect. His mother supposed that he was serving on a schooner somewhere on Lake Erie He ought to have informed her of his whereabouts. And his thoughts were busy during his lonely journey home. It was nearly dark when he left the boat, so that he did not reach home until eleven o'clock at night.

As he drew near the house, he could see the light of the fire through the window. His heart beat quick and strong ; he knew that it would be a glad surprise to his mother. Looking in at the window, he beheld her kneeling in the corner, with a book open in the chair before her. Was she reading ? He looked again : her eyes were turned heavenward , she was praying. He listened, and he distinctly heard, " Oh, turn unto me, and have mercy upon me ! Give Thy strength unto Thy servant, and save the son of thine handmaid ! " That was enough ; he waited to hear no more. Mother and son were united again in loving embrace ; and the tears that were shed were tears of joy.

XIV

THE TURNING-POINT

"WHY, James!" exclaimed his mother, when the excitement of their meeting was over, " you look sick."

" I am sick ; and that's the reason I came home. It's been a very hard walk for me, I am so weak."

" How long have you been sick ? " inquired his mother, with much anxiety.

" Not long. I've got the ague , had it a week or more."

" The ague ! " answered his mother, astonished ; " I didn't know that they ever had the ague on a ship."

" I have not been on a ship, but on the canal."

" On the canal ! " rejoined his mother, still more surprised. " I thought you was on the lake all this time. How did it happen that you was on the canal ? "

James rehearsed his experience on the schooner that he boarded, especially narrating his encounter with the captain, and his haste to escape from such a demon ; how he met his cousin, Amos Letcher, of the canal boat " Evening star " and bargaining with him for the position of driver, not omitting his hair-breadth escapes on the boat ; concluding by a description of the exposures of the business, in consequence of which he was attacked by the ague.

His mother listened to the narration, which was more interesting to her than a novel, remarking at the close of it :

" God has wonderfully preserved you, and brought you back in answer to my prayer as

James was too full to make much reply. He managed, however, to say, " Nobody saved me from drowning, that dark night, but God." This brief remark sent a thrill of pleasure through his mother's heart. With all his obedience and excellence of character, James had not given before so much evidence as this that he recognised his personal obligations to God. His mother construed it into genuine religious conviction, and she was rejoiced beyond measure by the revelation.

" You must say no more to-night ; you must go to bed, and get some rest," added his mother. " In the morning I will see what can be done for you."

Both retired ; his mother to a restless bed, being too full of joy and grateful thoughts to sleep. She lived over her whole life again during that night, with all its chequered scenes ; and she penetrated the future, in imagination, and beheld her dear boy dignifying his manhood by an honourable and useful career. " If he could only become a preacher ! " The thought grew upon her in the " night watches." It became a source of real delight to her ; and she thanked God again and again for His goodness She found more enjoyment in wakefulness and her thoughts on that night, than she could have had in the sweetest sleep It was the silent communings of a truly Christian heart.

Very early in the morning Mrs. Garfield was at the side of her son, anxious to learn how he was. He was in a sound sleep. She waited until the sunlight was bathing his brow, when she entered his room again. Her presence awoke him.

" You've had a sweet sleep, James ? " she said, inquiringly.

" The best sleep I've had for a week," James answered. " I was dreadful tired last night. I feel better this morning."

The ague is a fitful disease, and attacks its victims periodically, leaving them comparatively comfortable and strong on some days. James was really very comfortable on that morning—there was no visible appearance of the ague upon him—and he proposed to get up, dress himself, and look about the home that seemed more pleasant to him than ever. Returning to the kitchen, Mrs. Garfield prepared some simple remedy for him, such as pioneers were wont to administer to ague-patients. Pioneers were more or less familiar with the disease, and understood somewhat how to manage it. In severe cases a physician was called in to administer calomel—that was considered a specific at that time—until salivation was produced.

James was not comfortable long. On the following day a violent attack of the disease prostrated him completely.

" There's a hard bunch on my left side, and pain," said James to his mother.

" That's the ague-cake," replied his mother, on examining the spot " That always appears in severe cases." The name was given by pioneers to the hardness ; perhaps physicians called it by some other name

" You are pretty sick, my son," continued Mrs Garfield, " and I think you must have the doctor Don't you think you had better have the doctor ? "

" Perhaps so ; just as you think about it," was James's reply.

The physician of a neighbouring village was sent for, and he put the patient through the usual calomel treatment, salivating him, and really causing him to suffer more by the remedy than by the disease. For weeks, the big, strong boy lay almost as weak and helpless as a child. It was a new and rough experience for James. it was the first sickness he had ever had ; and to lie in bed and toss with fever, and shake with ague, by turns, was harder for him than chopping wood or planing boards. But for the wise management and tender care of his mother. his experience would have been much more trying for.

" How fortunate it was, James, that you came home when you did ! " remarked his mother.

" It was so ; though I should have come home before long if I had been well," replied James.

" Then you thought of giving up work on the canal ? " continued Mrs. Garfield.

" Yes ; I got about enough of it. Amos told me that I was a fool to follow such business when I am capable of something better," replied James, dropping just a word concerning his interview with Captain Letcher.

" I should agree with Amos on that," remarked his mother, smiling. " You knew that before."

" If God saved my life on that night, I didn't know but He saved it for something," added James, another indication of higher aspirations that gratified his mother very much.

" If God did not save your life, it would be hard telling who did," responded Mrs Garfield. " None of us should be blind to the lessons of His Providence. It's my opinion that the Lord didn't mean you should go to sea, and so he headed you off by that monster of a captain."

" Perhaps so," James answered, in a tone that might indicate either indifference or weakness.

" If God answers my prayers, James, you'll get an education, and be a teacher or preacher. My cup will run over when I see you in such a position."

" What if I should be a lawyer ? " remarked James

" Well, I shall not object to that if you are a good man. A wicked lawyer is almost as bad as a sailor. Above all things, I want you should feel that the Lord has the first *claim* upon your love and service Don't you ever think, James, that you ought to give your heart to Him, and try for a more useful life ? "

This question was unexpected to James, at the time, although such interrogatories had been put to him formly. It had been inquired until Mrs. Garfield put was unexpected to herself, for she did not intend to put such a question when the conversation began. She expected to come to it sometime, however. She was feeling her way along, and leading her boy as best she could; yet James answered:

" I've thought more about it lately."

" I hope you will continue to think about it, my son. It is the greatest thing you can think about. If you will only consecrate your powers to God, I know that you will make the best possible use of them; and you won't make such use of them unless you do that."

Mrs Garfield was very discreet, and thought it not best to press the matter too persistently, but leave James to his own reflections. She was confident that the Lord had taken him in hand, and was leading him in a way the son knew not. She was greatly encouraged, and her prayers were more earnest than ever for his conversion to Christ.

The weeks dragged heavily along, and winter set in. James was still sick, but convalescent. A few weeks more, according to his improved symptoms, and he would be well enough for business or school

The winter school near Mrs. Garfield's began the first week in December, and it was taught by a young man by the name of Samuel D. Bates. He was a young man of ability; a very earnest Christian, looking forward to the ministry in connection with the Disciples' Church. He was, also, an energetic, working young man, possessing large common sense, and intensely interested in benefiting the young people, intellectually and spiritually. From the commencement of the school he was very popular, too.

Mrs. Garfield made his acquaintance, and at once concluded that he was just the person to influence James to aspire to an education. She could not help him herself, but her faith that God would open the way for him to go to school was undiminished. She improved the first opportunity to tell Mr. Bates about James—his sickness, frame of mind, and aspirations. She frankly announced to him that she wanted he should bring all his influence upon James to induce him to strive for an education. The teacher readily consented, for that was a kind of business in which he delighted, to help young men onward and upward. His first call upon James was immediate, though he did not announce the real object he had in view, thinking it would not be wise

" Mr. Bates is a very interesting man, James," remarked Mrs. Garfield, after the teacher left. I don't wonder the scholars like him."

" I like him very much," replied James. " I hope he will come in here often. I wish I was able to go to school to him."

" I wish you could, but Providence orders otherwise, and it will be all for the best, I have no doubt Mr Bates is working his way into the ministry. He teaches school in order to earn money to pay his bills. That is what you could do If you could go to school a few months, you could teach school next winter, and, in that way, earn money for further schooling"

" I don't know as I should be contented in that occupation," responded James. " Once in a while, mother, I have a strong desire to go to sea again There is something about the water that fascinates me. The sight of a ship fills my eye ; indeed, the *thought* of a ship awakens a strong desire within to tread its deck and handle its ropes"

" But you are not disposed to return to the canal, or to follow a seafaring life ? " inquired his mother, surprised at his frank avowal. She had begun to think that he had abandoned all thoughts of the sea.

" I should like it if I thought it was best," he answered.

" It is not best, James ; I can see that plainly."

" Since I have got better, my desire for the sea has
reti   ¹,   me to

ask myself if I shall not be disappointed if I abandon the purpose altogether."

"Not at all," responded Mrs. Garfield. "When you once get engaged in study, you will like it far better than you can the sea, I am sure; and teaching school is a business that will bring you both money and respect. I think we can manage to scrape together money enough for you to start with."

"I will think it over," added James; "I shan't decide in a hurry."

"If you work on the canal, or become a sailor on the lake, you will have work only part of the year," continued his mother. "You will find little to do in the winter. How much better it will be for you to go to school, and qualify yourself for a teacher! Then you can sail in the summer, and teach school in the winter."

Mrs. Garfield feared that a total abandonment of the idea of going to sea would be quite impossible for James at present; and so her policy was to lure him into the way of knowledge by degrees. She suggested sailing in summer and teaching in winter, hoping that, when he had qualified himself to teach, he would be so much in love with books as to banish all thoughts of a ship.

There was a sort of mystery in James's strong desire for a seafaring life, to his mother. And yet there was no mystery about it. Many are born with an adventurous, daring spirit, which the reading of a book may set strongly in a given direction. There is no doubt that the books James read at the black-salter's were the spark that kindled his adventurous spirit into a flame. We have seen a sailor who enjoys life on the ocean with the keenest relish, and his attention was first turned in that direction by a book presented to him by his uncle.

It is related of a traveller, that he sought lodgings one night at a farm-house in Vermont. He found an aged couple, well-to-do in this world's goods, living there alone. In the course of the evening he learned that they had three sons following the sea   It was an inexplicable affair to them, that their sons, living far away from the sea, should have so strong a desire to be sailors, from boyhood.   One after the other, when they attained the age of twelve or fifteen, an almost incontrollable desire for the sea had taken possession of them.   In each case, too, the parents gave their consent to entering upon a seafaring life not until they feared the sons would go without it.   While the father was rehearsing the story of their lives, the traveller was observing a painting on the ceiling, over the mantel-piece.   It was an ocean scene—a ship sailing over a tranquil sea—painted after the manner of the olden times.   When the father ceased his remarks, the traveller said :

" There is the cause of your sons' sailor-life (pointing to the painting).   From infancy they have had that painting before their eyes, and it has educated them for the sea.   In the earliest years, when their hearts were most impressible, that ocean scene set them in that direction ; and finally their hearts were made to burn with unconquerable desire."

This explanation was perfectly satisfactory to the aged couple, and, no doubt, it was the correct one. The fact shows that there is no mystery about such a love for the ocean as James possessed.   Such a fervent nature as his would readily be ignited by a random spark from a glowing book or a glowing speech.   Nor did he ever outgrow this delight in the sea.   Although more than thirty years had elapsed since his conflict with the ague, he once said : " The sight of a ship fills me with a strange fascination.   When upon the water, and my fellow-men are suffering sea-sickness, I am as tranquil as when walking the land in serenest weather. The spell of ' Jack Halyard ' has not yet worn off."

Mr. Bates continued his calls at the Garfields', always aimir to draw out James in re pect to his religious con   and his plans for the futur   All these in terviews were very profitable to James. His mother saw clearly that in the skilful hands of the teacher he was being moulded, and her heart rejoiced. She was satisfied that he was making progress in religious purpose. He was frank to confess his need of Divine grace and renewing, and to express a purpose to become a Christian. At the last interview which we have space to notice, Mr. Bates brought him to a final decision.

" Look here, young man," he said ; " the difference between a scholar and a sailor is the difference between somebody and nobody." And he rung the changes on the words SCHOLAR and SAILOR, until the latter appeared almost beneath the notice.

" Go to school with me at Chester on the first week in March," said Mr. Bates. " Settle that first, that you will go with me to school at that time. That will be the first step, and the most important."

" I will go," answered James, unexpectedly at that moment to his mother. He said it with emphasis, indicating that the matter was settled

" That's business," continued Mr. Bates " I have no concern about the details, as to how you will raise money to pay your way, or whether you will have to relinquish the attempt to acquire an education after you have begun your studies. All these things will come right at the time, and the way will be provided. You have said, ' *I will go*,' and that commits you to the great purpose of your life. It is the *turning-point* of your career. You have set your face towards ' Geauga Seminary,' and I have no idea that you will look back, or hanker for a ship, or do any other unmanly thing. I consider that the turning-point of *my* life was when I finally decided to be educated for the ministry , and from that moment I have felt it was the great decision of my life."

These words exerted a profound influence upon James, and that influence deepened from year to year, as he

M

grew older. Years afterwards, as we have seen, when addressing the audience of young men, he bore strongly upon this point, and said, " It is a great point gained when a young man makes up his mind to devote several years to the accomplishment of a definite work."

A mother's prayers and love had triumphed. Was she not a happy woman ?

" I have a little money, and I know where I can get a little more, and that will be enough to start on," his mother remarked

" I can find work to do out of school, and on Saturdays, when school don't keep, and so earn money to pay my way," responded James.

" Yes, I've no doubt of it. You know that Mr Bates said all these things would come around right when you had decided to go," remarked Mrs Garfield.

" I mean to see if William and Henry will not go, too ; we can room together," continued James. These were his two cousins, who lived close by, sons of his uncle, Amos Boynton. They were members of his Spelling Club a few years before, when, together, they mastered Noah Webster's Spelling Book.

" That will be a good idea, James ; and I think they will go," responded his mother, encouragingly " There is no reason why they should not go."

It was only three weeks before the school at Chester would begin. James announced to his cousins that he had resolved to attend Geauga Seminary, and wanted they should go too. The subject was discussed in the family for a week ; Mr. Bates was consulted, and was glad to influence two other boys to take so wise a step ; and finally it was settled that William and Henry should go with James.

While matters were progressing thus favourably, James heard that Dr. J. P Robinson, of Bedford, was coming into the neighbourhood on a professional visit, and with a companion young, he resolved to consult

him concerning the practicability of his decision to acquire an education.   It was not because he was wavering
at all, but it was more of a curiosity on his part.   So he
called upon the doctor after his arrival at the neighbour's, and the interview, as narrated by Dr. Robinson
to a writer, recently, was as follows :—

" He was rather shabbily clad, in coarse satinet
trousers, far outgrown, and reaching only half-way
down the tops of his cowhide boots , a waistcoat much
too short, and a threadbare coat, whose sleeves went
only a little below the elbows.   Surmounting the whole
was a coarse slouched hat, much the worse for wear ;
and as the lad removed it, in making his obeisance to
the physician, he displayed a heavy shock of unkempt
yellow hair that fell half-way down his shoulders

" ' He was wonderfully awkward,' " says the good
doctor, ' but had a sort of independent, go-as-you-
please manner, that impressed me favourably.'

" ' Who are you ? ' was his somewhat gruff salutation.

" ' My name is James Garfield from Orange," replied
the latter

" ' Oh, I know your mother, and knew you when you
were a babe in arms ; but you have outgrown my knowledge   I am glad to see you.'

" ' I want to see you alone,' said young Garfield.

" The doctor led the way to a secluded spot in the
neighbourhood of the house, and there, sitting down on
a log, the youth, after a little hesitation, opened his
business.

" ' You are a physician,' he said, ' and know the fibre
that is in men.   Examine me, and tell me with the
utmost frankness whether I had better take a course of
liberal study.   I am contemplating doing so ; my desire is in that direction.   But if I am to make a failure
of it, or practically so, I do not desire to begin.   If you
advise me not to do so, I shall feel content.'

" In speaking of this incident, the doctor has remarked recently : ' I felt that I was on my sacred honour, and the young man looked as though he felt himself on trial I had had considerable experience as a physician, but here was a case much different from any other I had ever had. I felt that it must be handled with great care. I examined his head, and saw that there was a magnificent brain there. I sounded his lungs, and found that they were strong, and capable of making good blood. I felt his pulse, and saw that there was an engine capable of sending the blood up to the head to feed the brain I had seen many strong physical systems with warm feet, but cold, sluggish brain ; and those who possessed such systems would simply sit around and doze. Therefore I was anxious to know about the kind of an engine to run that delicate machine, the brain At the end of a fifteen minutes' careful examination of this kind, we rose, and I said, " Go on, follow the leadings of your ambition. and ever after I am your friend. You have the brain of a Webster, and you have the physical proportions that will back you in the most herculean efforts All you need to do is to work. Work hard, do not be afraid of overworking, and you will make your mark." ' "

" I wish you had a better suit of clothes, James." remarked his mother, " but we shall have to make these do, I guess." It was the same suit he had on when he called upon Dr. Robinson. Indeed, he possessed no other suit. The trouseres were nearly out at the knees, but under the skilful hand of his mother they were made almost as good as new.

" Good enough, any way," said James, in reply to his mother's wish. It was fortunate that he was not the victim of a false pride : if he had been, he would not have consented to attend a " seminary " in that plight.

It was settled that the boys should board themselves, each one carrying his own outfit in utensils and provisions, doing it as a matter of economy.

When Mrs. Garfield had scraped together all the money she could for James, the amount was only about eleven dollars.

" That will do to begin with," he remarked " I can earn more."

XV

GEAUGA SEMINARY

ON the fifth day of March, the day before the school opened, James and his cousins travelled to Chester, on foot, quite heavily loaded with cooking utensils and provisions. The distance was ten miles, over roads that were poor, indeed, at that season of the year. They carried dippers, plates, a knife and fork each, a fry-pan, kettle, and other things to match, with a quantity of ham, or " bacon," as the settlers called it. James was arrayed in the suit of clothes in which he appeared before Dr. Robinson, and the other boys were clad about ditto. No one would have charged them with pride, on their way to the " Seminary." At this day, some faithful constable would arrest such a troupe for tramps, who had robbed a farmer's kitchen, and were taking " leg bail." Nevertheless, they were three as jolly boys as Cuyahoga County could boast Their errand was nobler and grander than that of any aspirant who was fishing for an office in the State of Ohio. Why should they not be jolly ?

They proceeded directly to the house of the principal, Mr. Daniel Branch, an eccentric man, though a very respectable scholar in some departments.

"We've come to attend your school," said James, addressing himself to Mr. Branch. "We came from Orange."

"Wh t' y u ish " i r . d t . ; i i l.

"*My* name is James A. Garfield ; and these are my cousins (turning to the boys) , their names are William and Henry Boynton."

"Well, I'm glad to see you, boys ; you might be engaged in much worse business than this. I suppose you are no richer than most of the scholars we have here."

The last remark of Mr. Branch is good evidence that he had surveyed the new-comers from head to foot, and that the remark was prompted by their poor apparel

"No, sir," answered James, drily ; " we are not loaded down with gold or silver, but with pots, and kettles, and provisions for housekeeping."

"Going to board yourselves, then ? " replied the teacher, by way of inquiry.

"Yes, sir ; can you tell us where we can find a room ? " answered James.

"Yes ; near by," answered Mr. Branch ; " a good deal of that business is done here. Scores of our boys and girls would never stay here if they could not board themselves Look here," and stepping out from the door-way, he pointed to an old, unpainted house, twenty or thirty rods away. "You see that old house there, do you ? " he said James assented. " I think you will find a room there , an old lady, as poor as you are, lives in one part of it You will go to her to inquire.' "

"Thank you, sir, thank you," repeated the boys, politely, as they started for the antique habitation. They found the old lady, and hired a room, for a pittance, in which there were a fireplace, three old chairs, that corresponded with the building, and two beds on the floor or what the good woman of the house was bold enough to call beds. Here they unpacked their goods, and set up housekeeping by cooking their first meal.

The "Geauga Seminary" was a Free-will Baptist institution, in quite a flourishing condition, having a hundred students, of both sexes, drawn thither from the towns in that region. The town in which it was ed,

Chester, was small, but pleasant, the academy furnishing the only attraction of the place.

School opened, and James devoted himself to grammar, natural philosophy, arithmetic, and algebra. He had never seen but one algebra before he purchased the one he used. The principal advised him to take this course of study.

It was a new scene for James, a school of one hundred pupils, male and female, most of them better clad than himself. He was awkward and bashful, especially in the presence of young ladies, whom he regarded as far superior to young men of the same age and attainment. Still he broke into the routine of the school readily, and soon was under full headway, like a new vessel with every sail set.

Singularly enough, he encountered an unexpected difficulty in the grammar-class within a very few days.

James said, " *But* is a conjunction."

" Not so ; *but* is a *verb*, and means *be out*," replied the teacher.

" A *verb ! but a verb ?* " exclaimed James, in reply, without scarcely thinking that he was calling the teacher's opinion in question. He had Kirkman's grammar at his command, even to its preface, which he could glibly repeat, word by word ; and he knew that *but* was a conjunction, according to Kirkman and all the teachers whose pupil he had been. Could his teacher be joking, or did he make a blunder ?

" Yes , *but* is a verb, no matter what the books say, young man ; whose grammar have you studied ? " the teacher answered.

" Kirkman's," replied James.

" Kirkman ! and he is just like all the rest of them, wrong from beginning to end," said Mr. Branch. " That's not the grammar you will learn in this school, I can tell you, by any means. I teach a grammar of my own, the grammar f common en e."

James thought it was the grammar of nonsense, though he did not say so. At that time he did not know that Mr. Branch was at war with all the grammarians, and had introduced a system of instruction in that study peculiarly his own.

" Besides Kirkman, all the teachers I ever have had called *but* a conjunction," added James, directly implying that he did not accept Branch's grammar.

" You don't believe it, I clearly see, young man ; but you *will* long before you have spent twelve weeks in this school," remarked Mr. Branch. " You will have sense enough to see that I am right, and the old grammarians wrong.' '

" If *but* is a verb, I don't see why *and* is not a verb also," remarked James, being quite inclined to array Kirkman against Branch.

" It is a verb, James ! *and* is a verb, I want you to understand, in the imperative mood, and means *add ;* that is all there is to it," was the emphatic answer of Mr. Branch

James looked at the boys, and smiled in his knowing way. The teacher saw the unbelief which pervaded that look, and he continued :

" See here, young man, *and* does something more than connect two things ; it *adds.* I want to speak of you and Henry, two of you together, and I say James and Henry ; that is, *add* Henry to James : don't you see it now ? It is clear as daylight."

There was no daylight in it to James, and he so expressed himself. Each day brought discussion in the class between the principal and James. The former's system of grammar was all of a piece with *and* and *but*, so that the hour for the grammar class was an hour of contention, very spicy to the members of the class, but rather annoying to the teacher. The latter was not long in discovering that he had a remarkable scholar in James —one who would in in truth, without the most substantial reason or proof. His respect for James's talents somewhat reconciled him to his annoying contradictions.

The boys had much sport over Branch's grammar ; we mean James and his cousins

"If *but* is a verb, then but*ler* must be an *adverb*, since it only adds three more letters and one more syllable," said James.

"You ought to have told him so," replied Henry , "it's a good point , it is carrying out his system exactly."

"Not much system about it any way," responded James, "but a good deal of egotism and stubbornness"

"You can be as stubborn as he is," remarked Henry "He don't hardly know how to get along with Kirkman ; it's tough for him."

We will not follow the grammar class. It should be said, however, that James never adopted Branch's grammar He contended against it, so long as he continued in the class ; and it is our private opinion that the author of Branch's Grammar was well pleased when James exchanged it for another study.

The boys succeeded tolerably well at housekeeping though they did not extract quite so much fun from it as they expected. After a short time, they hired the old lady in the house to cook some of their food. She did their washing also. It was only a very small amount they paid her weekly. Still, buying his books, and incurring some other unavoidable expenses, James saw his eleven dollars dwindling away quite rapidly

"I must look up work, or I shall become bankrupt soon," remarked James. "I can see the bottom of my purse now, almost."

"What sort of work do you expect to find in this little place ? " inquired William.

"Carpenter s work, I guess," answered James. "I've had my eye on that carpenter's shop yonder (pointing) for some time They seem to be busy there I never

lived anywhere yet that I couldn't find work enough. I
shall try them to-morrow."

"What is that carpenter's name ? " inquired William.

"Woodworth—Heman Woodworth. I have had my
eye on him for some time."

Before school, on the following morning, James applied to Mr. Woodworth for work

"What do you know about this business ? " Mr.
Woodworth inquired.

"I have worked for Mr. Treat, of Orange," James
replied.

"I know him ; what can you do ? " said Mr. Woodworth.

"I can build a barn, if you want I should," answered
James, laughingly. "I have helped in building five or
six barns. I can plane for you."

"You look as if you might be a good, strong fellow for
planing," continued Mr Woodworth. "You pay your
own way at school ? "

"Yes, sir ; I had only eleven dollars to begin with, and
that won't last long."

"Not long, I shouldn't think, as board is here "

"I board myself," added James, by way of enlighten-
ing the carpenter.

"Board yourself ?   That is rather tough, though many
do it."

"Many things are tougher than that," remarked
James.

"Perhaps so ; but that is tough enough. You may
come over after school, and I'll see what I can do for
you."

"And what you can do for yourself," quickly responded James. "If I can't work so as to make it an
object for you to hire me, then I don't wish to work for
you. I don't ask you to let me have work as a matter
of charity "

Mr Woodworth admired the pluck of the boy, and he

repeated, " Come over after school, and I will see what I can do for you."

" I can work two or three hours a day, and all day on Saturdays ; and you needn't put a price on my work until you see what I can do," added James, as he turned away.

The result was that Mr. Woodworth hired James, who worked at the shop before school in the morning, and then hurried to it at the close of school, at four o'clock ; and, on Saturdays, he made a long day's labour. He continued this method through the term, denying himself of the games and sports enjoyed by the scholars, excepting only an occasional hour. No boy loved a pastime better than he, but to pay his bills was more important than sport. At the close of the term he had money enough to pay all his bills, and between two and three dollars to carry home with him.

One of the chief attractions of the seminary to James was its library, although it was small. It contained only one hundred and fifty volumes ; but to James that number was a spectacle to behold. He was not long in ascertaining what books it contained ; not that he read a great many of them, for he had not time ; but he examined the library, and found it destitute of books of the " Jack Halyard " style ; nor was he sorry. He found a class of books just suited to aid students like himself in their studies, and he was well satisfied. He made as much use of them as possible in the circumstances, and often read far into the night. It was a luxury to him, rather than a self-denial, to extend his studies into the night, in order to be perfect in his lessons, and secure a little time for reading.

The regulations of the school made it necessary for James to write a composition twice a month, sometimes upon a subject announced by the Principal, and sometimes upon a topic of his own selection. Occasionally, the authors of the essays were required to read them to

the whole school, from the platform. The first time
that James read an essay, he trembled more than he
did before rebel cannon twelve or fourteen years thereafter

"Lucky for me," said James to his room mates
that there was a curtain in front of my legs," alluding to
a narrow curtain on the edge of the platform.

"How so?" inquired William.

"No one could see my legs shake ; you would have
thought they had the shaking palsy."

"I never would have thought that of you," added
William.

"It's true, whether you thought it of me or not. I
never trembled so in my life."

"Then you was scared?" remarked William

"I guess that was the name of it," replied James.

"Your essay wan't scared, Jim , it was capital," continued William. "I should be willing to shake a trifle,
if I could write such an essay. Some of them were
astonished that such a suit of clothes as yours should
hide such a production."

"Much obliged," answered James ; "you seem to
praise my essay at the expense of my clothing. I can
afford a better essay than suit of clothes. It costs only
thought and labour to produce the essay, but it costs
money to get clothes."

James had taken from the library the " Life of Henry
C Wright," and had become deeply interested in its
perusal. He learned of the privations and denials of
Mr. Wright, as well as his methods in acquiring an education ; and he was captivated by the spirit of the man.

"We can live cheaper than we do," he remarked to
his cousins. "Another term we must adopt Mr.
Wright's diet."

"What was that?" inquired Henry.

"Milk."

"Nothing but milk?"

" Bread and milk ; a milk diet wholly."

" How long ? "

" Right through his course of study."

" Was it cheaper than we are living—thirty-five cents a week, apiece ?"

" Yes ; but better than that, it was healthier."

" How did he know that ? "

" Because he was better than ever before, and had a clearer head for study."

" It may not suit us, though," remarked William, who had been listening to the conversation.

" We shan't know till we try," answered James " I propose to try it next term. We are a little too extravagant in our living now ; we must cut down our expenses. I have had the last cent that I shall take from my friends I shall pay my own way here after."

" You can't do it," said Henry.

" Then I will quit study. I know I can do it. My mother needs all the money she can get without helping me."

" I admire your pluck," added Henry ; " but I think you will find yourself mistaken."

" As I am earning money now, I can pay my way," continued James ; " and on a milk diet I can scrimp a little more."

" And if you should conclude not to eat anything, you could live at very small expense," retorted Henry, by way of making fun of his milk diet.

" Laugh at it as much as you please," replied James ; " meat is not necessary to health—I am satisfied of that. There is more nourishment in good bread and milk than there is in roast beef."

" Well, I should take the roast beef if I could get it," interrupted William. " Milk for babes ; and I am not a baby."

" Milk for scholars," responded James ; " I actually

believe that a better scholar can be made of milk than
of beef."

"If you will say 'bacon' instead of beef, perhaps I
shall agree with you," said William, playfully. "I
don't think that bacon can produce high scholarship."

"Jim's essay was made out of it chiefly," remarked
Henry, "that was scholarly Bacon has contributed
too much to my comfort for me to be-rate it now."

And so the boys treated with some levity a subject
over which James became an enthusiast He was
thoroughly taken with Mr. Wright's mode of living, and
thoroughly resolved to adopt it the next term.

The Debating Society, also, interested James very
much; it was the first one he had ever become acquainted with The Principal recommended it highly
as a means of self-culture, and James accepted his
recommendation as sound and pertinent. He engaged
in debate hesitatingly at first, as if he had grave doubts
of his ability in that direction; but he soon learned to
value the Society above many of his academical privileges. The trial of his powers in debate disclosed a
facility within him that he had not dreamed of He
possessed a ready command of language, could easily
express his thoughts upon any question under discussion, and was really eloquent for one so ungainly in
personal appearance. He studied each question before
the club as he would study a lesson in algebra, determined to master it. He could usually find books in the
library that afforded him essential aid in preparing for
debates, so that he appeared before the school always
well posted upon the subject in hand. His familiarity
with them often evoked remarks of surprise, from both
scholars and teachers. It was here, probably, that he
laid the foundation for that remarkable ability in debate that afterwards distinguished him in Congress.
He began by preparing himself thoroughly for every
discussic:, and the pai de cc . red with in the h-

out his political life. It made him one of the most
prompt, brilliant, and eloquent disputants in the national
legislature.

It was not strange that James won enviable notoriety
in the Debating Society of the Geauga Academy. The
debates became important and attractive to the whole
school because he was a disputant. Scholars hung upon
his lips, as, afterwards, the listening multitude were
charmed by his eloquence. Teachers and pupils began
very soon to predict for him a brilliant future as a
public speaker. In their surprise and admiration of the
young orator they forgot the jean trousers, that were
too short for his limbs by four inches.

Henry Wilson discovered his ability to express his
thoughts, before an audience in the village debating
society of Natick, Mass, in early manhood. Here he
subjected himself to a discipline that ensured his eminence as a debater in Congress. The celebrated English philanthropist Buxton had no thought of becoming
an orator or a statesman until he learned, in the debating society of the school which he attended, that he
possessed an undeveloped ability for the forum. The
distinguished English statesman, Canning, declared that
he qualified himself for his public career in the school of
his youth, where the boys organized and supported a
mock parliament, conducting the debates, appointing
committees, enforcing rules, and pitting one party
against the other, precisely as was done by Parliament.
In like manner, the hero of this volume really began his
distinguished public career in the lyceum of Geauga
Seminary.

XVI

AFTER VACATION

A VACATION of two months in the summer gave James ample opportunity for manual labour. Thomas was at home, and he decided to build a frame-barn for his mother. He could have the assistance of James, who really knew more about barn-building than Thomas did.

"I s'pose you can frame it, Jim?" said Thomas.

"I suppose that I can, if algebra and philosophy have not driven out all I learned of the business."

"You can try your hand at it, then. I should think that algebra and philosophy would help rather than hinder barn-building," added Thomas.

"Precious little they have to do with barns, I tell you," responded James. "They are taking studies, though."

"It won't take you long to find out what you can do," continued Thomas; "it spoils some boys to go to school too much."

Thomas had prepared sufficient timber when he was at home, at different times, for the barn. It was all ready to be worked into the building; and the brothers proceeded to the task resolutely, James leading off in framing it. No outside help was called in, Thomas and James considering themselves equal to the task.

We need not delay to record the details of the job. It will answer our purpose to add, simply, that the barn was built by the brothers, and thus one more convince

was added for the comfort of their mother. The day of
log buildings was now over to the Garfield family. Times
had wonderfully changed since Mr. Garfield died, and the
population of the township had increased, so that " the
wilderness and solitary place" had disappeared.

As soon as the barn was completed, James sought
work elsewhere among the farmers. He must earn
some money before returning to Chester, for a portion of
his doctor's bill remained unpaid, and then, a new suit of
clothes, shirts, and other things would require quite an
outlay.

He found a farmer behind time in getting his hay.

" Yes, I want you," the farmer said ; " and I wish you
had been here two weeks ago : it seems as if haying
would hold out all summer."

" You are rather behind time, I judge," replied James.
" Better late than never, though "

" I don't know about that, James. I rather have it
read, *better never late*," remarked the sensible man.

" That is my rule," answered James. " At school we
are obliged to be in time. Tardiness is not allow-
able."

" It never should be allowed anywhere. It seems as
if we can never catch up when we once get behind," continued the farmer ; " and then there is no comfort in it
It keeps one in torment all the while to feel that he is
behindhand ; I don't like it."

" Neither do I," answered James. " It is worse to be
behindhand in school than it is on a farm ; much worse,
I think   A scholar behind his class is an object of
pity."

The farm work did not continue behindhand long,
however. The remainder of the haying was accomplished in a week, and James had opportunity for other
jobs. He found work clear up to the close of his vacation not having even a day for pastime. Thus he was
able to pay off his doctor's bill, provide a better outfit

for another school term than he had the first term, and to aid his mother also.

James was not idle during the evenings of his vacation. Algebra occupied a portion of his time ; and two or three reading books which he brought from the Chester library beguiled many of his evening hours. If he had any leisure hours during his vacation, they were not idle hours. Every hour told upon the new purpose of his life. He had ceased to talk about going to sea, or even coasting on Lake Erie, in his enthusiasm for an education. His mother, of course, never reverted to the subject, and she was rejoiced to find that James was aspiring after something higher and nobler. He was too much absorbed in his course of study to talk about a seafaring life, or even to think about it.

" I wish you had some money to take back with you, James," remarked his mother, the day before he left for the seminary.

" I don't know as I care for more," answered James. " I have a *ninepence* (showing the bit, and laughing), and that will go as far as it is possible for a ninepence to go. I have it all arranged to work for Mr. Woodworth, out of school, and I can easily pay my way."

" That may be true , but a few dollars to begin the term with would be very convenient," responded Mrs. Garfield.

" Better begin with nothing and end with something, than to begin with something and end with nothing," added James.

" I suppose, then, that you expect to end the term with more money than you begin it with ? " said his mother, inquiringly.

" Yes, I do ; for I shall want a little change in my pocket in the winter, if I teach school," replied James.

" Then you really expect to be qualified to teach school next winter do you ? "

" I design to ; perhaps I shall be disappointed, though "

" I hope not," continued his mother. " By teaching school in the winter you can get together money enough to pay your school bills all the rest of the year , and that will make it easy for you. I want to see you able to earn enough in winter to pay all your school bills, so that you will not be obliged to work before and after school to earn money."

" I don't expect to see that time, mother. I am content to work my way along as I have done," was James's brave reply. " Nobody can be healthier than I am ; so that it don't wear upon me much."

James returned to Geauga Seminary at the opening of the fall term, with the solitary ninepence in his pocket. He playfully suggested to Henry that " the bit must be very lonesome," and thought he might provide a " companion " for it ere long. The circumstances remind us of the experience of the late Horace Mann, of Massachusetts. Born in poverty, though not so poor as James, he had little hope of gratifying his strong desire for an education. Providence, however, opened the way for him to prepare for college, which he did in six months, not knowing whether he would be able to enter or not. By dint of perseverance, he scraped together money enough to get him into college, although he could not tell where the money was coming from to keep him there. After a few weeks he wrote to his sister, " My last two ninepences parted company some days ago, and there is no prospect of their ever meeting again." That is, he had a solitary ninepence in his pocket.

On the Sabbath after James's return to the seminary he was at public worship, when the contribution-box was passed through the audience. Whether James's sympathy for the lonely bit in his pocket got the better of his judgment, or whether it was the generosity of his soul (we suspect it was the latter) he dropped the ninepence into the box, thereby creating as great an emptiness as possible in his pocket. He was now upon an equality with the widow of the Scriptures, who cast her two mites (all she had) into the treasury of the Lord.

James and his cousins boarded themselves during the fall term, adopting Wright's milk diet at first, thereby reducing their expenses a very little, though not much.

"Just thirty-one cents each, per week," remarked James, after the trial of that method of living four weeks. He had kept a careful account, and now found the result to be as indicated.

"I feel as if it had not cost us more than that," answered Henry. "My physical constitution is reduced quite as much as our expenses, I think." He said this humorously in part, although he was not much captivated with their mode of living.

"That which costs the least is not always the cheapest," remarked William, whose opinions coincided with those of his brother. "I feel as if we were having pretty *cheap* living;" and he emphasized the word cheap in his peculiar way.

"Well, I feel as if I had been living on the fat of the land," responded James. "I think I could handle you both," he added, laughingly.

"There's no doubt of it," replied Henry; "you would grow fat on sawdust pudding, only have enough of it; but this sticking to one article of diet right along don't suit me."

"You are one of the philosophers who maintain that 'variety is the spice of life,' in eating as well as in pleasure, I suppose," answered James. "For my part, one thing at a time will do for me, if it is only *good* enough."

"I don't know of one thing alone that is good enough for me," remarked Henry. "I go for increasing our expenses a little We can go up to fifty cents a week without damaging anybody

"That's what I think," added William. "I think I can be pretty well satisfied with that."

"Just as you choose, boys; I can make way with nineteen cents' worth of luxuries more, in case of necessity," replied James. "Sawdust pudding or plum pudding is all the same to me; I can thrive on either."

"Now, Jim," said Henry, very philosophically, "I believe, after all, that you are as anxious as we are for better living, only you don't want to own it, and back down. You are the last fellow to back out of anything." Henry was about right in his remark. James was not at all unwilling to adopt a more expensive fare, although his iron will would carry him through his work with almost any sort of diet. His health was so robust, and his power of endurance so great, that he could eat much or little, apparently, and thrive.

The upshot of this interview was, that James assented to the increase of expenses to fifty cents per week, each. Milk was continued chiefly as their diet, but other things were added for variety. The last half of the term their board cost them fifty cents per week

James had never spoken with the principal about becoming a teacher, although he was intending to do it. But Mr. Branch opened the subject about the middle of the term. He well knew the poverty of James, and took additional interest in him for that reason. He felt that a youth of his talents ought to acquire an education; and he could see no better way of accomplishing it than by teaching school in the winter.

"How would you like to try your hand at school keeping, James?" inquired Mr. Branch.

"I *intend* to try my hand at it next winter, if I can get a school," answered James. "My mother has always said that I could get an education if I would qualify myself to teach school."

"A good plan. James: [· ~ith ·~ · other,

exactly. Glad to see that you mind your mother, for
such boys usually come out all right." Mr. Branch was
in a happy frame of mind when he said this, and his
real kindness to James appeared in every word.

"Then," he continued, " what is better than all, you
can do a great deal of good by teaching school. You
will not only find it the best way to help yourself, but
you will find it the best way to help others ; and that is
the highest of all considerations. We don't live for ourselves in this world, or *ought not* to live for ourselves
alone. That is too selfish and contemptible to be
tolerated."

"Do you think I can obtain a school, without any
doubt ? " inquired James.

"Unquestionably," answered Mr Branch. " Teachers
are more numerous than they were ten years ago, and
so it is with schools. More than that, I think you will
succeed in the business. Every one will not be successful in the calling."

"Why do you think I shall succeed ? " asked James,
who was curious to understand what particular qualities
would win in the school-house

"You will be well qualified ; that is one thing. You
possess ability to express your thoughts readily , that is
very important for a teacher. Your mind is discriminating and sharp to analyze and see the reason of things ,
that is also an indispensable qualification for a successful teacher You will govern a school well, I think,
without much trouble A young man who is popular
with associates in study usually makes a good teacher."
This was the honest reply of the principal to the last
inquiry of James ; all of which was a substantial
encouragement to the latter He began to look forward
to the new occupation with much pleasure

One incident occurred at this term of school, relating
to its discipline, in which James played a conspicuous
part. Al ui du ''r : i m . r. av i u s in

a school of one hundred pupils as there are to-day. Human nature averaged about as it does now among pupils. There was the same need of wise government and watchfulness, on the part of the principal, to maintain order. In this respect the principal was well qualified for his position ; and roguish pupils could not rebel against his government with impunity. This was quite well understood ; and still there were occasional scrapes, in which a class of pupils engaged as the best way, in their estimation, to dispose of a surplus fund of animal spirits.

A youth of considerable pertness insulted one of the townspeople, and it came to the ear of the principal. Indeed, the citizen entered a complaint against the pupil, rehearsing the facts to Mr. Branch. The credit of the school, and the credit of the principal himself, demanded that he should take notice of the matter, rebuke the act, and lecture the whole school, that there might not be a repetition of the act.

As often happens in large schools, the pupils took sides with the author of the naughty deed. The sympathies of young people, especially in school, unite them together as by strong cords. Without regard to the merits of the case, they decide for the accused party, and sustain him.

" If Bell goes, I go," exclaimed one of the boys, meaning, that if the principal expelled Bell, he would be one to leave the school also. The fact shows that feeling played a more prominent part in the affair than judgment.

" And I'll be another to go," answered a smart young fellow ; that is, smart in his own estimation.

" Will you take me along with you ? " asked a third, who was more disposed to show humour than passion. " I'll add one to the company."

" Me, too ! " exclaimed a fourth. " Put me down for that scrape. A great many folks think that school-boy v. · n ti.bts."

In this way the subject was discussed among a class of the boys, and even some girls signified a willingness to express their indignation in some such way as that proposed. It was claimed that as many as "twenty" pupils would quit school if Bell was expelled. But when, at last, they came around to James with their proposition, they met with a serious embarrassment.

"Why should I leave the school because another fellow is sent away?" answered James. "Can you tell me?"

Of course they could not give a reason why he should. One boy did venture to reply.

"We want to show our indignation."

"Indignation about what?" asked James.

"At sending Bell away."

"But he is not sent away yet, and he may not be."

"Well, I don't believe in treating a fellow so."

"How?" persisted James.

"Well, call a fellow up, and make such a touse over his way of speaking to a man."

"How did he speak?"

"The citizen claims that he insulted him. But that's not the thing for us boys to look at; we ought to stand by our fellows."

"Stand by them, right or wrong?" inquired James.

"Yes, if necessary."

"Well, I shall not," answered James, emphatically. "If one of our fellows gets into a scrape, I will not help him out unless it can be done honourably; you can depend on that."

"I think it is mean," continued the boy, "for a citizen to complain of a scholar just because he did not use his tongue quite right."

"I don't agree with you," answered James; "Bell ought to use his tongue as well as he does his hands, for all that I can see; and if it gets him into trouble, he has no one to blame except himself."

"That may all be true," added Bell's persistent friend ; "but if he gets into trouble thoughtlessly, I am willing to help him out."

"So am I," quickly responded James, "provided he is sorry, and is willing to be helped out of it in a proper way "

"I suppose by that, you have not a good opinion of our method of helping him ? "

"No, I have not If Bell will apologize to the citizen, and signify to Mr. Branch that he is sorry, and will not repeat the insult, I will be among the first to intercede for him ; but he must help himself before I am willing to help him."

This ended the proposed rebellion in school. Bell did make all suitable amends for his misconduct, and remained in the school. The incident illustrates a prominent trait of character in James thus far through his life. He had an opinion of his own, and maintained it, in his youth, as he did in later life. He would not knowingly defend even a school-companion in wrong doing. He repudiated the so-called "code of honour " in schools, requiring boys to support each other, whether right or wrong.

The fall term was a very profitable one to James His scholarship became fully established He led the school in talents and progress. He paid all his bills, also, by his daily labour in the carpenter's shop, and had several dollars left for pocket-money at the close of the term.

XVII

KEEPING SCHOOL

THE next day after James reached home at the close of the term, he started out to find a situation as teacher

"When will you return?" inquired his mother.

"When I get a school. Somehow I feel as if it would be a hard matter to get a school"

"I hope not, my son," answered his mother, rejoicing in her heart that James was going to be a teacher, and not a sailor.

"*I* hope not," responded James; but I don't seem to feel so elated over the prospect as I did once. I shall do my best, however, and I may be gone several days."

James took the most favourable route, on foot, and made his first application about ten miles from home.

"You are too young," replied the committee to his application; "we don't want a *boy* to teach our school."

"I have a recommendation from Mr. Branch, Principal of the Geauga Seminary;" and he proceeded to exhibit his testimonials.

"No matter about that," replied the committee-man. "No doubt you know enough, but you can't make yourself any older than you be; that's the trouble. We've had boys enough keep our school"

This was quite a damper upon the ardour of James; and he left the man, and continued his journey, reflecting upon the value of age in profession

The next school district that he reached had engaged a teacher.

" If you had come a week ago, I'd hired yer," the man said.

It was encouraging to James that he had found a district where age was not an absolute requirement. He thought better of youth now.

" Possibly in the Norton District they've not a teacher yet," the man added.

" Where's that ? " inquired James.

" About three miles north of here," pointing with his finger. " Go to Mr. Nelson ; he's the man you want ter see He'll hire yer, if he's no teacher."

James posted away to the Norton District, and found Mr. Nelson, just about dark

" Just found a teacher, young man, and hired him." Mr. Nelson said. " Can't very well hire another "

" Of course not," answered James ; " and perhaps the one you hired needs the chance as much as I do "

" Perhaps so ; he's trying to get an education."

" So am I," responded James.

" Where ? "

" At Geauga Seminary."

" Ah ! we had a teacher from that seminary two years ago, and he was as good a teacher as we ever had."

" That is fortunate for me," remarked James, pleasantly. " If he had not proved a good teacher, you would not want another from that institution."

" Very like," replied Mr. Nelson. " But come, you can't look after more schools to-night ; it is getting dark Come in, and stop over night with us."

James accepted the cordial invitation, stopped with the family over night, and, on the following day, continued his school-hunting trip. But he did not find a school. He met with one committee-man who declined to hire him because " We had one feller from Gaga

Siminary, and he made sich a botch of it that we don't want another."

After two days of hard work in the vain search for a school, James reached home more thoroughly discouraged than his mother ever knew him to be before

"It is impossible to find a school; most of them have teachers engaged," said James. And he gave a full account of his travels and disappointments.

"Perhaps the Lord has something better for you in store, James," answered his mother. "It is not best for you to be discouraged, after you have overcome so many obstacles."

James did not tell his mother that if the Lord had anything better in store for him he would be obliged if He would make it known; but he thought so.

"You are tired enough to go to bed," added his mother; "and to-morrow you can talk with your uncle Amos about it."

Uncle Amos was their counsellor in all times of trial; and James accepted the suggestion as a kind of solace, and retired.

The next morning, before he was up, he heard a man call to his mother from the road.

"Widow Garfield!"

She responded by going to the door.

"Where's your boy Jim?"

"He is at home. He is not up yet," Mrs Garfield replied, a little curious to know what he wanted of James so early in the morning.

"I wonder if he'd like to keep our school at the Ledge this winter?" the man continued

James bounded out of bed at the sound of the word *school*, beginning to think that Providence had sent an angel in the shape of a man, to bring the "something better" which his mother told about. He stood face to face with the man in an incredibly brief period. The caller was a well-known neighbour living only a mile away, and the school for which he wanted a teacher was not much farther than that.

"How is it, Jim? Will you keep our school at the Ledge this winter?" he inquired.

"I want a school," was James's indirect reply. He knew the character of the school—that it was rough and boisterous—and he hesitated.

"Reg'lar set of barbarians, you know, Jim, down there," the man continued.

"Yes; I know it is a hard school to teach. Do you think I can manage it? All the scholars know me." This reply of James showed what thoughts were passing through his mind. The committee-man replied:

"They all know you, of course, and they know that you can lick the whole of them without any trouble, if you set about it; and you are just the chap to run the school. The boys have driven out the master for two winters now; and I want somebody to control the school this winter, if he don't do a thing but stand over them with a cane. A thrashing all around would do them an immense amount of good. Now, what do you say? Give you twelve dollars a month and board"

This pourtrayal of the character of the school rather discouraged James than otherwise; but his mother spoke, by way of helping him out of the difficulty:

"This is an unexpected call to James, and he'd better consider it to-day, and let you know his decision to-night."

"I will do that," said James.

"That will answer; but I hope you won't fail me," the man responded, and drove off.

"Go over and consult your Uncle Amos after breakfast," advised his mother. "It is a very difficult school to undertake for the first one."

"I should prefer to teach among strangers, at least my first school," responded James. "Do you think this is
tl   l ng ho   r P: . .., w e had in store for me?"

"Perhaps so If you should be successful in thi school, your reputation as a teacher would be established; you would have no more trouble in finding schools to keep."

"I see that; and still, if I had a chance to take a school among strangers, I should decline this one," said James.

"Perhaps that is the very reason you did not find a school. Providence means you shall take this one. I really think, James, that this is the correct view of the case"

James could not suppress a laugh over this turn of affairs, nor could he fail to respect his mother's moral philosophy. He really began to think that Providence was forcing him to take this school, and he mentally decided to take it before he saw Uncle Amos.

"Tough school," remarked Uncle Amos, when James sought his advice. "Those rough fellows have had their way so long in school that it will be a hard matter to bring them into subjection. How do you feel about it yourself?"

"I would prefer to teach where the scholars are not acquainted with me," replied James.

"That might make a difference with some teachers, James; but the boys have nothing against you. Perhaps they will behave better because they know you so well. I think they respect you, and that will be a great help."

"Then you think I had better teach the school?" remarked James, understanding the drift of his uncle's remarks to mean that.

"On the whole, I am inclined to think you had better teach the school."

"If I had an opportunity to teach a better school, you would not advise me to take the one at the Ledge: I understand you to mean this"

"About that," his uncle answered. Pri l, t l w

moments, as if to reflect upon the matter, he continued ·

" It is just here, James ; you will begin that school as ' Jim Garfield ' ; now, if you can leave it, at the close of the term, as Mr Garfield, your reputation as a teacher will be established, and you will do more good than you can in any other school in Ohio."

Uncle Amos was a very wise man, and James knew it. His opinion upon all subjects was a kind of rule to be followed in the Garfield family. In this case his counsel was wise as possible ; its wisdom appeared in every word.

" I shall take the school," said James, decidedly, as he rose to go

" I think it will prove the best decision," added his uncle.

The committee-man was notified according to agreement, and within two days it was noised over the district that " Jim Garfield" would teach the winter school. At first, remarks were freely bandied about pro and con, and the boys, and girls too, expressed themselves very decidedly upon the subject, one way or the other. Before school commenced, however, the general opinion of the district, parents and pupils, was about as one of the large boys expressed it .

" Me like Jim : he's a good feller, and he knows more'n all the teachers we ever had. I guess we better mind. He can lick us easy 'nuf if we don't ; and he'll do it."

This hopeful schoolboy understood that the committee-man had instructed James to keep order and command obedience, " if he had to lick every scholar in school a dozen times over."

It was under these circumstances that James entered upon his new vocation. He dreaded the undertaking far more than he confessed ; and when he left home, on the morning his school began, he remarked to his m '

" Perhaps I shall be back before noon, through with school-keeping," signifying that the boys might run over him in the outset.

" I expect that you will succeed, and be the most popular teacher in town," was his mother's encouraging reply. She saw that James needed some bracing up in the trying circumstances.

James had determined in his own mind to run the school without resorting to the use of rod or ferrule, if possible. He meant that his government should be firm, but kind and considerate. He was wise enough to open his labour on the first morning without laying down a string of rigid rules. He simply assured the pupils he was there to aid them in their studies, that they might make rapid progress ; that all of them were old enough to appreciate the purpose and advantages of the school, and he should expect their cordial co-operation. He should do the best that he could to have an excellent school, and if the scholars would do the same, both teacher and pupils would have a good time, and the best school in town.

Many older heads than he have displayed less wisdom in taking charge of a difficult school. His method appeared to be exactly adapted to the circumstances under which he assumed charge. He was on good terms with the larger boys before, but now those harmonious relations were confirmed.

We must use space only to sum up the work of the winter. The bad boys voluntarily yielded to the teacher's authority, and behaved creditably to themselves and satisfactorily to their teacher. There was no attempt to over-ride the government of the school, and former rowdyism, that had been the bane of the school, disappeared. The pupils bent their energies to study, as if for the first time they understood what going to school meant. James interested the larger scholars in spelling-matches, in which all found much enjoyment as well as

O

profit. He joined in the games and sports of the boys at noon, his presence proving a restraint upon the disposition of some to be vulgar and profane. He was perfectly familiar with his scholars, and yet he was so correct and dignified in his ways that the wildest boy could but respect him.

James " boarded around," as was the universal custom ; and this brought him into every family in the course of the winter. Here he enjoyed an additional opportunity to influence his pupils He took special pains to aid them in their studies, and to make the evenings entertaining to the members of the families. He read aloud to them, rehearsed history, told stories, availing himself of his quite extensive reading to furnish material. In this way he gained a firm hold both of the parents and their children.

His Sabbaths were spent at home with his mother during the winter. The Disciples' meeting had become a fixed institution, so that he attended Divine worship every Sabbath. A preacher was officiating at the time in whom James became particularly interested. He was a very earnest preacher, a devout Christian, and a man of strong native abilities. He possessed a tact for " putting things," as men call it, and made his points sharply and forcibly. He was just suited to interest a youth like James, and his preaching made a deep impression upon him. From week to week that impression deepened, until he resolved to become a Christian at once ; and he did. Before the close of his school he gave good evidence that he had become a true child of God. And now his mother's cup of joy was overflowing. She saw distinctly the way in which God had led him, and her gratitude was unbounded. James saw, too, how it was that his mother's prophecy was fulfilled · " Providence has something better in store for you."

The verdict of parents and pupils at the close of the term was · " THE BEST TEACHER WE EVER HAD." So

James parted with his scholars, sharing their confidence and esteem , and his Uncle Amos was satisfied, because he left the school as MR. GARFIELD.

He returned to Geauga Seminary, not to board himself, but to board with Mr Woodworth, the carpenter, according to previous arragement. Mr. Woodworth boarded him for one dollar six cents per week, including his washing, and took his pay in labour. It was an excellent opportunity for James, as well as for the carpenter His chief labour in the shop was planing boards. On the first Saturday after his return he planed fifty-one boards, at two cents apiece ; thus earning on that day one dollar and two cents,—nearly enough to pay a week's board.

We shall pass over the details of his schooling that year, to his schoolkeeping at Warrensville the following winter, where he was paid sixteen dollars a month and board It was a larger and more advanced school than the one of the previous winter, in a pleasanter neighbourhood, and a more convenient school-house. We shall stop to relate but two incidents connected with his winter's work, except to say that his success was complete.

One of the more advanced scholars wanted to study geometry, and James had given no attention to it. He did not wish to let the scholar know that he had never studied it, for he knew full well that he could keep in advance of his pupil, and teach him as he desired. So he purchased a text-book, studied geometry at night, sometimes extending his studies far into the night, and carried his pupil through, without the latter dreaming that his teacher was not an expert in the science. James considered this a clear gain ; for he would not have mastered geometry that winter but for this necessity laid upon him. It left him more time in school for other studies.

This fact is a good illustration of what James said

after he had entered on public, viz : " A young man should be equal to more than the task before him ; he should possess reserved power." He had not pursued geometry, but he was equal to it in the emergency. His reserved force carried him triumphantly over a hard place.

One day he fell when engaged in outdoor sports with his big boys, the result of which was a large rent in his pantaloons. They were well worn, and so thin that it did not require much of a pressure to push one of his knees through them. He pinned up the rent as well as he could, and went to his boarding place, after school, with a countenance looking almost as forlorn as his trousers. He was boarding with a Mrs. Stiles at the time, a motherly kind of a woman, possessing considerable sharpness of intellect.

" See what a plight I am in, Mrs. Stiles ! " showing the rents in his pants.

" I see ; how did you do that ? " said Mrs Stiles

" Blundering about, as usual," James replied " I hardly know what I shall do."

" What ! so scared at a rent," the good lady exclaimed ; " that's nothing "

" It is a good deal, when it is all the pantaloons a fellow has," answered James. " This is all the suit I possess in the world, poor as it is."

" It's good enough, and there's enough of it as long as it lasts," replied the good woman ; " make the best of things."

" I think I could make the best of an extra suit," responded James ; " but this making the best of a single suit, and a flimsy one at that, is asking too much." He said this humorously

" Well," continued Mrs. Stiles, " I can darn that rent so that it will be just as good as new, if not better. That's easy enough done "

" On me ? " asked James, in his innocence

" Mercy, no ! When you go to bed, one of the boys will bring down your trousers, and I'll mend them.   In the morning no one will know that you met with such an accident   You mustn't let such matters trouble you   You'll forget all about them when you become President."

James's wardrobe was not much more elaborate at this time than it was when he began attending school at Chester. He had no overcoat nor underclothing, preferring to expose his body to the cold rather than rob his mind of knowledge.

At the close of his school in Warrensville James returned home, where an unexpected change in his programme awaited him

XVIII

THIRD YEAR AT SCHOOL

JAMES spent three years at Geauga Seminary, including school-keeping in winter. It was during his last term there that he met a young man who was a graduate of a New England college. James had never thought of extending his education so far as a college course He scarcely thought it was possible, in his extreme poverty, to do it

"You can do it," said the graduate "Several students did it when I was in college. I did it, in part, myself"

"How could I do it?" inquired James.

"In the first place," answered the graduate, "there is a fund in most of the New England colleges, perhaps in all of them, the income of which goes to aid indigent students. It is small, to be sure, but then every little helps when one is in a tight place. Then there is a great call for school-teachers in the winter, and college students are sought after."

"How much is the annual expense, to an economical student?" asked James.

"It varies somewhat in different colleges, though two hundred dollars a year, not including apparel, could be made to cover the running yearly expenses, I think A young man would be obliged to be very saving in order to do it."

"I am used to that," added James. "They say that

' necessity is the mother of invention,' and I have invented a good many ways of living cheaply "

" I have known students to obtain jobs of work in term time—those who know how to do certain work," continued the graduate. " I knew a student who took care of a man's garden two summers, for which he received liberal pay. I knew one who taught a gentleman's son in the place an hour or so every day, for which he was paid well. The boy was in delicate health, not able to enter a school for hard study. I have known students to get jobs of the faculty, about the college buildings. I knew one student who sawed wood for his fellow-students in the fall and winter terms, and he was one of the best scholars in his class. He was very popular, too, and was honoured for his perseverance in acquiring an education I think that he must have paid half his bills by sawing wood "

James began to see further than he did. In his imagination he began to picture a college building at the end of his career. It was further off than he had intended to go in the way of study, but the way before him seemed to open up to it. What he supposed was impossible now appeared among possibilities.

" What is the shortest time that it would require me to prepare and get through college ? " James asked further.

" The necessary time is four years in preparation, and four years in college," the graduate answered. " Some students shorten the preparatory course, and enter college one year in advance."

" *I* should have to *lengthen* it in order to earn the money to pay my way," responded James. " I would be willing to undertake it, if I could get through in twelve years, and pay all my bills."

" You can get through in less time than that, I know I forgot to tell you that students sometimes enter college with money enough to carry them through the first two years; then they stay out a year and teach an academy or high school, for which they receive sufficient remuneration to carry them through the remainder of the course. It is a better plan, I think, than to teach a district school each winter; it don't interfere so much with the studies of the college, and it is easier for the student Then I have known several students who borrowed the money of friends to pay bills, relying upon teaching, after getting through college, to liquidate the debt. By waiting until their college course was completed they obtained a more eligible situation, at a higher salary, than would have been possible before."

"Well, I have no friends having money to loan," remarked James. "I shall have to content myself with working my own way by earning all my money as I go along; and I am willing to do it I had never thought it possible for me to go to college, but now I believe that I shall try it."

"I hope you will," answered the graduate, who had learned of James's ability, and who had seen enough of him to form a high opinion of his talents "You will never regret the step, I am sure. You get something in a college education that you can never lose, and it will always be a passport into the best society."

From that time James was fully decided to take a college course, or, at least, to try for it; and he immediately added Latin and Greek to his studies.

During the last year of his connection with Geauga Seminary, James united with the Disciples' Church in Orange. He took the step after much reflection, and he took it for greater usefulness. At once he became an active, working Christian, in Chester. He spoke and prayed in meeting; he urged the subject of religion upon the attention of his companions, privately as well as publicly, he seconded the religious efforts of the principal, and assisted him essentially in the conduct of religious meetings. In short, the same earnest spirit pervaded his Christian life that had distinguished his secular career.

In religious meetings his simple, earnest appeals, eloquently expressed, attracted universal attention. There was a naturalness and fervour in his addresses that held an audience remarkably   Many attended meetings to hear him speak, and for no other reason. His power as a public speaker began to show itself unmistakably at that time.   No doubt his youthful appearance lent a charm to his words.

" He is a born preacher," remarked Mr. Branch to one of the faculty, " and he will make his mark in that profession."

" One secret of his power is, that he is wholly unconscious of it," answered the member of the faculty addressed   " It seems to me he is the most eminent example of that I ever knew   He appears to lose all thought of himself in the subject before him.   He is not a bold young man at all ; he is modest as any student in the academy, and yet, in speaking, he seems to be so absorbed in his theme that fear is banished.   He will make a power in the pulpit, if present appearances foreshadow the future."

" It cannot be otherwise," responded Mr Branch, " if cause and effect follow each other.   He develops very rapidly indeed   I wish it were possible for him to have a college education."

All seemed to take it for granted that James would be a preacher, although he had not signified to any one that he intended to be.   He had given no thought to that particular subject   He was too much absorbed in his studies, too much in love with them, to settle that question.   But his interest in religious things, and his ability as a speaker, alone led them to this conclusion. The same feeling existed among the pupils.

" Jim will be a minister now," remarked one of his companions to Henry.

"Perhaps so," was Henry's only reply.

"He will make a good one, sure," chimed in a third "By the time he gets into the pulpit, he will astonish the natives."

"That will be ten years from now," said the first speaker.

"Not so long as that," rejoined Henry. "Five or six years is long enough"

"He won't wear trousers of Kentucky jean then," added the second speaker, in a jocose manner

"He won't care whether he does or not," remarked Henry. "He would wear Kentucky jean just as quick as broadcloth ; such things are wholly unimportant in his estimation"

So the matter of his becoming a preacher was discussed, all appearing to think that he was destined to become a pulpit orator. Doubtless some thought it was the only profession he would be qualified to fill

During the summer vacation of his last year at Geauga Seminary, in connection with a schoolmate, he sought work among the farmers in the vicinity He found no difficulty in securing jobs to suit his most sanguine expectations An amusing incident occurred with one of the farmers to whom he applied for work.

"What do you know about work ? " inquired the farmer, surveying them from head to foot, and seeming to question their fitness for his farm.

"We have worked at farming," answered James, modestly

"Can you mow ? "

"Yes, sir."

"Can you mow *well ?* " emphasizing the last word.

"You can tell by trying us," answered James, not wishing to praise his own ability at labour

"What wages do you want ? "

"Just what you think is right "

"Well that is fair ; where did you come from ? "

James enlightened him on this subject, and informed him, also, that they were trying to get an education.

" You are plucky boys," the farmer added ; " I think you may go to work "

He conducted them to the hay-field, where they were provided with scythes, remarking to the three men already mowing, " Here are two boys who will help you."

James exchanged glances with his companion, and the imitated might have discovered in their mutual smiles an inkling of what was coming. Their glances at each other said, as plainly as words, " Let us beat these fellows, though we are *boys* " James thought that the farmer emphasized the word *boys* more than was justifiable.

The boys had mowed an hour, the farmer being an interested witness, when the latter cried out to the three men :

" See here, you lubbers , those *boys* are beatin' you all holler Their swaths are wider, and they mow better than you do. You ought to be ashamed of yourselves."

The men made no reply, but bent their energies to work more resolutely. The boys, too, were silent, although they enjoyed the praise of their employer very much They comprehended the situation fully, and their labours were pushed accordingly. One day, while at work with the men, one of them said to James :

" Yer are schoolboys, I understand."

" Yes, we are," answered James.

" Where's yer larn to farm it ? "

" At home, and all about. We've had to earn our living," was the reply of James.

" Yer are no worse for that ; it won't damage your larnin "

" I expect not ; I should say good-bye to the scythe if I thought so," replied James. " If there had been no work, there would have been no education for me."

" What yer goin' to make—a preacher ? "

" That is an unsolved problem," answered James, in a playful way " I have undertaken to make a man of myself first. If I succeed, I may make something else afterwards ; if I don't succeed, I shall not be fit for much, any way "

" Yer in a fair way to succeed, I guess," responded the labourer, who seemed to have the idea, in common with other people, that James was aiming to be a minister.

When the day of settlement with the boys came, the farmer said

" Now, boys, what must I pay you ? "

" What you think is right," replied James, at the same time thinking that the farmer's emphasis of the word *boys* indicated boys' pay.

" I s'pose you don't expect men's wages ; you are only boys."

" If boys do men's work, what's the difference ? "

" Well, you see, boys never have so much as men · there's a price for boys, and there's a price for men Some boys will do more work than others, but the best of them only have boys' pay."

" But you told the men that we mowed wider swaths and mowed better than they, and beat them. Now admit that we are boys, if we have done men's work, why should we not have their pay ? I told you at first to pay us what was right, and I say so now ; and if we have worked as well as your men, or better, is it not *right* that we should have their pay ? "

James's plea was a strong one, and the farmer felt its force. There was but one honourable course out of the difficulty, and that was to pay the boys just what he did the men.

" Well, boys, I can't in justice deny that you did as much work as the men." he said. " and so I'll pay you men's wages; but you are the first boys I ever paid such wages to."

" I hope we are not the last ones," added James, who was never in a strait for a reply.

The farmer paid them full wages, and parted with them in good feeling, wishing them success in their struggles for an education, and saying to James:

" If, one of these days, you preach as well as you mow, I shall want to hear you."

When they left the farmer, James remarked to his companion:

" Everybody seems to think that I am going to be a preacher; why is it? " He was so unconscious of his abilities for that profession that he was actually puzzled to know why it was.

" I suppose it is because they think you are better qualified for that than any other calling," his companion replied " I never heard you say what profession you should choose."

" No, I don't think you have; nor any one else When the time comes I shall choose for the best. I should like to be a preacher, and I should like to be a teacher. I don't know but I should like to be a lawyer. I shouldn't want to be a doctor "

James stated the matter here just about as it was at that time. He was going to make the most of himself possible, in the first place—a very sensible idea for a youth—and then devote himself to the manifest line of duty

At this time the anti-slavery contest ran high throughout the country. In Ohio its friends were as zealous and fearless as they were anywhere in the country. The question of the abolition of slavery was discussed. not only in pulpits and on public rostrums, but in village and school lyceums It was discussed in the Debating Society of the Seminary " OUGHT SLAVERY TO BE ABOLISHED IN THIS REPUBLIC? " This was a question that drew out James in one of his best efforts. From the time his attention was drawn to the subject, he was a thorough hater of slavery. It was such a monstrous wrong, that he had no patience with it.

"A disgrace to the nation," he said. "People fighting to be free, and then reducing others to a worse slavery than that which they fought! It is a burning shame!"

"The founders of the government didn't think so," answered the schoolmate addressed. "If they had thought so, they would have made no provision for it"

"So much more the shame," replied James "The very men who fought to break the British yoke of bondage legalized a worse bondage to others! That is what makes my blood boil. I can't understand how men of intelligence and honour could do what is so inconsistent and inhuman"

"Slavery wouldn't stand much of a show where you are, I judge," added his schoolmate "You would sweep it away without discussing the question whether *immediate* emancipation is safe or not."

"Safe!" exclaimed James, in a tone of supreme contempt; "it is always *safe* to do right, and it is never safe to do wrong, especially to perpetrate such a monstrous wrong as to buy and sell men."

It was this inborn and inbred hostility to human bondage that James carried into the discussion of the question named, in their school lyceum. He prepared himself for the debate with more than usual carefulness He read whatever he could find upon the subject, and he taxed his active brain to the utmost in forging arguments against the crime.

Companions and friends had been surprised and interested before by his ability in debate; but on this occasion he discussed his favourite theme with larger freedom and more eloquence than ever. There was a

manly and exhaustive treatment of the question, such
as he had not evinced before. It enlisted his sympathies and honest convictions as no previous question
had done , so that his fervour and energy were greater
than ever, holding the audience in rapt and delighted
attention.

Commenting upon his effort afterwards, one of his
schoolmates said to a number of his companions present :

"We'll send Jim to Congress one of these days."
James was present, and the remark was intended both
for sport and praise

"I don't want you should send me until I have
graduated at Geauga Academy," retorted James, disposed to treat the matter playfully.

"We'll let you do that , but we can begin the campaign now, and set the wires for pulling by-and-by,"
replied the first speaker. "I'll stump the District for
you, Jim, and charge only my expenses "

"And who will you charge your expenses to ? "
inquired James

"To the candidate, of course, Hon. James A Garfield,"
the schoolmate answered, with a laugh, in which the
whole company joined, not excepting James. The
incident illustrates the place that James held in the
opinions of his school-fellows Not the immature
opinions of partial friends, but the well-considered and
honest estimate of faculty and pupils.

In the fall term of that year there came to the school
a young lady by the name of Lucretia Rudolph, a
modest, unpretentious, talented girl. James soon discovered that she was a young lady of unusual worth
and intellectual ability. He was not much inclined to
the company of schoolgirls ; he was too bashful to make
much of a display in that line. He was not very companionable in their society, for he was not at home
there. But he was unconsciously drawn to this new

and pretty pupil, Miss Lucretia Rudolph. First, her modest, lady-like demeanour attracted his attention There was a grace in her movements, and evidence of intellectual strength in her conversation. Her recitations were perfect, showing industry and scholarship These things impressed James sensibly. No female student had attracted his attention at all before. Nor was there any such thing as falling in love with her on his part. He regarded her with more favour than he had ever regarded a young lady in school ; and it was her worth and scholarship that drew him. They were intimate, mutually polite, helpers of each other in study, real friends in all the relations of schoolmates. Further than that, neither of them had thoughts about each other. They associated together, and parted at the close of the term with no expectation, perhaps, of renewing their acquaintance again. We speak of the matter here, because the two will meet again elsewhere

James made rapid progress in Latin after he decided to go to college. It was the study that occupied his odd moments especially Every spare hour that he could snatch was devoted to this. The following winter he taught school, and Latin received much of his attention in evening hours He enjoyed the study of it, and, at the same time, was stimulated by the consideration that it was required in a college course of study.

Late in the autumn James met with a young man who was connected with the Eclectic Institute, a new institution just established in Hiram, Portage County, Ohio. James knew that such an institution had been opened, and that was all ; of its scope and character he was ignorant.

" You can fit for college there," he said to James ; " there is no better place in the country for that business. The school opened with over one hundred scholars, and the number is rapidly increasing."

" Any fitting for college there now ? " James inquired.

" Yes, several ; I am one of them."

" How far along are you ? "

" Only just begun. I have to work my own way, so that it will be slow."

" That is the case with me. So far I have had but eleven dollars from my friends, and I have more than returned that amount to them."

" A fellow can do it if he only has grit enough."

" How expensive is the school ? " continued James.

" Not more expensive than Geauga Seminary. It is designed to give a chance to the poorest boy or girl to get an academical education. Besides, it is conducted under the auspices of the Disciples, and the teachers belong to that sect."

" I belong to the Disciples' Church," said James

" So do I That would not take me there, however, if it was not a good school. I think it is one of the best schools to be found "

" The teachers are well qualified, are they ? "

" They are the best of teachers ; no better in any school."

" I am glad that you have called my attention to the school," added James. " I think I shall go there next year."

Here was the second casual meeting with a person, in a single term, that had much to do with the future career of James His mother would have called it PROVIDENTIAL. Meeting with one of them led to his decision to go to college ; meeting with the other carried him to the Hiram Eclectic Institute.

James closed his connection with the Geauga Seminary at the expiration of the fall term, leaving it with a reputation for scholarship and character of which the institution was justly proud. As we have said, he taught school during the following winter. It was at Warrensville, where he had taught before He received

P

eighteen dollars a month, and board, with the esteem
and gratitude of his patrons.

We should not pass over the oration that James
delivered at the annual exhibition of Geauga Seminary,
in November, 1850 It was his last task performed at
the institution, and the *first* oration of his literary life.
The part assigned to him was honorary ; and he spent
all the time he could spare, amid other pressing duties,
upon the production. He was to quit the institution,
and he would not conceal his desire to close his course
of study there with his best effort. He kept a diary at
the time, and his diary discloses the anxiety with which
he undertook the preparation of that oration, and the
thorough application with which he accomplished his
purpose. Neither ambition nor vanity can be discovered,
in the least degree, in his diary ; that was written for no
eyes but his own. His performance proved the attraction of the hour. It carried the audience like a surprise,
although they expected a noble effort from the ablest
student in the academy. It exceeded their expectations,
and was a fitting close of his honourable connection
with the school.

Returning home, he found his mother making preparations to visit relatives in Muskingum County, eighteen
miles from Zanesville.

" You must go, James ; I have made all my arrange-
ments for you to go with me," said his mother

" How long will you be gone ? "

" All the spring, and into the summer, perhaps "

" I had concluded to go to the Eclectic Institute, at
Hiram, when the spring term opens."

" You have ? Why do you go there ? "

" To prepare for college."

" Do you expect you can work your way through
college ? "

" I expect I can, or I should not undertake it." And
James then rehearsed the circumstances under which

he decided to go to college, if possible, and to take a preparatory course at Hiram

"I shall be glad, James, to have you accomplish your purpose," remarked his mother, after listening to his rehearsal, in which she was deeply interested. "I think, however, that you had better go with me, and enter the Eclectic Institute at the opening of the fall term."

"It will be wasting a good deal of time, it seems to me," said James.

"I don't mean that you shall go there to idle away your time. Take your books along with you. You can find *work* there, too, I have no doubt. Perhaps you can find a school there to teach."

"Well, if I can be earning something to help me along, perhaps I had better go It will give me an opportunity to see more of the world——"

"And some of your relations, also," interrupted the mother.

It was settled that James should accompany his mother on her visit ; and they started as soon as they could get ready. The journey took them to Cleveland first, where James was sensibly reminded of his encounter with the drunken captain, and his providential connection with the canal boat. The Cleveland and Columbus railroad had just been opened, and James and his mother took their first ride in the cars on that day. James had not seen a railroad before, and it was one of the new things under the sun, that proved a real stimulus to his thoughts. He beheld in it a signal triumph of skill and enterprise.

The State capitol had been erected at Columbus, and the legislature was in session. It was a grand spectacle to James. He had scarcely formed an idea of the building, so that the view of it surprised him. He visited the legislature in session, and received his first impression of the law making power It was a great treat to him, and the impressions of that day were never obliterated.

From Columbus they proceeded by stage to Zanesville. On their way James remarked :

" I never should have made an objection to this trip, if I had expected to see the capitol, or the legislature in session. That alone is equal to a month's schooling to me. It has given me an idea about public affairs that I never had before."

" It is fortunate that you came," replied Mrs Garfield " It does boys who *think* much good to see things which set them to *thinking* "

" I guess that is so," replied James, with a roguish smile, as if he thought his mother had exerted herself to compliment him. " *Thinking* is needed in this world about as much as anything."

" *Right* thinking," suggested his mother.

" Mr Branch says a young man had better think erroneously than not think at all," responded James

" I don't think I should agree with Mr Branch. It is safer not to think than to think wrong," said Mrs. Garfield

" I suppose that Mr. Branch meant to rebuke dull scholars, who never think for themselves, and take every assertion of the books as correct, without asking *why*," added James

James and his mother thus discussed the scenes and the times on their way to Zanesville, enjoying the change and the scenery very much. From the latter place they floated down the Muskingum River, in a skiff, to their destination, eighteen miles distant. Here they found their relatives the more rejoiced to see them because their visit was unexpected.

As soon as they were fairly settled among their relations within four or five days after their arrival, James began to cast about for something to do.

Perhaps he did not attend to keep with Harrison, four miles from here," said his aunt. " I heard they were looking after a teacher "

" Who shall I go to there to find out ? " inquired James.

" I can't tell you, but your uncle can, when he gets home."

James learned to whom application should be made, and posted away immediately, and secured the school, at twelve dollars a month, for three months.

" You are fortunate," said his mother, on hearing his report. " You will be contented to stay now until I get ready to go home What kind of a school-house have they ? "

" A log-house ; not much of an affair."

" How large is the school ? "

" About thirty ; enough to crowd the building full."

" When do you begin ? "

" Next Monday."

" Board round, I suppose ? "

" Yes ; and some of the families are between two and three miles away."

James commenced his school under favourable auspices, so far as his relations to the pupils were concerned The conveniences for a school were meagre, and the parents were indifferent to the real wants of their children. Most of them failed to appreciate schooling It was quite cold weather when the school opened, and there was no fuel provided Near by the school-house, however, there was coal, in a bank, and James proposed to his pupils to dig fuel therefrom ; and, in this way, their fire was run until it became so warm that fire was not needed.

The pupils were so far advanced as the pupils at Warrensville, but not so rough as those at the Ledge. The neighbourhood was not so far advanced in the arts of civilization as the region with which James had been familiar. Yet he enjoyed school-keeping there : and his connection with the families was pleasant. At the close of the term he received many expressions of affection and confidence from the pupils, and separated from them with the best of feeling

Mrs. Garfield was ready to return to Orange at the close of the school, nor was James sorry to start on the journey home. After an absence of over three months, James found himself at the homestead with more money than he had when he left.

XIX

THE ECLECTIC INSTITUTE

SEVERAL weeks would intervene before the commencement of the term at Hiram , and James looked about for work, that he might add to his funds for an education. He was planning now to lay up money to assist himself through college. He found jobs to occupy his time fully until he would leave to enter the Eclectic Institute.

It was the last of August, 1851, when James reached Hiram. The board of trustees was in session. Proceeding directly to the institution, he accosted the janitor

" I want to see the principal of the Institute," he said.

" He is engaged with the board of trustees, who are in session now," replied the janitor.

" Can I see him, or them ? "

" Probably ; I will see " And the janitor went directly to the room of the trustees, and announced

" A young man at the door, who is desirous to see the board at once."

" Let him come in," answered the chairman.

James presented himself politely, though, perhaps, awkwardly

" Gentlemen," he said, " I am anxious to get an education, and have come here to see what I can do."

" Well, this is a good place to obtain an education,"

231

answered the chairman, without waiting for James to proceed further "Where are you from ? "

"From Orange. My name is James Abram Garfield. I have no father; he died when I was an infant My mother is widow Eliza Garfield."

"And you want what education this institution can furnish ? "

"Yes, sir, provided I can work my way."

"Then you are poor ? "

"Yes, sir; but I can work my way I thought, perhaps, that I could have the chance to ring the bell, and sweep the floors, to pay part of my bills."

"How much have you been to school ? "

"I have attended Geauga Seminary three years, teaching school in the winter."

"Ah! then you are quite advanced ? "

"No, not very far advanced I have commenced Latin and Greek."

"Then you think of going to college ? "

"That is what I am trying for."

"I think we had better try this young man," said one of the trustees, addressing the chairman. He was much impressed by the earnestness and intelligence of the applicant, and was in favour of rendering him all the aid possible.

"Yes," answered the chairman; "he has started out upon a noble work, and we must help him all we can "

"How do we know that you can do the sweeping and bell-ringing to suit us ? " inquired another trustee of James.

"Try me—try me two weeks, and if it is not done to your entire satisfaction, I will retire without a word."

James's honest reply settled the matter.

James was nineteen years old at this time , he became twenty in the following November. So he was duly installed bell-ringer and sweeper-general

Hiram was a small, out of the way town twelve

miles from the railroad, the "centre" being at a cross-roads, with two churches and half a dozen other buildings. The institution was located there to accommodate the sons and daughters of the Western Reserve farmers. President Hinsdale, who now presides over the college (it was elevated to a college twelve or fifteen years ago), says "The Institute building, a plain but substantially built brick structure, was put on the top of a windy hill, in the middle of a corn-field. One of the cannon that General Scott's soldiers dragged to the city of Mexico in 1847, planted on the roof of the new structure, would not have commanded a score of farmhouses. Here the school opened at the time Garfield was closing his studies at Chester. It had been in operation two terms when he offered himself for enrolment. Hiram furnished a location, the board of trustees a building and the first teachers, the surrounding country students, but the spiritual Hiram made itself Everything was new. Society, traditions, the genius of the school had to be evolved from the forces of the teachers and pupils, limited by the general and local environment Let no one be surprised when I say that such a school as this was the best of all places for young Garfield There was freedom, opportunity, a large society of rapidly and eagerly opening young minds, instructors who were learned enough to instruct him, and abundant scope for ability and force of character, of which he had a super-abundance

"Few of the students who came to Hiram in that day had more than a district-school education, though some had attended the high schools and academies scattered over the country; so that Garfield, although he had made but slight progress in the classics and the higher mathematics previous to his arrival, ranked well up with the first scholars. In ability, all acknowledged that he was the peer of any; soon his superiority to all others was generally conceded."

James sought an early opportunity to confer with the principal.

"I want your advice as to my course of study," he said. "My purpose is to enter college, and I want to pursue the best way there."

"You want to make thorough work of it as you go along?" the principal answered, by way of inquiry.

"Yes, sir, as thorough as possible. What I know, I want to know *certainly*"

"That is a good idea; better take time, and master everything as you go along. Many students fail because they are satisfied with a smattering of knowledge. Be a scholar, or don't undertake."

"I agree with you perfectly, and I am ready to accept your advice, and will regulate my course accordingly"

"Our regular preparatory course of study cannot be improved, I think," continued the principal. "You can pursue higher studies here, and enter college in advance if you choose. But that can be determined hereafter At present, you can go on with the branches undertaken, and time will indicate improvement and changes necessary"

"It will be necessary for me to labour some out of school hours, in order to pay all my bills," added James "Then I would like to be earning something more to help me through college."

"What do you propose to do?"

"I can work on a farm, or in a carpenter's shop, or do odd jobs at most anything that offers. I have already seen the carpenter here."

"Well, what prospect for work?"

"After a few days he will have work for me, mostly planing; and that I have done more than anything in the carpenter's line."

"You are fortunate to find work at once"

"I never have failed to find work since I have been dependent upon my own exertions"

" I hope you always will find work, that you may realize the accomplishment of your object. I shall do everything in my power to assist you, and do it with all my heart."

" Thank you," responded James, grateful for the deep interest the principal appeared to manifest in his welfare.

He secured quarters in a room with four other students , rather thick for the highest comfort, but " necessity multiplies bedfellows." Here he set about his literary work with a zeal and devotion that attracted attention. The office of bell-ringer obliged him to rise very early ; for the first bell was rung at five o'clock. The office of sweeper compelled him to be on the alert at an early hour, also. Promptness was the leading requirement of the youth who rang the bell It must be rung on the mark. A single minute too early, or too late, spoiled the promptness. *On the mark precisely*, was the rule. Nor was it any cross to James. Promptness, as we have seen, was one of his born qualities. It was all the same to him whether he arose at four or five o'clock in the morning, or whether he must ring the bell three or a dozen times a day. He adapted himself to circumstances with perfect ease. Instead of bending to circumstances, circumstances bent to him. He made a good bell-ringer and sweeper, simply because it was a rule with him to do everything well. One of his roommates said to him :

" Jim, I don't see but you sweep just as well as you recite."

" Why shouldn't I ? " James responded promptly.

" Many people do important things best," replied his schoolmates ; " and a lesson is more important than sweeping."

" You are heretical," exclaimed James. " If your views upon other matters are not sounder than that, you will not make a very safe leader Sweeping in its place, is just as important as a lesson in Greek is, in its place, and, therefore, according to your own rule, should be done as well."

" You are right, Jim ; I yield my heresy, like the honest boy that I am."

" I think that the boy who would not sweep well would not study well," continued James. " There may be *exceptions* to the rule ; but the rule is a correct one."

" I guess you are about right, Jim ; but my opinion is that few persons carry out the rule. There are certain things about which most people are superficial, however thorough they may be in others."

" That may be true , I shall not dispute you there," rejoined James ; " and that is one reason why so many persons fail of success. They have no settled purpose to be thorough. Not long ago I read, in the life of Franklin, that he claimed, ' thoroughness must be a principle of action.' "

" And that is why you sweep as well as you study ? " interrupted the room-mate, in a complimentary tone

" Yes, of course. And there is no reason why a person should, not be as thorough in one thing as in another. I don't think it is any harder to do work well than it is to half do it. I know that it is much harder to recite a lesson poorly than to recite it perfectly."

" I found that out some time ago, to my mortification," rejoined the room-mate, in a playful manner " There is some fun in a perfect lesson, I confess, and a great amount of misery in a poor one."

" It is precisely so with sweeping," added James. " The sight of a half-swept floor would be an eyesore to me all the time. It would be all of a piece with a poor lesson."

" I could go the half-swept floor best," remarked the room-mate.

" I can go neither best," retorted James, " since there is no good end to it "

James had told the trustees to try him at bell-ringing and sweeping two weeks. They did ; and the trial was perfectly satisfactory. He was permanently installed in the position.

A person, now an esteemed clergyman, who acted in the same capacity six or eight years after James did, writes · " When I did janitor work, I had to ring a bell at five o'clock in the morning, and another at nine o'clock in the evening, and I think this had been an immemorial custom during school sessions. The work was quite laborious, and much depended upon the promptness and efficiency of the person who handled the bell-rope, as the morning had to be divided into equal portions, after a large slice had been taken out of it for the chapel exercises, which were always protracted to uncertain lengths It was annoying, tedious work."

A lady now living in the State of Illinois was a member of the school when James was inaugurated bell-ringer, and she writes . " When he first entered the Institute, he paid for his schooling by doing janitor's work—sweeping the floor and ringing the bell. I can see him even now standing, in the morning, with his hand on the bell-rope, ready to give the signal calling teachers and scholars to engage in the duties of the day. As we passed by, entering the school-room, he had a cheerful word for every one. He was the most popular person in the Institute.˙ He was always good-natured, fond of conversation, and very entertaining. He was witty and quick at repartee ; but his jokes, though brilliant and striking, were always harmless, and he never would willingly hurt another's feelings "

The young reader should ponder the words, " most popular person in the Institute,"—and yet bell-ringer and sweeper ! Doing the most menial work there was to do with the same cheerfulness and thoroughness that he would solve a problem in algebra ! There is an important lesson in this fact for the young They can afford to study it. The youth who becomes the most "popular" student in the institution, notwithstanding he rings the bell and sweeps the floors, must possess unusual qualities. Doubtless he made the office of bell-ringer and sweeper very respectable. We dare say that some students were willing to serve in that capacity thereafter who were not willing to serve before Any necessary and useful employment is respectable ; but many youths have not found it out. The students discovered the fact in the Eclectic Institute. They learned it of James He dignified the humble offices that he filled. He did it by putting *character* into his work.

There were nearly two thousand volumes in the library belonging to the school. From this treasury of knowledge James drew largely. Every spare moment of his time was occupied with books therefrom. He began to be an enthusiastic reader of poetry at Geauga Seminary. "Young's Night Thoughts," which he found there, was the volume that particularly impressed his mind, just before he became a Christian under the preaching of the Disciples' minister at Orange. His tenacious memory retained much that he read, both of poetry and prose. Here he had a wider field to explore, more books to occupy his attention, though not more time to read. He began to read topically and systematically.

"What are you doing with that book ? " inquired a room-mate ; " transcribing it ? "

" Not exactly, though I am making it mine as much as possible," James replied. " Taking notes "

" I should think that would be slow work."

" Not at all, the way I do."

" What way are you doing ? "

" I note the important topics on which the book treats, with the pages, that I may turn to any topic of which I its, should I h casion hereafter. I mean to do the same with every book I read, and preserve the notes for future use."

"A good plan, if you have the patience I want to dash through a book at double-quick, I couldn't stop for such business," added the school-mate

"I spend no more time over a book than you do, I think," answered James. "I catch the drift, and appropriate the strong points, and let all the rest slide. But taking notes serves to impress the contents upon my memory. Then, hereafter, when I speak or write upon a given topic, my notes will direct me to necessary material"

"Your ammunition will be ready, all you will have to do will be to load and fire," suggested his room-mate. "That is not bad. I think the plan is a good one."

"It will save much time in the long run. Instead of being obliged to hunt for information on topics, I can turn to it at once." James remarked thus with an assurance that showed his purpose was well matured. He could testify afterwards that the method adopted was one of the most helpful and important rules of his life Many scholars have pursued a similar course, and their verdict respecting the usefulness of the plan is unanimous It is an excellent method for the young of both sexes, whether they are contemplating a thorough education or not, for it will promote their intelligence, and increase their general information. This result is desirable in the humblest as well as in the highest position. An intelligent, well-informed citizen adorns his place. That honoured and lifted into respectability the office of bell-ringer and sweeper at Hiram Institute, as we have seen.

When James had completed his collegiate course, and became Principal of Hiram Institute, he wrote to a youth whom he desired should undertake a liberal course of education :

"Tell me, Burke, do you not feel a spirit stirring within you that longs *to know, to do, and to dare*, to hold converse with the great world of thought, and holds before you some high and noble object to which the vigour of your mind and the strength of your arm may be given? Do you not have longings like these, which you breathe to no one, and which you feel must be heeded, or you will pass through life unsatisfied and regretful? I am sure you have them, and they will for ever cling round your heart till you obey their mandate. They are the voice of that nature which God has given you, and which, when obeyed, will bless you and your fellow-men."

Whether Burke felt this "spirit stirring within him" or not, it is certain that it moved James, as some mysterious power, when he entered this new field, and long before, impelling him onward and upward in a career that could have been denied him without inflicting an everlasting wound upon his soul

In the spring, after James became connected with the school, the principal proposed that the pupils should bring trees from the forest, and set them out on the Campus, to adorn the grounds, and provide a lovely shade for those who would gather there twenty and thirty years hence.

"A capital idea!" exclaimed James to Baker, with whom he was conferring upon the subject. "If each male student will put out one tree for himself, and one for a female student, we can cover the Campus with trees, and the streets near by as well, and do it next Saturday, too"

"That is real gallantry, Jim," answered Baker "The girls, of course, can't set out trees."

"And the boys will take pride in setting them out for them," interrupted James

"And calling them by their names," added Baker, su. ·· ` \ ˙

" A bright idea is that, to name the trees after those for whom they are set out," responded James. " You are an original genius, George ; I should not have thought of that It must be because you think more of girls than I do "

" But the plan to plant a tree for each girl is yours, Jim. I can't claim the patent for that."

" I am not ashamed to own it. It is worthy of the boys of the Western Reserve. We can have a rich time in carrying out the plan, better than a ride or party."

" I think so," said Baker

" The satisfaction of knowing we are doing something that will be a great blessing thirty years from now, adding beauty and comfort to the Institute and town, is stimulus enough," continued James.

This enterprise was nobly prosecuted, and the trees were planted and named as above. James enjoyed it hugely He was a great admirer of nature, and a tree or a flower afforded him genuine pleasure. To plant trees about his favourite institution, that would furnish shady walks in future days, was to him a privilege that he would not willingly miss.

During his first year's connection with the school, a female student of considerable brightness and scholar-ship violated some rule of the institution, for which the principal thought she should be publicly rebuked. The rebuke would be administered after chapel exercises on the following morning. The affair caused much discussion among the pupils Their sympathies were wholly enlisted for the girl, as she was deservedly quite popular.

" It is most too bad," remarked James to a lady student. " It will well-nigh kill her ; I pity her."

" I think it is a shame to make a small affair like that so public," replied the young lady " If it was one of the boys it would not be half so bad."

" You think boys are used to it, or are of less consequence than girls ? " retorted James, in a vein of humour.

" Not exactly that I think the worst way of rebuking a young lady should not be selected "

" I agree with you exactly , but I suppose there is no help for it now "

" Unless we get up a petition asking that the rebuke be privately administered "

" I will sign it," said James ; " but it must be done immediately."

" I will see some of the girls at once." And, so saying, the young lady hastened away.

In many groups the matter was discussed on that day, and much excitement prevailed ; but the movement for a petition failed, and the following morning dawned with the assurance that the rebuke would be administered before the whole school. The scholars assembled with hearts full of pity for the unfortunate girl. No one felt more keenly for her than James. He expected to see her overcome and crushed.

The principal called upon her to rise and the rebuke was administered, while all the scholars dropped their heads in pity for her. She survived the ordeal. She neither wept nor fainted. On retiring from the chapel, with the crowd of scholars, she remarked to James, in the hearing of many :

" It seems to me that Uncle Sutherland was rather personal."

The jocose remark created a laugh all round, and none laughed more heartily than James, who concluded that their profound sympathies had been sadly wasted.

James had not been at Hiram long before the students discovered one prominent trait of his character, viz , a keen sense of justice. He was fond of ball-playing, and he wanted everybody to enjoy it. One day he took up the bat to enjoy a game, when he observed veral of

the smaller boys looking on wistfully, seeming to say in
their hearts, " We wish we could play."

" Are not those boys in the game ? " he asked.

" What ! those little chaps. Of course not ; they
would spoil the game."

" But they want to play just as much as we do. Let
them come in ! "

" No ; we don't want the game spoiled. They can't
play ! "

" Neither shall I, if they cannot," added James, decidedly. And he threw down his bat.

" Well, let them come then," shouted one of the play-
ers, who wanted the game to go on " Spoil it, if you
will "

" We shall make it livelier," responded James, taking
up his bat, and calling upon the little boys to fall in.
" We may not have quite so scientific a game, but then
all hands will have the fun of it ; and that is what the
game is for "

XX

STUDENT AND TEACHER

JAMES ceased to be janitor at the close of his first
year at Hiram, and was promoted to assistant
teacher of the English department and ancient languages.
His rapid advancement is set forth by Dr. Hinsdale,
who is now president of the institution.

"His mind was now reaching out in all directions;
and all the more widely because the elastic course of
study, and the absence of traditionary trammels, gave
him room. He was a vast elemental force, and nothing
was so essential as space and opportunity. Hiram was
now forming her future teachers, as well as creating her
own culture. Naturally then, when he had been only
one year in the school he was given a place in the corps
of teachers. In the catalogue of 1853-54 his name
appears both with the pupils and teachers 'James A.
Garfield, Cuyahoga County,' and ' J. A. Garfield, Teacher
in the English Department, and of the Ancient Languages.' His admission to the faculty page may be an
index to a certain rawness in the school, but it gave
to his talents and ambition the play that an older
school, with higher standards, could not have afforded
him."

Now he was filling three important positions—student, teacher, and carpenter. He had become nearly
as indispensable to the carpenter's business as to that of
the Institute. The sound of his hammer, before and

after school, was familiar to the students and the citizens

"See there !" exclaimed Clark, pointing to James on the roof of a house, building near the academy. "Jim has taken that house to shingle."

"Alone ?" inquired Jones.

"Yes, alone, and it won't take him long, either, if he keeps his hammer going as it goes now. Jim's a brick "

"Very little brick about him, I should say ; more brain than brick."

"With steam enough on all the while to keep his brain running. Did you ever see such a worker ? "

"Never. Work seems as necessary to him as air and food. If he was not compelled to work, in order to pay his way, his brain would shatter his body to pieces in a year. He is about the only student I ever thought was fortunate in being poor as a stray cat "

"I declare, I never thought of that. Poverty is a blessing sometimes. I had thought it was a curse to a student always."

"It is Jim's salvation," added Jones. "I have thought of it many times. I suppose that this carpentering business is better exercise for him than our ball-playing or pitching quoits."

"Minus the *fun*," added Clark, quickly, really believing that James was depriving himself of all first-class sport "Have you not observed how he enjoys a game of ball or quoits when he joins us ? "

"Of course, but he does not seem to me to enjoy these games any more than he enjoys study, reading, and manual labour. He studies just as he plays ball, exactly, with all his might ; and I suppose that is the way we all ought to do."

"That is what Father Bentley said in his sermon on 'Whatsoever thy hand findeth to do, do it with thy might.' You remember it ? "

"Certainly; and who knows but Father Bentley has engaged Jim to illustrate his doctrine? He preaches, and Jim practises. Nobody in the Eclectic Institute will dispute such a sermon while Jim's about, you can count on that." That remark was made jocosely, and, at the same time, a compliment was intended for James.

This conversation discloses the facts about James's manual labour while connected with the Institute. We have not space for the details of his work with the plane and hammer during the whole period. We can only say, here, once for all, that he continued to add to his money by manual labour to the end of his three years at Hiram. He planed all the siding of the new house that he was shingling when the foregoing conversation took place. His labour was expended upon other buildings, also, in the place, during that period. Several jobs of farming also, were undertaken at different times. He was laying up money to assist himself in college, in addition to paying his way at the Institute.

When James entered the school his attention was attracted to a class of three in geometry. As he listened to the recitation in this study, which was animated and sharp, he became particularly impressed. Since that time he said, 'I regarded teacher and class with reverential awe." The three persons in the class were William B. Hazen, who became one of our most distinguished major-generals in the late rebellion, and who is now on the Indian frontier; Geo A. Baker, now a prominent citizen of Cleveland, Ohio, and Miss Almeda A Booth, a very talented lady of nearly thirty years, who was teaching in the school, and at the same time pursuing her studies in the higher mathematics and classics. As this Miss Booth exerted a more powerful influence upon James than any other teacher, except Dr Mark Hopkins, of Williams College, we shall speak of her particularly, and her estimate of our hero. She was the daughter of a Methodist preacher whose circuit extended a thousand

miles on the Reserve, a man of marked mental strength,
and of great tact and energy The daughter inherited
her father's intellectual power and force of character, so
that when the young man to whom she was betrothed
died, she resolved to concentrate herself to higher intellectual culture, that her usefulness might be augmented
This resolution brought her to the Eclectic Institute.
She died in 1875, and afterwards General Garfield said
of her talents "When she was twelve years of age she
used to puzzle her teachers with questions, and distress
them by correcting their mistakes. One of these, a male
teacher, who was too proud to acknowledge the correc-
tions of a child, called upon the most learned man in
town for help and advice in regard to a point of dispute
between them He was told that he was in error, and
that he must acknowledge his mistake. The teacher
was manly enough to follow this wise advice and thereafter made this little girl his friend and helper. It was
like her to help him quietly, and without boasting.
During her whole life none of her friends ever heard an
intimation from her that she had ever achieved an intellectual triumph over anybody in the world."

It was fortunate for James that this accomplished
lady became deeply interested in his progress and
welfare.

"The most remarkable young man I ever met," she
said to the principal. "There must be a grand future
before him."

"True, if he does not fall out of the way," answered
the principal

"I scarcely thought that were possible when I spoke
His Christian purpose is one of the most remarkable
things about him His talents, work, everything,
appear to be subject to this Christian aim. I feel that
he will make a power in the world"

"I agree with you such are my feelings in regard to
him, notwithstanding the prevalence of temptations that

lure and destroy so many of our hopeful young men."
The principal had seen more of the world than Miss
Booth, so he spoke with less confidence.

James had not been connected with the school but a
few months before his studies were the same as those of
Miss Booth, and they were in the same classes. " I was
far behind Miss Booth in mathematics and the physical
sciences," he once said , " but we were nearly in the
same place in Greek and Latin " She could render him
essential aid in his studies, and she delighted to do it.
Their studies were nearly the same until he ceased to be
a member of the school. The librarian kept textbooks
for sale, and the following are his memoranda of sales to
them :

"January, 1852. Latin Grammar and Cæsar.
March, 1852. Greek Grammar.
April, 1852. French Grammar.
August, 1852. German Grammar and Reader.
November, 1852. Xenophon's Memorabilia and Greek
Testament."

All this in a single year.

"August, 1853. Sophocles and Herodotus
November, 1853. Homer's Iliad."

During the fall term of 1853, Miss Booth and James
read about one hundred pages of Herodotus, and one
hundred of Livy. They met two of the professors, also
on two evenings of each week, to make a joint translation of the book of Romans. His diary has this record
for December 15, 1853 · " Translation society sat three
hours at Miss Booth's room, and agreed upon the translation of nine verses " The record shows that these
studies were pursued critically, and therefore slowly.

Miss Booth was more or less familiar with the standard authors of English literature, both prose and poetry ;
and she aided James greatly in the selection of books,
many of which they read together, discussing their
merit   making notes   and also to her memory,

a few years since, General Garfield said : " The few spare hours which schoolwork left us were devoted to such pursuits as each preferred, but much study was done in common I can name twenty or thirty books, which will be doubly precious to me because they were read and discussed in company with her. I can still read between the lines the memories of her first impressions, of the page, and her judgment of its merits. She was always ready to aid any friend with her best efforts "

James was appointed to prepare a thesis for an exhibition day One evening he repaired to the room of Miss Booth

" I want your help, Miss Booth," he said. " I am afraid that I shall make a botch of it without your assistance."

" I will risk you," Miss Booth replied ; " but I will render you all the assistance in my power."

" That will be all I shall need," remarked James, facetiously ; " and I hardly see how I can get along with less I like to talk over subjects before I write ; it is a great help to me."

" It is an essential help to everybody," answered Miss Booth " Two heads may be better than one in canvassing any subject. Discussion awakens thought, sharper and more original ; and it often directs the inquirer to new and fresher sources of information. I am at leisure to discuss your thesis at length."

So James opened the subject by stating some of his difficulties, and making inquiries. Both were soon absorbed in the subject before them, so thoroughly absorbed as to take no note of time, nor dream that the night was gliding away, until surprised by the morning light coming in at the window.

In 1853 Miss Booth proposed that twelve of the advanced pupils—James and herself among the number—should organize a literary society for the purpose of spending the approaching vacation of four weeks in a more thorough study of the classics. The society was formed, and the services of one of the professors were secured, to whom they recited statedly. During that vacation they read " the Pastorals of Virgil, the first six books of the Iliad, accompanied by a thorough drill in the Latin and Greek grammars at each recitation " It proved a very profitable vacation to James, a season to which he always looked back with pride and pleasure. He regarded Miss Booth as the moving and controlling spirit of that society, increasing his sense of obligation to her.

Perhaps the chief reason of Miss Booth's confidence in the Christian purpose of James, as expressed to the principal, was found in his consistent Christian life. From the time he became a member of the Institute he took an active part in the religious meetings, identifying himself with the people of God in the village. His exhortations and appeals were examples of earnestness and eloquence, to which the students and citizens listened in rapt attention No student of so much power in religious meetings had been connected with the school. Indeed, it was the universal testimony that no such speaker, of his age, had ever been heard

Father Bentley, pastor of the Disciples' Church in Hiram, was wonderfully drawn to James. After a few months, he felt that James's presence was almost indispensable to the success of a meeting. He invited him specially to address the audience. Often he urged him to take a seat upon the platform, that he might address the assembly to better advantage. In his absence he invited James to take charge of the meeting. The last year of his stay at Hiram, Father Bentley persuaded him several times to occupy his pulpit on the Sabbath, and preach, which he did to the gratification of the audience.

His gift at public speaking was so remarkable, that a demand was frequently made upon him for a speech on .id and public occasions It i related that, at a

weekly prayer-meeting, he was on the platform with
Father Bentley, waiting to perform his accustomed part,
when a messenger came for him to address a political
meeting, where speakers had failed them. Father
Bentley scarcely noticed what was going on, until James
was half-way down the aisle, when he called out ·

" James, don't go ! " then quickly, as if thinking his
request might be unreasonable, he said to the congregation, " Never mind, let him go , that boy will yet be
President of the United States."

" I remember his vigorous exhortations now," remarked a Christian woman before his death, who was
connected with the Institute at that time ; " they were
different from anything I was accustomed to hear in
conference meetings "

" How were they different ? " she was asked.

" They were original and fresh beyond anything I
had ever heard in such meetings , nothing common-
place or stale about them, making one feel that they were
not the thoughts of some commentator he was giving
us at secondhand, but the product of his own genius
and great talents, uttered with real earnestness and
sincerity."

" He must have possessed a wonderful command of
language," remarked her friend

" That was one thing that charmed us. His flow of
language, appropriate and select, was like a river. It
seemed as if he had only to open his mouth, and thoughts
flowed out clothed in language that was all aglow
Many, many times I heard the remark ' He speaks as
easily as he breathes.' Well," she continued after a
pause " he was substantially just such a speaker then
as he is now, bating the dignity that age and experience
impart."

In this connection we should speak of him as a debater
in the lyceum. He was older and more experienced
at Hiram than he was at Chester, and his efforts in debate

were accordingly more manly. The Illinois lady, from whom we have already quoted, says, " In the lyceum he early took rank far above the others as a speaker and debater." His interest in public matters was growing with the excitement of the times. The infamous fugitive slave-law, for the restoration of runaway slaves to their masters, had been enacted by Congress, as a compromise measure, and no people of the country felt more outraged by the attempts to enforce the Act than the people of the Western Reserve The excitement became intense. Young men partook of it in common with older citizens. It pervaded the higher schools. It was as strong in the Eclectic Institute as elsewhere Schools and village lyceums received an impetus from it. James was an uncompromising foe to slavery before , if possible, he was more so now. The excitement fired him up in debate He was more denunciatory than ever in slavery. He had been a great admirer of Daniel Webster, but his advocacy of the Fugitive-Slave Bill awakened his contempt. He was not a young man to conceal his feelings, and so his utterance was emphatic

" A covenant with death, and an agreement with hell," he exclaimed, quoting from Isaiah, " that will destroy the authors of it. The cry of the oppressed and downtrodden will appeal to the Almighty for retribution, like that of the blood of Abel. The lightning of Divine wrath will yet shiver the old, gnarled tree of slavery to pieces, leaving neither root nor branch ! "

When James became assistant-teacher, he had for a pupil, in his Greek class, Miss Lucretia Rudolph, the young lady in whom he was so much interested at Chester. Her father removed to Hiram, in order to give her a better opportunity to acquire a thorough education.

James was glad to meet her ; and he was happy to welcome so talented a scholar as pupil. He had no expectation that she would ever stand in a closer relation to him than pupil. But the weeks and months rolled on, and she became one of his permanent scholars, not only in Greek, but in other branches as well , in all of them developing a scholarship that won his admiration.   At the same time her many social and moral qualities impressed him, and the impression deepened from month to month.   The result was, before he closed his connection with the school, that a mutual attachment grew up between them, and she engaged to become his wife when he completed his course of study, and was settled   He was twenty-two years of age, and Miss Rudolph was one year his junior.

This was one of the most important steps that James had taken, and it proved to be one of the most fortunate. Those who prophesied that the engagement would interfere with his studies did not fully understand or appreciate the solidity of his character nor the inflexibility of his purpose   Such love affairs are often deprecated because so many young men allow them to interfere with their life purpose, thus disclosing weakness and puerile ideas.   With James the love affair became an aid to the controlling purpose of his life, and at the same time served to refine his coarser qualities by passing them through the fire of a pure and exalted passion   True love is sweeter and higher than the brightest talents, and when its pure and elevating influence refines the latter they shine with a fairer lustre than ever. This was eminently true of James

Notwithstanding James was so bashful and retiring when he first went to Chester to commence his studies, he became one of the most social and genial students at Hiram.   He was the life of the social circle.   Unlike many ripe students, whose minds are wholly absorbed in their studies, he could unbend himself, and enter into a social occasion with zest, bringing his talents, his acquisitions, his wit and humour, to contribute to the enjoyment of all.   The lady in Illinois, from whom we have twice quoted, says on this point.

" During the month of June the entire school went in carriages to their annual grove-meeting, at Randolph, some twenty-five miles away On this trip he was the life of the party, occasionally bursting out in an eloquent strain at the sight of a bird, or a trailing vine, or a venerable giant of the forest. He would repeat poetry by the hour, having a very retentive memory "

The reader learns from this, that it was not "small talk," nor mere slang and folly, that he contributed to a social time, but sensible, instructive material. He had no sympathy for, or patience with, young men who dabbled in silly or trifling conversation and acts, to entertain associates. To him it was evidence of such inherent weakness and absence of common sense that aroused his contempt. One who was intimate with him in social gatherings at Hiram makes a remark that discloses an important element of his popularity. " There was a cordiality in his disposition which won quickly the favour and esteem of others He had a happy habit of shaking hands, and would give a hearty grip, which betokened a kind-hearted feeling for all " The same writer says, what confirms the foregoing statements respecting his recognised abilities, " In those days, both the faculty and pupils were in the habit of calling him ' the second Webster,' and the remark was common, ' He will fill the White House yet.' "

There was one branch of the fine arts that he pursued to gratify a taste in that direction, which should receive a passing notice. It was mezzotint drawing He became so proficient in the art that he was appointed teacher of the same The lady from whom we have quoted was one of his pupils, and she writes :—

" One of his gifts was that of mezzotint drawing, and he gave instruction in this branch I was one of his pupils in this, and have now the picture of a cross, upon which he did some shading and put on the finishing touches Upon the margin is written in the hand of the

noted teacher, his own name and his pupil's.   There are,
also, two other drawings, one of a large European bird
on the bough of a tree, and the other a churchyard scene
in winter, done by him at that time "

Thus the versatility of his talents, enforced by his
intense application, appeared to win in almost any undertaking.   Without his severe application, his versatility
would not have availed much.   He reduced that old
maxim thoroughly to practice, " Accomplish, or never
attempt," because his application was invincible.   Here
was the secret of his success in teaching—just as good
a teacher as scholar.   Before the completion of his aca-
demic course the trustees made his success a subject of
serious consideration.

" We must secure his return to Hiram as soon as he
gets through college," said the chairman.   " He will
make a popular and successful professor "

" That is true," replied another trustee   " In what
department would you put him ? "

" Any department that is open   He will fill any position admirably.   I have noticed that when we conclude
that he is particularly suited to one position, he soon
surprises us by filling another equally well "

" It will certainly be for the popularity of the school
to instal him over a prominent professorship here,"
added the chairman ; and I daresay it will be agreeable
to his feelings."

The subject was not dropped here.   Both the principal and chairman of the board interviewed James
upon the subject ; and when he left the Institute for
college, it was well understood that he would return at
the close of his college course.   The present president of
the institution says :—

" I shall not here speak of him as a teacher further
than to say, in two years' service he had demonstrated
his great ability in that capacity, had won the hearts of
the students generally, and had wrought in the minds of

the school authorities the conviction that his further services would be indispensable on his return from college "

On his success as a teacher, when preparing for college, the Illinois lady who was his pupil writes :—

" He was a most entertaining teacher—ready with illustrations, and possessing, in a marked degree, the power of exciting the interest of the scholars, and afterwards making clear to them the lessons In the arithmetic class there were ninety pupils, and I cannot recollect a time when there was any flagging in the interest. There were never any cases of unruly conduct, or a disposition to shirk With scholars who were slow of comprehension, or to whom recitations were a burden, on account of their modest or retiring disposition, he was specially attentive, and by encouraging words and gentle assistance would manage to put all at their ease and awaken in them a confidence in themselves "

A leading lawyer of Cleveland, Ohio, Hon. J H. Rhodes, referring to his connection with the school, at the time James was studying and teaching, in a public assembly, said :

" I remember a circumstance that had much to do with my remaining at Hiram. I was a little home-sick, and one day I went into the large hall of the college building, and the tall, muscular, tow-headed man in charge there, who was teaching algebra, came up to me, and, seeing a cloud over my face, threw his arms about me in an ardent way. Immediately the home-sickness disappeared The tow-headed man has not so much hair to-day as he had then. Hard knocks in public life have uprooted a heap of his hair."

" Going to Bethany College, I suppose ? " remarked the principal to him. That was the college established by Alexander Campbell, founder of the sect called Disciples

" I had intended to go there until recently," James answered

" What has changed your purpose ? That college is of our denomination, you know."

" Yes, I know ; but I have been thinking that it might be better for me to enlarge my observation by going beyond our sect."

" That may be ; you want more room, do you ? "

' I know the Disciples' Church pretty well   Perhaps I had better know something outside of it.   It seems narrow to me to tie myself down to the limits of my own denomination.   Besides, will it not be of real value to me to connect myself with a New England college ? "

" Perhaps so ; I agree with you in the main ; too contracted a sphere will not be well for you.   That idea is well worth considering.   You will be qualified to enter college two years in advance ; at least, you can enter some colleges two years in advance   What college have you in mind ? "

" I have not decided upon any particular one yet   I am going to write to Yale College, Williams College, and Brown University, stating the ground I have been over, and inquiring whether I can enter Junior, learning the expense, and other things."

" That is a good plan.   Then you will know definitely where to go, and you can prepare accordingly "

James did write to the presidents of Yale College, New Haven, Ct , Williams College, Williamstown, Mass , and to the president of Brown University, Providence, R I., also , and each one of the presidents replied to his inquiries.   The substance of the answers, together with his decision, may be learned from a letter James wrote to a friend one week before he started for college, as follows —

" There are three reasons why I have decided not to go to Bethany : First, the course of study is not so extensive or thorough as in eastern colleges ; second, Bethany leans too heavily towards slavery ; third, I am the son of Disciple parents, and one myself and have had

P

but little acquaintance with people of other views, and having always lived in the west, I think it will make me more liberal, both in my religious and general views and sentiments, to go into a new circle, where I shall be under new influences. These considerations led me to conclude to go to some New England college. I therefore wrote to the presidents of Brown University, Yale, and Williams, setting forth the amount of study I had done, and asking how long it would take me to finish their course

"Their answers are now before me. All tell me I can graduate in two years They are all brief, business notes, but President Hopkins concludes with this sentence : ' If you come here, we shall be glad to do what we can for you ' Other things being so nearly equal, this sentence, which seems to be a kind of friendly grasp of the hand, has settled the question for me I shall start for Williams next week."

James always did like to have people carry their hearts in their hands, as he did , and Dr Hopkins came so near to it that he put his heart into his pen, when he wrote, and James accepted his hearty hand-shake

"How is it, James, about funds ? You cannot have enough money laid up for your college expenses " His brother said this to him several weeks before he closed his studies at Hiram, just at the time when James was revolving the subject with some anxiety True, he had trusted to Providence so much, and Providence had provided for him so unexpectedly at times, and so generously always, that he was disposed to trust for the wherewithal to pay expenses in college His brother's question was timely He always thought that Providence managed the affair.

"No, I have not more than half enough," James replied ; " but I shall teach in the winter, and perhaps I can find some kind of labour to perform in term time. I alw · ' ave been able to pay my w '

" But if you enter two years in advance, I would not advise you to labour in term-time. You will have enough to do."

" How can I pay my way unless I do work ? "

" I will loan you money to pay your expenses—

" And wait long enough for me to pay it ? "

" Yes When you get through college you can teach, and it will not take you long to pay the debt "

" Suppose I should die ; where will you get your pay ? "

" That is my risk "

" It ought not to be your risk It is not right that you should lose the money on my account."

" It is if I consent to it."

" It occurs to me," continued James, after a pause, " that I can arrange it in this way. You can loan me the money, and I will get my life insured for five hundred dollars. This will protect you in case of my death."

" I will agree to that, if it suits you any better."

' Well, it does I shall be satisfied with that method ; and I shall be relieved of some anxiety. I want to make my two years in college the most profitable of any two years of my course of study."

James took out an insurance upon his life, and when he carried it to his brother, he remarked :—

" If I live I shall pay you, and if I die you will suffer no loss "

What James accomplished during the three years he was at Hiram Institute may be briefly stated thus :—

The usual preparatory studies, requiring four years, together with the studies of the first two years in college —the studies of six years in all—he mastered in three years At the same time he paid his own bills by janitor and carpenter work, and teaching, and, in addition, laid up a small amount for college expenses

XXI

IN COLLEGE

AT the close of the summer term at Williams College, candidates for admission, who presented themselves, were examined James presented himself to Dr Hopkins very different, in his personal appearance, from the well-worded and polished letter that he wrote to him. One describes him " As a tall, awkward youth, with a great shock of light hair, rising nearly erect from a broad, high forehead, and an open, kindly, and thoughtful face, which showed no traces of his long study with poverty and privation " His dress was thoroughly western, and very poor at that It was evident to Dr. Hopkins that the young stranger before him did not spend much time at his toilet ; that he cared more for an education than he did for dress. Of course Dr Hopkins did not recognize him

"My name is Garfield, from Ohio," said James That was enough. Dr. Hopkins recalled the capital letter which the young man wrote. His heart was in his hand at once, and he repeated the cordial hand-shake that James felt when he read in the doctor's letter, " If you come here, we shall be glad to do what we can for you." James felt at home at once. It was such a kind, fatherly greeting, that he felt almost as if he had arrived *home* He never had a natural father whom he could remember, but now he had found an intellectual father sure and he was never happier in his life Yet a   before the president of the college, whose massive head and overhanging brow denoted a giant in intellect. James was perfectly satisfied that he had come to the right place now, he had no wish to be elsewhere. He had read Dr. Hopkins's Lectures on the "Evidences of Christianity," and now the author impressed him just as the book did when he read it The impression of *greatness* was uppermost

James passed the examination without any difficulty, and was admitted to the Junior class. Indeed, his examination was regarded as superior. He was qualified to stand abreast with the Juniors, who had spent Freshman and Sophomore years in the colleges. And this fact illustrates the principle of *thoroughness*, for which we have said James was distinguished In a great measure he had been his own teacher in the advanced studies that he must master in order to enter the Junior class, yet he was *thoroughly* prepared.

"You can have access to the college library if you remain here during the summer vacation," said Dr Hopkins to him "If you enjoy reading, you will have a good opportunity to indulge your taste for it."

"I shall remain here during vacation, and shall be thankful for the privilege of using the library," answered James. "I have not had the time to read what I desire, hitherto, as I have had to labour and teach, to pay my bills It will be a treat for me to spend a few weeks in reading, with nothing else to do"

Dr Hopkins gave him excellent advice and words of encouragement, not only for vacation, but for term time as well, and James found himself revelling among books within a few days. He had never seen a library of such dimensions as that into which he was now introduced, and his voracious mental appetite could now partake of a "square meal" One of the authors whom he desired to know was Shakespeare. He had read only such extra ... ... other volumes. Therefore he took up a volume containing Shakespeare's entire works with peculiar satisfaction. He read and studied it, studied and read it, committing portions of it to memory, and fairly made the contents of the book his own. His great familiarity with the works of Shakespeare dates from that period Certain English poets, also, he read and studied for the first time ; and he committed a number of poems to memory Works of fiction he rejected, from principle When he joined the Disciples' Church, he resolved to read no novels His decision was in accordance with the practice of that Church On the whole, that vacation in the college library was a very profitable one to James. It was just what he needed after so many years of hard study in the sciences and classics.

It was well for him, too, to be relieved from strain of study and pecuniary support, that had taxed him heavily from the outset. He had no carpenter's job on hand, or class to teach for his support For exercise, the beauty and grandeur of the scenery lured him into the fields and over the mountains The wild, mountainous country around presented a striking contrast with the level, monotonous landscape of the Western Reserve. He enjoyed explorations of the region , climbing Greylock to its summit that he might take in the view, plunging into forests, and ranging fields, until the country for miles around was almost as familiar to him as Orange township, Ohio By the time the college term opened, he was as familiar with the locality as any of the students

" Hill, what do you think of that westerner ? " said one of the juniors to his classmate, Hill, a few days afte the term began. " Got acquainted with him ? "

" Not exactly ; haven't had time yet Have you ?

" A little acquainted ; not much, though "

" He is not a slave to the fashions I conclude , " alluding

" No ; he gives tailors a wide berth, in my judgment :
but he is none the worse for that   Put him into a tasty
garb, and he would be a splendid-looking fellow."

" That's so ; but neither his character nor scholarship would be improved by the change.   If dress would
improve these, some of our fellows would patronize
tailors more than butchers, a great deal."

" I think I shall like him, judging from a slight acquaintance.   A little western in his speech "

" Western provincialisms ? "

" Yes ; though not bad   Evidently he is one of the
fellows who will go through thick and thin to acquire
an education   There must be considerable in him, or
he never could enter a New England college two years
in advance, expecially if he prepared at the west."

" Do you know where in the west he fitted for college ? "

" At a little place on the Western Reserve somewhere ;
an academy that belongs to a sect called Disciples.   So
one of the boys says "

" Disciples !   I never heard of that sect before, except
the one in New Testament times.   A disciple will work
in well here , " trying to be humorous.

This conversation shows quite well the circumstances
in which James was brought into contact with the students   That they should scrutinize his apparel and
appearance is not strange.   James expected that, and
the thought caused him some embarrassment   He
knew very well that his dress must appear shabby to
young men who consulted tailors, and that his speech
was marred by provincialisms that must sound queerly
to them.   So he very naturally dreaded the introduc-
tion to college life.   Yet he proved as much of a philosopher here as elsewhere, and made the best of the situation.   He was happily disappointed with his intercourse
with students   He found no pride or caste among them.
They to ... Hindly ... at him the ... welcome

to their companionship. Within a few weeks he ranked among the " best fellows " of the college The college boys soon found that the " Great West," had turned out a great scholar ; that the student who had the least to do with tailors was a rare fellow , and they treated him accordingly James never had any reason to complain of his treatment by the faculty and students of Williams College

" He is one of the most accurate scholars I ever knew," said Hill to Leavitt, some weeks after James entered college ; " he never misses anything, and he never fails to answer a question."

" That is because he knows it all," replied Leavitt " He gave me some account of his methods of study in preparing for college. He did it all himself, pretty much. He sticks to anything until he understands it fully ; that gives him the advantage now. He is one of the best-read students in college, and all that he ever read is at his tongue's end."

" He showed *that* in the debate last Saturday," continued Hill. " His ability as a debater is superior , nobody in this college can compete with him " Reference here was made to a debate in the Philologian society of the college."

" A born speaker, I think It is just as easy for him to speak as it is to recite ; and that is easy enough "

" I predict," continued Hill, " that he will stand at the head of our class, notwithstanding he entered two years in advance "

" It looks so now. ' All signs fail in a dry time,' it is said, but the signs certainly point that way."

That these young men were not partial, or mistaken, in their estimate of James, is evident from the following communication, penned by a class-mate, after the lapse of twenty-five years :—

" In a class of forty or more he immediately took a stand above all others for accurate scholarship in

every branch, but particularly distinguishing himself as a
writer, reasoner, and debater He was remarkable for
going to the bottom of every subject which came before
him, and seeing and presenting it in entirely a new
light His essays written at that time, not of the
common-place character too common in college compositions, can even now be read with pleasure and
admiration. While an indefatigable worker, he was by
no means a bookworm or recluse, but one of the most
companionable of men, highly gifted, and entertaining
in conversation, ready to enjoy and give a joke, and
having a special faculty for drawing out the knowledge
of those with whom he conversed, thus enriching his
own stock of information from the acquirements of
others Even then he showed that magnetic power,
which he now exhibits in a remarkable degree in public
life of surrounding himself with men of various talents,
and of employing each to the best advantage in his
sphere. When questions for discussion arose in the
college societies, Garfield would give each of his allies a
point to investigate ; books and documents from all the
libraries would be overhauled ; and the mass of facts
thus obtained being brought together, Garfield would
analyze the whole, assign each of the associates his part,
and they would go into the battle to conquer He was
always in earnest, and persistent in carrying his point,
often against apparently insurmountable obstacles ; and
in college election contests (which are often more intense
than national elections) he was always successful.

James had taxed himself so long to his utmost capacity by advanced and extra studies, crowding six years'
labour into three, that it was easy for him now to lead
his class He added German to the regular studies
of the college, and he became so proficient in it within
one year that he could converse considerably in the
language. But all this was little labour in comparison
with his work at Hiram He found much time to read,

and to engage in the sports of the Campus. The latter he enjoyed with a keen relish ; no one entered into them more heartily than he did   His college mates now recall with what enthusiasm he participated in their games This was indispensable for his health now, as he had no labour with plane or hammer to perform

The " Williams Quarterly " was a magazine supported by the college.   James took great interest in it, and his compositions frequently adorned its pages, both prose and poetry   The following was from his pen in 1854 :- -

" AUTUMN.

" Old Autumn, thou art here !   Upon the earth
And in the heavens the signs of death are hung ,
For o'er the earth's brown breast stalks pale decay,
And 'mong the lowering clouds the wild winds wail,
And sighing sadly, shout the solemn dirge
O'er Summer's fairest flowers, all faded now
The Winter God, descending from the skies,
Has reached the mountain tops, and decked their brows
With glittering frosty crowns, and breathed his breath
Among the trumpet pines, that herald forth
His coming

" Before the driving blast
The mountain oak bows down his hoary head,
And flings his withered locks to the rough gales
That fiercely roar among his branches bare,
Uplifted to the dark, unpitying heavens
The skies have put their mourning garments on,
And hung their funeral drapery on the clouds
Dead Nature soon will wear her shroud of snow,
And he entombed in Winter's icy grave !

" Thus passes life.   As heavy age comes on
The joys of youth—bright beauties of the Spring—
Grow dim and faded, and the long, dark night
Of death's chill winter comes   But as the Spring
Rebuilds the ruined wrecks of Winter's waste,
And cheers the gloomy earth with joyous light,
So o'er the tomb the star of hope shall rise
And t h   h   ver during da

' Garfield, what are you going to do with yourself this vacation ? " inquired Bolter, just as the fall term was closing.

" I am considering that question now. How should I make it teaching penmanship, do you think ? "

" You would do well at it , and the vacation is long enough for you to teach about ten lessons "

James was a good penman for that day, and he had taken charge of a writing-class in school for a time. The style of his penmanship would not be regarded with favour now by the teachers in that department ; nevertheless, it was a broad, clear, business style, that country people, at least, were then pleased with

" Think I could readily get a class ? " continued James.

" No doubt of it. Strike right out into the country, almost anywhere, and you will find the way open "

" I am quite inclined to take a trip into New Hampshire, to see what I can do. I have some distant relatives there my mother was born there "

" Well, if you go where your mother was born, you will not be likely to get into bad company, though there s enough of it in New Hampshire "

' Acquainted there ? "

" As much as I want to be There is too much of the pro-slavery democracy there for me , but they need to improve their penmanship awfully, Garfield It won't interfere with *your* business."

The conversation proceeded in a kind of semi-jovial way until the bell rang for recitation The upshot was that James opened a writing-school in Pownal, Vermont, instead of in New Hampshire He met with some party who directed his steps to this small town, where he taught a large class in penmanship, in the village schoolhouse. It proved a profitable venture to him, both financially and socially He added quite a little sum to his private treasury besides if in many warm friends and inlarging the sphere of his observation and experience.

As he spent the next winter vacation in New York State, we may relate the circumstances here. He went to Poestenkill, a country village about six miles from Troy, N. Y., where there was a Disciples' Church, over which a preacher by the name of Streeter was settled. Here he opened a school of penmanship, thereby earning a few dollars in addition to paying his expenses His efforts in the religious conference meeting were so marked that the pastor invited him to occupy his pulpit on the Sabbath, and the invitation was accepted. Having preached once, the people demanded that he should preach again ; and he did. It was the common opinion that "he would become the most renowned preacher in the Disciples' Church," no one doubting that he was expecting to fill the sacred office.

James became acquainted with several of the teachers and school committee at Troy, and when he was there one day, Rev. Mr. Brooks, one of the committee, surprised him by saying :

"We have a vacancy in the high-school, and I would like to have you take the situation. It is an easy place. and a good salary of twelve hundred dollars."

"You want me to begin now, I suppose ? "

"Yes ; next week the term begins "

"I should be obliged to relinquish the idea of graduating at Williams."

"That would be necessary, of course ; and perhaps that may be best for you "

"No, it seems best for me to graduate, at any rate, that has been my strong desire for several years, and to abandon the purpose now, when I am just on the eve of realizing my hopes, would be very unwise "

' You understand your own business best," continued Mr. Brooks, "but we should be very glad to employ

"There is another difficulty in the way," James replied. "I feel under some obligations to Hiram Institute, where I prepared for college. There was no bargain with me, and yet the trustees expect me to return, and take a postion as teacher. That is a young institution struggling to live, and I have a desire to give my small influence to it"

"You need not decide to-day; think of it longer; you may view the matter differently after a little thought," Mr. Brooks urged.

"No, I may just as well decide now. Your offer is a tempting one, I could soon pay my debts on that salary. I cannot expect any such salary at Hiram, and I thank you with all my heart for the offer. But my ambition has been to win an honourable diploma at an Eastern college, and then devote my energies to the institute that has done so much for me. I must decline your alluring offer"

James arrived at this decision quickly, because accepting the offer would interfere with the accomplishment of the great purpose of his life. He had no difficulty, at any time, in rejecting any proposition that came between him and a collegiate education.

His refusal of the tempting offer was the more remarkable because he was in straitened circumstances at the time. His brother, who had promised to loan him money, had become embarrassed, so that further aid from that quarter was out of the question. He needed a new suit of clothes very much, but he had not the money to purchase them. One of his friends in Poestenkill, knowing this, went to a tailor of his acquaintance in Troy, Mr P. S. Haskell, and said.

"We have a young man in our village, a rare fellow, who is poor, but honest, and he wants a suit of clothes He is struggling to go through Williams College, and finds it . . . . ?"

"Ye . . . . to a

suit of clothes. I will let him have a suit of clothes on credit," the tailor replied promptly

" You will get every cent of your pay in time, I'm sure of that The young man preaches some now, and he preaches grandly."

" What is his name ? "

" James A Garfield His home is in Ohio "

" Well, send him along "

On the following day James called upon the tailor, frankly told him his circumstances, and promised to pay him for the clothes as early as possible. He could not fix the date.

" Very well," said Mr Haskell, who was thoroughly pleased with James's appearance " Take your own time ; don't worry yourself about the debt Go on with your education , and when you have some money that you have no other use for, pay me " James got his suit of clothes, returned to college, and paid the debt in due time, to the entire satisfaction of the tailor.

After returning to college, James looked about for pecuniary relief. Debts on his second year had already accumulated, and now it was certain that he would receive no loans to meet them from his brother. He thought of the cordial and friendly doctor who examined him about six years before, and encouraged him to acquire an education,—Dr. J. P Robinson, now of Cleveland, Ohio. He sat down and wrote to the jolly doctor, stating his pressing wants and future purposes, telling him of his life insurance, and of his expected connection with Hiram Institute as teacher, when he would be able to liquidate the debt. It is enough to say that Dr Robinson cheerfully loaned him the money.

At the close of his first collegiate year James visited his mother in Ohio. She was then living with her daughter, who was married and settled in Solon. It is not . . . . the . . . . in this year . the rea . . . . much

better than we can describe it. Imagination cannot
exaggerate the satisfaction his mother found in meeting
her son again, so near the ministry, where she had come
to think his field of usefulness would be found.

In college James's anti-slavery sentiments grew
stronger, if possible. Charles Sumner was in Congress,
dealing heavy blows against slavery, assailing the fugitive slave-bill with great power and effect, claiming that
" freedom is national, and slavery sectional," denoun-
cing the " crime against Kansas," and losing no opportunity to expose the guilt and horrors of Southern bondage   Outside of Congress he made speeches, urging that
the Whig party should attack and overthrow American
slavery. James admired the fearless, grand public
career of Sumner, and also despised the criminal support
the Democratic party gave to slavery, and the truck-
ling, timid, compromising course of the leaders of the
Whig party.   Then, in the fall of 1855, John Z Good-
rich, who was a member of Congress from Western
Massachusetts, delivered a political address in Williamstown upon the history of the Kansas-Nebraska struggle,
and the efforts of the handful of Republicans then in
Congress to defeat the Missouri compromise   James
was profoundly impressed by the facts and logic of that
speech, and he said to a class-mate, on leaving the hall .

" This subject is new to me , I am going to know all
about it "

He sent for documents, studied them thoroughly,
and was fully prepared to join the new Republican party,
and the nomination of John C Fremont for President
of the United States.   The students called a meeting in
support of Fremont, and James was invited to address
them.   The scope and power of his speech packed with
facts and history showed that he had canvassed the
subject with his accustomed ability, and even his class-
mates, who knew him so well, were surprised

" The   ntry will .. t tru . . et and l . , i, will

get some hard knocks from him," remarked a class-mate.

Just afterwards the country was thrown into the greatest excitement by the cowardly attack of Preston Brooks, of South Carolina, upon Charles Sumner. Enraged by his attacks upon slavery, and urged forward, no doubt, by Southern ruffians, Brooks attacked him with a heavy cane while Sumner was writing at his desk in the United States Senate. Brooks intended to kill him on the spot, and his villainous purpose was nearly accomplished

On receipt of the news at Williams College the students called an indignation meeting, at which James, boiling over with indignant remonstrance against such an outrage, delivered the most telling and powerful speech that had fallen from his lips up to that time. His fellow-students listened with wonder and admiration. They were so completely charmed by his fervour and eloquence that they sat in breathless attention until he closed, when their loud applause rang through the building, repeated again and again in the wildest enthusiasm.

" The uncompromising foe to slavery ! " exclaimed one of his admirers.

" Old Williams will be prouder of her student than she is to-day, even," remarked another.

And many were the words of surprise and gratification expressed, and many the prophecies concerning the future renown of young Garfield.

We said that James rejected fiction from his reading, on principle. When about half through his college course he found that his mind was suffering from excess of solid food. Mental dyspepsia was the consequence His mind was not assimilating what he read, and was losing its power of application. He was advised to read fiction moderately. " Romance is as valuable a part of intellectual food as salad of a dinner. In its place, its discipline to the mind is equal to that of science in its place " He finally accepted the theory read one volume of fiction each month, and soon found his mind returning to its former elasticity. Some of the works of Walter Scott, Cooper, Dickens, and Thackeray, not to mention others, became the cure of his mental malady. His method of taking notes in reading was systematically continued in college. Historical references, mythological allusions, technical terms, and other things, not well understood at the time, were noted, and afterwards looked up in the library, so that nothing should remain doubtful or obscure in his mind. " The ground his mind traversed he carefully cleared and ploughed before leaving it for fresh fields "

James graduated in 1856, bearing off the honours of his class Dr. Hopkins had established the " metaphysical oration " as the highest honour at Commencement, and James won it, by the universal consent of the faculty and students. In the performance of his part at Commencement, he fully sustained the well-earned reputation for scholarship and eloquence. Both teachers and class-mates fully expected, when he left college, that his name would appear conspicuously in the future history of his country.

Dr. Hopkins wrote of him, eight years after James graduated :—

" The course of General Garfield has been one which the young men of the country may well emulate. . . . A rise so rapid both in civil and military life is, perhaps, without example in the country. . . . Obtaining his education almost wholly by his own exertions, and having reached the age when he could fully appreciate the highest studies, General Garfield gave himself to study with a zest and delight wholly unknown to those who find in it a routine. A religious man, and a man of principle, he pursued, of his own accord, the ends proposed by the institution. He was prompt, frank, manly, social in his tendencies ; combining active exercise with habits of study, and thus did for himself what it is the object of a college to enable every young man to do—he made himself a MAN. There never was a time when we more needed those who would follow his example."

Mr. Chadbourne, who is now president of Williams College, and who was professor when James was a student, writes :—

" He graduated in 1856, soon after I began my work here as professor. The students who came under my instruction then made a much stronger impression upon me than those of a later day, since my attention has been called to other interests than those of the lecture-room. But Garfield, as a student, was one who would at any time impress himself upon the memory of his instructors, by his manliness and excellence of character. He was one whom his teachers would never suspect as guilty of a dishonest or mean act, and one whom a dishonest or mean man would not approach College life is, in some respects, a severe test of character. False notions of honour often prevail among students, so that, under sanction of " college custom," things are sometimes done by young men which they would scorn to do in other places. There was a manliness and honesty about Garfield that gave him power to see and do what was for his own good and the honour of the college. His life as a student was pure and noble. His moral and religious character, and marked intellectual ability, gave great promise of success in the world. His course since he entered active life has seemed to move on in the same line in which he moved here. He has been distinguished for hard work, clear insight into great questions of public interest, strong convictions, and manly courage. I know of no better example among our public men of success fairly won."

XXII

RETURN TO HIRAM

THE trustees of Hiram Institute elected Garfield " Teacher of Ancient Languages and Literature " before his return to the school. His welcome back was a hearty one. His acceptance of the position was equally hearty

His position was now a high and honourable one, although he was but nine years removed from the tow-path of the Ohio and Pennsylvania Canal. Into that nine years was crowded labours, struggles, and triumphs, the like of which we can scarcely find in the annals of human effort.

" I have attained to the height of my ambition," he said to a friend. " I have my diploma from an Eastern college, and my position here as instructor ; and now I shall devote all my energies to this Institute "

He had no intention of entering the ministry perma-nently, as many supposed, nor had he aspirations for a political career. He was content to be a teacher at Hiram, ambitious to make the school the pet of the Western Reserve if possible. He might have secured positions where double the salary was paid , but he was satisfied to teach at Hiram for eight hundred dollars a year No board of trustees could lure him away by the offer of a princely income. His heart was at Hiram and he meant that his best efforts should be there.

He brought from Williams College a profound rever-ence for Dr Hopkins, the president, as an instructor and scholar of great ability He profited by the les-

275

sons he learned at his feet, and augmented the value of his own labours by imitating him as far as practicable. He was not long in convincing the board that, successful as he was in teaching before entering Williams College, his ability in that sphere was largely increased by his collegiate course. At the end of the first year he was placed at the head of the institution with the title, " Chairman of the Board of Instructors," and one year later was made PRINCIPAL In eleven years from the time he left the tow-path of the canal he was installed Principal of the " Eclectic Institute of the Western Reserve," where three hundred young ladies and gentlemen were pursuing a course of education.

One of his successful points, as instructor, was to discover young men of superior talents and persuade them to acquire a liberal education. Sometimes their fathers would put a veto upon such a project, when he was forced to try his logic and persuasive powers upon them. He called this " capturing boys," and he enjoyed it hugely. There are many bright intellects now adorning the learned professions of the country that would have been unknown to fame but for his persistent efforts in "capturing them." President Hinsdale, who now presides over Hiram College, was one of them—one of the ablest and most remarkable scholars of the land. Garfield tells the story of the capture of two boys as follows :

" I have taken more solid comfort in the thing itself, and received more moral recompense and stimulus in after life, from capturing young men for an education than from anything else in the world

As I look back over my life thus far, I think of nothing that so fills me with so much pleasure as the planning of these sieges, the revolving in my mind of plans for scaling the walls of the fortress ; of gaining access to the inner soul life, and at last seeing the besieged party won to a fuller appreciation of himself, to a higher

conception of life, and of the part he is to bear in it.
The principal guards which I have found it necessary to
overcome in gaining these victories are the parents or
guardians of the young men themselves. I particularly remember two such instances of capturing young
men from their parents. Both of those boys are to-day
educators, of wide reputation—one president of a college,
the other high in the ranks of graded-school managers.
Neither, in my opinion, would to-day have been above
the commonest walks of life unless I, or some one else,
had captured him. There is a period in every young
man's life when a very small thing will turn him one way
or the other. He is distrustful of himself, and uncertain as to what he should do. His parents are poor,
perhaps, and argue that he has more education than
they ever obtained, and that it is enough. These
parents are sometimes a little too anxious in regard to
what their boys are going to do when they get through
with their college course. They talk to the young man
too much, and I have noticed that the boy who will make
the best man is sometimes most ready to doubt himself.
I always remember the turning period in my own life,
and pity a young man at this stage from the bottom of
my heart. One of the young men I refer to came to me
on the closing day of the spring-term, and bade me
good-bye at my study. I noticed that he awkwardly
lingered after I expected him to go, and had turned to
my writing again. ' I suppose you will be back again
in the fall, Henry ? ' I said, to fill in the vacuum. He
did not answer, and turning towards him I noticed that
his eyes were filled with tears, and that his countenance
was undergoing contortions of pain.

" He at length managed to stammer out, ' No, I am
not coming back to Hiram any more. Father says I
have got education enough, and that he needs me to
work on the farm ; that education don't help along a
farmer any '

" ' Is your father here ? ' I asked, almost as much affected by the statement as the boy himself. He was a peculiarly bright boy, one of those strong, awkward, bashful, blonde, large-headed fellows, such as make men He was not a prodigy by any means ; but he knew what work meant, and when he had won a thing by the true endeavour, he knew its value.

" ' Yes, father is here, and is taking my things home for good,' said the boy, more affected than ever

" ' Well, don't feel badly,' I said. ' Please tell him Mr. Garfield would like to see him at his study before he leaves the village. Don't tell him that it is about you, but simply that I want to see him.' In the course of half an hour the old gentleman, a robust specimen of a Western Reserve yankee, came into the room, and awkwardly sat down. I knew something of the man before, and I thought I knew how to begin. I shot right at the bull's-eye immediately.

" ' So you have come to take Henry home with you, have you ? ' The old gentleman answered ' Yes.' ' I sent for you because I wanted to have a little talk with you about Henry's future. He is coming back again in the fall, I hope ? '

" ' Wal, I think not. I don't reckon I can afford to sind him any more. He's got eddication enough for a farmer already, and I notice that when they git too much they sorter get lazy. Yer eddicated farmers are humbugs. Henry's got so far 'long now that he'd rother hev his head in a book than be workin'. He don't take no interest in the stock nor in the farm improvements. Everybody else is dependent in this world on the farmer, and I think that we've got too many eddicated fellows setting around now for the farmer to support.'

" ' I am sorry to hear you talk so,' I said , ' for really I consider Henry one of the brightest and most faithful students I have ever had. I have taken a very deep interest in him What I wanted to say to you was, that

the matter of educating him has largely been a constant
outgo thus far, but if he is permitted to come next fall
term, he will be far enough advanced so that he can
teach school in the winter, and begin to help himself and
you along. He can earn very little on the farm in the
winter, and he can get very good wages teaching How
does that strike you ? '

  " The idea was a new and good one to him. He simply
remarked, ' Do you really think he can teach next
winter ? '

  " ' I should think so. certainly,' I replied. ' But if he
cannot do so then, he can in a short time, anyhow.'

  " ' Wal, I will think on it He wants to come back
bad enough, and I guess I'll have to let him. I never
thought of it that way afore '

  " I knew I was safe It was the financial question
that troubled the old gentleman, and I knew that would
be overcome when Henry got to teaching, and could
earn his money himself He would then be so far along,
too, that he could fight his own battles He came all
right the next fall, and, after finishing at Hiram, graduated at an Eastern college."

  " Well. how did you manage the campaign for capturing the other young man ? " Garfield was asked

  " Well, that was a different case. I knew that this
youth was going to leave mainly for financial reasons
also, but I understood his father well enough to know
that the matter must be managed with exceeding deli-
cacy He was a man of very strong religious convictions, and I thought he might be approached from that
side of his character , so when I got the letter of the
son, telling me, in the saddest language that he could
master, that he could not come back to school any more,
but must be content to be simply a farmer, much as
it was against his inclination, I revolved the matter
in my mind, and decided to send an appointment to
preach in the little country church where the old gentle-

man attended. I took for a subject the parable of the talents, and in the course of my discourse dwelt specially upon the fact that children were the talents which had been entrusted to parents, and if these talents were not increased and developed, there was a fearful trust neglected. After church I called upon the parents of the boy I was besieging, and I saw that something was weighing upon their minds. At length the subject of the discourse was taken up and gone over again, and in due course the young man himself was discussed, and I gave my opinion that he should by all means be encouraged and assisted in taking a thorough course of study. I gave my opinion that there was nothing more important to the parent than to do all in his power for the child. The next term the young man again appeared upon Hiram Hill, and remained pretty continuously till graduation."

He was wonderfully magnetic He never failed to win students to himself President Hinsdale says of him :

" Naturally, Garfield, the teacher, drew his pupils to himself with extraordinary power. Never have I seen such devotion to another teacher. An old Hiram student, now holding a responsible office in the public schools of Cleveland, speaking of the old times before Garfield went to college, says in a private letter : ' Then began to grow up in me an admiration and love for Garfield that has never abated, and the like of which I have never known. A bow of recognition or a single word from him was to me an inspiration ' And such would be the general testimony. In all this there was method ; not the method of crafty art, as the cynical might say, but the method of nature, the method of a great mind and noble heart. I take my leave of this Hiram teacher with affirming my conviction that, other things being equal, Garfield has never been greater than he was in Hiram from 1857 to 1861. He left the

quiet of the academy for the roar of the field and the
forum at the age of thirty, but not until he had demonstrated his fitness for the highest educational work and
honours."

The following facts and incidents will illustrate some
of his methods and qualities as a teacher.

One day a pupil made a sad failure in the class,—
at least, on a portion of the lesson,—when Garfield
roguishly pointed to a soiled place in one corner of the
recitation room, where the water had trickled through
the plastering and run down upon the wall.

" Look there," he said, laughing at the same time,
and eliciting a smile from each member of the class.
That was all he said ; but the rebuke was keen and
sharp, coming in that way from him.   Such was his
usual method.   Occasionally, however, when he per-
ceived a really rebellious spirit that meant mischief,
he was severe and withering in his method of treatment.

He assigned a certain task to a student at one time,
when the latter said :

" I doubt whether I can do it.   I do not think I am
equal to it."

" Not equal to it ? "

" No, sir."

" Darsie ! " answered Garfield, " when I get into a
place that I can easily fill, I always feel like shoving
out of it into one that requires of me more exertion."

In this single sentence was one of the secrets of his
success , and Darsie saw it at once.   Garfield had risen
rapidly by setting his standard high, and bringing himself up to it.

Akin to this, he said to the students on one occasion :

" I shall give you a series of lectures upon history,
beginning next week.   I do this not alone to assist
you ; the preparation for the lectures will *compel* me to
study history."

It was not the mere announcement that was interesting ; it was a method of his to show his pupils the best plan of study. He could do more and better work under a necessity than otherwise ; and so can every one. It was his custom to lecture on the topics he desired to study particularly, that he might derive the benefit of a two-fold object. He wanted his pupils to appreciate the advantage of it

" How in the world can he time his steps so as to take the last one just as the bell stops ? " remarked a student, referring to his coming into the chapel-exercises and taking his seat precisely as the bell ceased

" Hard telling," replied Darsie ; " but he is always on the stairs in the last half of the last minute, and glides into his seat just as the last tap of the bell is struck." The last stroke of the bell was indicated by a little more vigorous pull of the rope.

" And what seems marvellous to me is, tha the never fails   I couldn't time my steps like that," added the student.

Garfield insisted on *punctuality* everywhere—at prayers, recitation, lectures, all engagements   He demanded *promptness* as an essential duty.   He made his pupils feel the importance of the qualities   But he would not require of them what he did not practise himself.   He was the last man to preach what he did not practise. So he illustrated, every day, by persona lexample, the lessons which he taught respecting these virtues.

Returning from a neighbouring town one morning, where he lectured on the previous evening, he entered his recitation room late.   Another teacher, supposing he would not return in season to hear the recitation, had taken his class.   As he entered, a pupil was answering a question.   While in the act of removing his overcoat, and precisely as the pupil's answer ceased, Garfield put another question in the same line, as if the previous question were put by himself   He smiled   the teacher laughed and bowed himself out of the room, and the class roared. It was a happy termination of a single act of tardiness.

He was accustomed to lecture to his pupils upon " manners," " elements of success," and kindred topics. One day his topic was the ' Turning Point of Life," in which he said .

" The comb of the roof at the court-house at Ravenna (capital of Portage county, of which Hiram was a town) divides the drops of rain, sending those that fall on the south side to the Gulf of Mexico, and those on the opposite side into the Gulf of St. Lawrence, so that a mere breath of air, or the flutter of a bird's wing, may determine their destiny. It is so with your lives, my young friends. A passing event, perhaps of trifling importance in your view, the choice of a book or companion, a stirring thought, a right resolve, the associations of an hour, may prove the turning point of your lives."

During his connection with the school as principal his lectures were numerous. He lectured upon the natural sciences, reading, books, government, and occasional " topics of the times." He delivered many lectures in Portage county, and in neighbouring counties, before literary societies ; lectures upon geology, illustrated by charts of his own making, " Character and Writings of Sir Walter Scott," " Character of the German People," and " Carlyle's Frederic the Great." He was the most popular lecturer in Ohio. Crossing swords with William Denton, the sceptic, brought him into great notoriety. " He held a debate with Denton on the question of Whether all life upon the earth was developed by processes of law, or had been introduced by successive creative acts. Denton held the development theory ; Garfield that of intelligent, providential action. The discussion lasted five days and evenings, embraced twenty speeches on the part of each of the disputants and was remarkable as a sustained and severe intellectual effort." It won laurels for Garfield as a debater and a man of intellect.

Says Rev. J. L. Darsie, who was one of his pupils, "His lectures to the school were on all sorts of subjects, and were generally the result of his readings and observation. One season he took a trip, and, on his return, gave a very interesting series on 'The Chain of Lakes,' including Niagara, Thousand Islands, and sub-historic points. One lecture on aerolites I shall never forget. He gave several upon Ordnance, about the time of the attack upon Fort Sumter. Æsthetics came in for a share of treatment, with others on the personal habits of the students; and they were very effective. He lectured upon any and every scientific subject."

A large number of students were always in attendance, who paid their way along by teaching school in the winter. To these he gave lectures on the art of teaching. Mr. Darsie says: "At each lecture he appointed one or two pupils to bring in a review of the lecture in writing on a succeeding morning, and these reviews were read to the school. I now recall one of the most successful journalists of our land, who began his training here. In all he said or did, Garfield had the remarkable power of impressing himself and his thoughts upon his hearers, by his manners, gestures, tone of voice, and the freshness of his style. It was customary to act plays on Commencement occasions, and the drama, in its moral and high-toned phases, was encouraged. Often the play was original, and always subject to the strictures of the faculty, as were all the public performances. Garfield, when a student, was one of the most successful in delineating character. He could impersonate almost any character, and was amazingly successful in this *rôle*."

He delivered, also, many extemporaneous speeches on social and literary occasions, and even in political campaigns. He studied law, also, while he was teacher at Hiram, doing it by the improvement of odd moments and by burning midnight oil. He was admitted to the bar before he exchanged the quiet of teaching for the roar of battle. He studied law, " not so much with the intention of becoming a lawyer, as to acquaint himself with the principles of law. He had no idea of abandoning his chosen profession to spend his energies in law-practice, but the principles of law were needed to round his knowledge and increase his power "

As a Christian man, his influence was grand and ennobling, and his labours as a preacher are to be added to the mass of his other labours. He often preached in the Disciples' Church at Hiram, and at one time he preached regularly at Solon and Newburg, whither he went on Saturday night, returning on Monday morning. He preached more or less throughout the county. Preaching and lecturing in other towns, near and remote, spread a knowledge of the school, and made it popular He required his pupils to observe the highest standard of moral conduct, and his counsel here was frequent and direct. His favourite hymn at chapel-service was, " Ho ! Reapers of Life's Harvest," etc., and he joined in the singing with a will He often requested the students to sing this hymn at morning devotions, allowing them to sit until they came to the last verse, when he would rap upon the desk with his knuckles, and the school would rise and sing the last verse standing.

He married Miss Rudolph, the lady to whom he was engaged before entering college, on November 11, 1858. Her efficient co-operation enabled him to accomplish so large an amount of labour. Often, in the preparation of a lecture or speech, his wife and Miss Booth would explore the library for him, or examine certain books which he designated. The number of books that he perused in a year was almost incredible. Going from the library with his arms full of volumes was a common spectacle. Mr Darsie has seen him on his way to the library in the rain, returning with ten or twelve volumes, a student walking by his side holding an umbrella over his head. Some books awakened his enthusiasm ; he read them more than once. Such books as " Tom Brown's Schooldays," won his admiration. He told his pupils that every one of them ought to read the work carefully. Macaulay's works, and Mills', and works of kindred ability and value, he particularly enjoyed and recommended.

In those days Commencement exercises brought together from five to ten thousand people. They came from fifty miles around. A large tent was pitched over a stage, on which the literary exercises were performed Booths for refreshments were erected here and there, and often showmen would appear on the ground. Roughs and intoxicated persons sometimes appeared in large numbers, causing disturbance, and sadly marring the harmony of the occasion. But after Garfield became principal, these scenes stopped. The pointing of his finger, or the waving of his hand, when disturbance broke out in any quarter, quelled it at once. Roughs appeared to understand that his authority could not be trifled with on such occasions.

We shall close this chapter by another quotation from Rev. Mr. Darsie :

" No matter how old the pupils were, Garfield always called us by our first names, and kept himself on the most familiar terms with all. He played with us freely, scuffled with us sometimes, walked with us in walking to and fro, and we treated him out of the class just about as we did one another. Yet he was a most strict disciplinarian, and enforced the rules like a martinet He combined an affectionate and confiding manner with respect for order, in a most successful way If he wanted to speak to a pupil, either for reproof or approbation, he would generally manage to get one arm around him and draw him up close to him He had a

peculiar way of shaking hands, too, giving a twist to
your arm, and drawing you right up to him. This
sympathetic manner has helped him to advancement.
When I was janitor, he used sometimes to stop me and
ask my opinion about this and that, as if seriously
advising with me   I can see now that my opinion
could not have been of any value, and that he probably
asked me, partly to increase my self-respect and partly
to show me that he felt an interest in me   I certainly
was his friend all the firmer for it.

" I remember once asking him what was the best way
to pursue a certain study, and he said : ' Use several
text-books, get the views of different authors as you
advance ; in that way you can plough a broader furrow.
I always study in that way.'   He tried hard to have us
observe carefully and accurately.   He broke out one
day in the midst of a lesson with, ' Henry, how many
posts are there under the building downstairs ? '   Henry
expressed his opinion, and the question went round the
class, hardly one getting it right.   Then it was, ' How
many boot-scrapers are there at the door ? '   ' How
many windows in the building ? '   ' How many trees in
the field ? '   ' What were the colours of particular rooms,
and the peculiarities of familiar objects ? '   He was
the keenest observer I ever saw.   I think he observed,
and numbered, every button on our coats.   A friend of
mine was walking with him through Cleveland one day,
when Garfield stopped and darted down a cellar-way,
asking his companion to follow, and briefly stopping to
explain himself   The sign, ' Saws and Files ' was over
the door, and in the depths was heard a regular clicking
sound   ' I think this fellow is cutting files," he said,
' and I have never seen a file cut.'   Down they went,
and, sure enough, there was a man re-cutting an old file,
and they stayed there ten minutes and found out all
about the process.   Garfield would never go by anything without understanding it."

XXIII

TOP OF THE LADDER

IT was impossible for a speaker of Garfield's power to keep out of politics. In political campaigns the public demand his efforts ; men will not take *no* for an answer. It was so with Garfield. He was impressed into the service by the leading citizens of his county In the autumn after his return to Hiram, before he hardly had time to become settled in his great work, his efforts on the platform were sought , and the new Republican party, on the anti-slavery basis, with its first candidate, John C. Fremont, a man of Garfield's stamp in vigour, courage, and force of character, was exceedingly taking to him. Nobody had to tease him long for a speech. Often he went in the evening to make a speech, five, six, ten miles distant, returning after the address. Usually he took a student with him for company and improvement. As soon as they started he would open conversation, seldom upon the subject of his discourse, but upon some topic of real value to the student. Going and returning his conversation was continued without the least abatement

Alphonso Hart, a stalwart Democrat of Ravenna, delivered a speech in Hiram, full of slavery and Democratic sophistries and errors. Garfield heard it, with many Republican citizens.

" Reply to it, Mr Garfield," appealed an influential citizen to him. " Floor him."

" That can easily be done," Garfield answered ; " but is it wise ? "

"It is always wise to refute error and wrong anywhere."

"I confess that I should enjoy handling him without gloves for an hour"

"Handle him, then," urged the citizen.   "It will do the Republican party a world of good."

Other citizens put in their pleas for him to answer Hart.

"You are just the one to do it."

"Everybody wants you should answer him."

"It will make votes for Fremont."

"Come now, do gratify the public desire"

In this way Garfield was beset with pleas to answer the Democratic orator ; and he consented   The meeting was in the Disciples' Church, and it was packed to its utmost capacity.   Garfield's reply was devoid of all bitterness, but it was powerful with logic and facts   He hauled over the record of the Democratic party, with its endorsement of slavery with all its horrors, and he made that record appear black enough   The effort was both able and triumphant, and the fame of it rapidly spread throughout the county.   Appeals for more speeches came in from all the region about, and finally a discussion was arranged between Garfield and Hart, to take place at Garrettsville on a given day.   Crowds flocked to hear the debate.   Garfield was in his element on that day, for he had posted himself throughly upon the history of the Democratic party, and the aims of its Southern leaders to make slavery national.   His antagonist was completely discomfited in the discussion.   He had counted without his host.   He was floored.   Garfield's success lifted him at once into enviable notoriety as a political debater and orator, and from that time, remarks like the following were common .—

"He must go to the legislature"

"We must send him to Congress."

"Just the man to follow that old anti-slavery warhorse, Giddings "

T

" You'll see him President yet "

And so the enthusiastic awakening expended itself, in a measure, upon Garfield's supposed future career One year later the position of representative to the State legislature was tendered him.

" No ; my work is here in the Institute. I have no ambition to enter political life. I must decline the proposition." Garfield thus replied out of an honest heart.

Again and again he was urged to accept the position, but to every one his answer was the same.

" My work is here, and my heart is here, and my DUTY is here." No appeals could move him.

In 1859 the faculty of Williams College invited him to deliver the master's oration on Commencement day. It was a rare compliment the faculty paid to him by this invitation, for it was but three years after he was graduated Accepting the invitation, and preparing himself carefully for the occasion, he left Hiram for Williamstown, Massachusetts, accompanied by his wife, taking the first pleasure-trip of his life. He descended the St. Lawrence River to Quebec, and then crossed the New England States to his destination A warm welcome awaited him there. Nor were the numerous friends who gathered disappointed in the orator of the day. His praises were on every lip.

On his return, when he had reached Mentor, in his own State, a delegation of citizens met him with an unexpected proposition.

" We want you to become a candidate for State senator."

" Indeed ! " exclaimed Garfield, very much surprised by the proposition. " I thought Mr. Prentiss was the man.

" Mr. Prentiss has just died, very suddenly."

" Mr. Prentiss was a man well advanced in life, a very popular citizen of Ravenna, whose re-election had been determined upon. But his sudden death frustrated their plans; and now all hearts turned to the young principal of the Hiram Institute.

" You are the first choice of the leading Republicans of the district."

" I thank you sincerely for thinking of me, and really, it is a temptation to receive this offer, but I do not see how I can consistently consent."

" Your name will enable us to carry the district for the Republicans easily," urged another of the delegation. " I hope you will not decline without giving the subject some thought."

" Yes, but my thought is of the Institute. How can I accept your proposition and discharge my duties to the school ? "

" Your duties in the senate will keep you away but a few weeks. Suppose you take the subject into considertion, confer with the faculty, and let us have your decision a week hence."

The last speaker knew that some members of the faculty and board of trustees were anxious that he should accept the nomination.

To this last suggestion Garfield yielded, and the matter was laid before the faculty and trustees. To his surprise all of them urged him to consent to the use of his name. Teachers volunteered to do extra work in his absence, and all were willing to contribute service, so as to make it possible for him to go.

Garfield was pressed into this political service, and received the nomination. He was present, by request, at the nominating convention, and while the business was in progress a delegate, who saw the youthful candidate on that day for the first time, remarked to a leading Republican :

" Don't you make a mistake in putting forward so young a man for senator ? "

" Only young in years; he is not young in ability," was the prompt reply.

" I don't know about that ; unless his looks belie him, his experience in public life must be rather limited "

· " You wait and see. We shall hear from him when this business is through, and you will be satisfied that his head is old, though his body is young."

After the nomination, according to the custom that prevailed, Garfield accepted it in a characteristic speech The delegate who doubted the wisdom of the nomination immediately said to the Republican to whom his doubts were expressed :

" I am perfectly satisfied ; he is a power "

Garfield was elected by a very large majority, and took his seat in the State senate, January, 1860. It was a time of great excitement. The South was threatening secession and civil war, if a Republican should be elected president in the approaching campaign. The North was fully aroused to check the incursions of slavery, by a bold and victorious advance. Garfield was just the man to occupy a seat in the State senate at such a time, though he was the youngest member of the body. There was another able young man in the senate with him, as radical as himself, Jacob D. Cox, afterwards major-general, governor of Ohio, and Secretary of the Interior. The two roomed together, and were as intimate as brothers Some of the members called them " Damon and Pythias." There was still another young man, Professor Munroe of Oberlin College, an institution that was founded on anti-slavery principles, and whose teachers were as one with Garfield on the great national question that over-topped all others—liberty. Cox himself was the son-in-law of an Oberlin professor. These three senators stood shoulder to shoulder against slavery and were called the " radical triumvirate."

Garfield took rank at once with the ablest speakers in that body. President Hinsdale says, " He was a valuable man on committees and in party counsels. No senator was more frequently called into the counsels by the president of the senate when knotty points of order were to be untied or cut."

In a previous chapter we learned that Garfield visited Columbus with his mother, and saw the legislature in session. Little did he dream, or his mother, that in less than ten years he would be a leading member of that senate, his eloquence ringing through those halls, and his wise counsels and patriotic efforts preparing the state to oppose rebellion with great power, yet so it was. One of the most marvellous examples of success on record!

During his second term in the senate, 1861, he was confronted by the gravest questions that State or nation ever have to deal with Lincoln had been elected president, the Southern States were preparing to secede, and civil war was imminent. "Shall Ohio prepare for war?" "Has a State the right to secede?" "Can a State be coerced?" "Shall we punish treason?" These were among the questions the young senator was compelled to discuss Almost night and day he laboured to qualify himself to discuss them intelligently and ably. Night after night, until eleven, twelve, and even one o'clock, he spent in the state library, studying these and kindred questions. Whenever he spoke upon them, he spoke pointedly, and with great power. He led the senate in its patriotic stand against secession and compromise with slavery. He denounced Buchanan, the Democratic president, who was favouring the secessionists, and characterized Cobb, who robbed the national treasury, and Floyd, who stole the arms from every Northern arsenal, and Toucy, who sent the ships of the navy as far away as possible—all members of the Democratic cabinet—he characterized them as traitors to their country. In a speech that blazed with fervid eloquence, he told a Democratic senator, Judge Key, of Cincinnati, "To remember whose cabinet it was that had embraced traitors among its most distinguished members, and sent them forth from its most secret sessions to betray their knowledge to their country's ruin ! "

When Congress very unwisely proposed a " Constitutional Amendment," prohibiting further legislation upon slavery in the States,—a measure designed to placate the secessionists,— Garfield denounced it in the Ohio senate as a compromise with traitors, an unpatriotic and base surrender to the slave oligarchy. He declared that his arm should wither in its socket before it should be lifted in favour of a measure that virtually abandoned liberty, and left slavery master of the situation. " The events now transpiring make it clear that this is no time for any such amendment," he exclaimed. " Would you give up the forts and other government property, or would you fight to maintain your right to them ? "

When the vote was taken, Garfield, with six others, recorded their names against the " base surrender." He opposed the meeting of the famous Washington Peace Commissioners until after the inauguration of Mr Lincoln ; he protested against all such " peace measures " as cowardly and futile, preferring himself to stand by the old flag, and *fight* for human rights.

Before this he was satisfied that war could not be averted. Late one night he said to his room-mate .

" Cox, war is inevitable."

" That is sure as you live," answered Cox.

" You and I must fight."

" Or prove ourselves cowards."

" Here, then, we pledge our lives to our country in this hour of peril." And they clasped hands silently, such emotions stirring their breasts as patriots only feel in the solemn hour of danger.

News of the firing upon Fort Sumter was followed immediately by a call from President Lincoln for seventy-five thousand men. The call was read in the Ohio Senate, crowded with patriotic spectators, whose tumultuous applause seconded the President's demand.

As soon as the deafening cheers had subsided, Garfield sprang to his feet, and in a short speech of almost surpassing eloquence and power moved :

"That Ohio contribute twenty thousand men, and three million dollars, as the quota of the State."

The motion was carried amid the wildest demonstrations of devotion to the country.

Governor Dennison, of Ohio, sent Garfield to Missouri to obtain five thousand stand of arms, a portion of those which General Lyon removed from the arsenal at St. Louis. He was successful in his mission, shipped the guns, and saw them safely delivered at Columbus.

After the fall of Sumter, Governor Dennison sent him to Cleveland, to organize the seventh and eighth regiments of Ohio infantry. Having organized them, the governor offered him the colonelcy of one of them ; but he declined the offer because he lacked " military experience." He promised to take a subordinate position, however, provided a West Point graduate was placed in command. The result was, that the governor appointed him lieutenant-colonel, and sent him to the Western Reserve to recruit a regiment, promising him a West Pointer to command it if one could be found   Garfield suggested his old friend and schoolmate, Captain Hazen, then in the regular army ; but when the governor sent to the war department for his transfer, General Scott refused to release him. So the forty-second Ohio regiment, recruited by Garfield, and embracing a large number of Hiram students, went into camp at Columbus without a colonel. It was in these circumstances and after repeated requests from officers and members of the regiment, that Garfield consented to take the command.

We have not space for details. Garfield proved himself as victorious in war as he had been successful in peace. In less than one month after he went into action with his regiment, under the orders of General Buell, he fought the battle of Middle Creek, January 10, 1862, driving the rebel general Marshall, whose forces largely outnumbered his, out of his entrenchments, compelling him to retreat into Virginia   Other victories followed, in what was called the " Sandy Valley campaign," eliciting from the commanding general a congratulatory order, in which he spoke of the expedition as " calling into action the highest qualities of a soldier—fortitude, perseverance, courage."   For his bravery and military skill in this campaign the authorities at Washington made Garfield a brigadier-general, dating his commission back to January 10, 1862, the day of the battle of Middle Creek   As Garfield was the youngest member of the Ohio Senate, so now he became the youngest brigadier-general in the army.

Subsequently he was made major-general " for gallant and meritorious services at the battle of Chickamauga." The antecedents of that famous battle, under General Rosecrans, show that the victory was due more to the sagacity, plans, and courage of General Garfield than to any other officer.   Within about one year and a half, he rose from a lieutenant-colonelcy to a major-general.

In the summer of 1862 leading republicans of the nineteenth Ohio congressional district nominated Garfield to represent them in Congress   They regarded him as the man above all others in the district qualified to succeed Joshua R Giddings, of whom they were justly proud.   Giddings was superseded four years before by John Hutchins, with whom the republicans were not satisfied   The movement for Garfield was undertaken without his knowledge.   He was at the head of his command in Kentucky.   The knowledge of his great abilities, and his military fame, led to his nomination   At first he thought he must decline the honour, and fight out the battles of his country.   He was very popular in the army, both with officer- and soldiers his pay, too, was double that of a congressman, and he was poor, and needed the greater salary—and there was no doubt that the highest honours awaited him should he continue on the field until the end of the war. The reader can readily see that to accept the nomination in these circumstances was an act of great self-denial. But President Lincoln signified his desire for Garfield to enter Congress, as a member of military experience and skill was much needed there. The wishes of Lincoln settled the doubts of Garfield, and he accepted the nomination, was triumphantly elected, and took his seat in the national house of representatives in December, 1863, after two years and three months of service in the army.

During this time the trustees of Hiram Institute had not abandoned the idea of his return to the institution. While a member of the Ohio Senate he continued his connection with the school, while the senate was not in session. One interesting item of his thoroughness in teaching belongs to this part of his career. He was teaching a class how to write letters, and having taught them how to address different classes of friends and relatives, how to superscribe letters, etc., illustrating the same on the blackboard, he requested each one to write a letter to him at Columbus. In due time the letters were written and forwarded. Subsequently they were returned to the authors, corrected.

During his first two years in Congress his name appeared on the catalogue of Hiram Institute as " Advisory Principal and Lecturer." He has been a member of the board of trustees ever since. For seventeen years he served his district as national representative. We have not space for any of the brilliant record of those seventeen years We can only say, that he became the acknowledged leader of the national house of representatives ; the pride of his native state, Ohio, and an honour to the Republic

His great popularity and usefulness as representative very naturally suggested his name to the Republicans of Ohio, when a United States Senator was to be elected by the legislature in January, 1880, to succeed Mr. Thurman. When the subject was opened to Garfield, he remarked :

" Just as you please ; if my friends think it best, I shall make no objection."

" We want you should go to Columbus when the election is pending."

" I cannot consent to any such plan. I shall not lift my finger for the office. I never sought an office yet, except that of Janitor at the Hiram Institute. If the people want me, they will elect me."

" Very true," urged his friends , " it is no engineering or finesse that we desire you to do at Columbus. We only want you to be where your friends can see you and confer with you."

" And that will be construed into work for the office, the very appearance of which is distasteful to me   I decline peremptorily to go to Columbus "   This was Garfield's characteristic decision and reply.

When the legislature assembled, the feeling was so strong for Garfield that all other candidates withdrew, and he was nominated by acclamation at the party caucus, and unanimously elected.

After the election was over he visited Columbus, and addressed both branches of the legislature in joint convention. The closing paragraph of his remarkable speech illustrates the courage and independence of the man—qualities that have recommended him to the confidence and support of the people. He said :

" During the twenty years that I have been in public life, almost eighteen of it in the Congress of the United States, I have tried to do one thing. Whether I was mistaken or otherwise, it has been the plan of my life to follow my conviction, at whatever personal cost to myself. I have represented for many years a district in Congress whose approbation I greatly desired ; but though it may seem, perhaps, a little egotistical to say it, I yet desired still more the approbation of one person, and his name was Garfield. He is the only man that I am compelled to sleep with, and eat with, and live with, and die with , and if I could not have his approbation, I should have bad companionship."

In view of this last triumph, President Hinsdale said :

" He has commanded success. His ability, knowledge, mastery of questions, generosity of nature, devotion to the public good, and honesty of purpose, have done the work. He has never had a political ' machine.' He has never forgotten the day of small things. It is difficult to see how a political triumph could be more complete or more gratifying than his election to the senate No bargains, no ' slate,' no ' grocery ' at Columbus He did not even go to the capital city. Such things are inspiring to those who think politics in a bad way. He is a man of positive convictions, freely uttered. Politically, he may be called a ' man of war ' , and yet few men, or none, begrudge him his triumph. Democrats vied with Republicans the other day, in Washington, in their congratulations ; some of them were as anxious for his election as any Republican could be. It is said that he will go to the senate without an enemy on either side of the chamber. These things are honourable to all parties. They show that manhood is more than party."

And so James, the hero of our tale, stands upon the highest round of the ladder of fame, save one !

The final step to the top of the ladder followed quickly—so quickly that he had not time to take his seat in the United States Senate He had but just planted his feet upon the highest round of the ladder, save one, when the call to come up higher—to the top —was l . ⸱ ⸱ la M. ⸱ ⸱ t⸱ the G⸱ lden Gate.

The National Republican Convention, five months later, assembled to nominate a candidate for the presidency of the United States. James A. Garfield was a member of that convention, and his magnetic presence was the occasion of much enthusiasm and applause. Although he was not a candidate for the position, whenever he arose to speak, or moved about in the vast audience, he was greeted with hearty cheers. He was, evidently *en rapport* with the crowded assembly. After thirty-four ineffectual ballots for a candidate about fifty members of the convention cast their votes for James A. Garfield in the thirty-fifth ballot. The announcement created a *furore* of excitement, as it indicated a breaking up of the factions, and a probable union of all upon the most popular Republican in the convention. Instantly the delegates of one State seized their banner with a shout (the delegates of each State sat together, their banner bearing the name of their State), bore it proudly forward, and placed it over the head of the aforesaid patriot and statesman, followed by other delegations, and still others, until seven hundred delegates upon the floor, and fifteen thousand spectators in the galleries joined in the remarkable demonstration, and cheer upon cheer rent the air, as the banners, one after another, were placed in triumph over the head of their hero, declaring to the world, without the use of language, that James A. Garfield was the choice of the convention for President of the United States ; the magnificent ovation terminating by the several bands striking up " Rally Round the Flag," fifteen thousand voices joining in the chorus, and a section of artillery outside contributing its thundering bass to the outburst of joy. It was a wild, tumultuous scene of excitement, the spontaneous outburst of patriotic devotion to the country, such as never transpired in any political assembly before and, probably, never will again. It was something more, and different from the usual excitement and passion of political assemblies ; it was an inspiration of the hour, begotten and moved by more than mortal impulse—the interposition of Him who has guided and saved our country from its birth !

That spontaneous burst of enthusiasm really nominated General Garfield for President. The thirty-sixth ballot, that followed immediately, was only a method of registering the decision of that supreme moment.

The news of General Garfield's nomination flew with the speed of electricity over the land, creating unbounded joy from Plymouth Rock to the Pacific Slope. The disappointments and animosities of a heated contest vanished at once before the conceded worth and popularity of the candidate. Partisans forgot the men of their choice, in their gladness that union and harmony signalized the close of the most remarkable political convention on record

HE WAS ELECTED PRESIDENT OF THE UNITED STATES ON THE SECOND DAY OF NOVEMBER, EIGHTEEN HUNDRED AND EIGHTY

He carried twenty of the thirty-eight states, securing 213 of the 369 electors. In his native town of Orange every ballot was cast for him.

The time between the election and inauguration of General Garfield was characterized by good feeling and general hopefulness. The almost unprecedented excitement of the political campaign subsided into national tranquillity and peace, in which the two great political parties seemed to be more harmonious then ever. Mr. Garfield's popularity won the esteem of leading men who opposed his election, and some of them publicly declared their entire confidence in the man, and their profound respect for his great talents. The striking change from the bitterness of an exciting campaign, for two or three months previous to the election, to the cheerful acquiescence in the result, and the general good-will towards the President-elect, was an event worthy of record.

XXIV

IN THE WHITE HOUSE

THE Fourth of March, 1881—the day of the inauguration of General Garfield as President of the United States—will be remembered for its bleak, uncomfortable, stormy morning, threatening to spoil the preparations for a grand military and civic display   About ten o'clock, however, the storm subsided, and the clouds partially broke. The city was crowded with visitors from different sections of the country, among them many civic organizations and military companies which had come to join in the procession   The wide-spread interest in the occasion was due to the fame of the President-elect and the era of good feeling that succeeded his election. Not only his personal friends, but many others in every part of the land, exerted themselves to make the occasion memorable beyond all similar demonstrations. General Garfield's college classmates were there, to the number of twenty, to congratulate him upon his remarkable public career.

The ceremony of inauguration was arranged for twelve o'clock, noon. Before that hour arrived, more than a hundred thousand people thronged the streets of the city to witness the unusual display   Every State of the Union was represented in the seething multitude ; and hundreds of public men were present—senators representatives, governors, judges, lawyers, clergymen, and authors. A large number of veterans of the late war were there to honour their beloved comrade of other days who was going up higher.

The ceremony was to take place at the Capitol and preparations were made at the White House, whence the presidential party would be escorted.

At half-past ten o'clock a chorus of bugles announced the arrival of President Hayes and President-elect Garfield from the hotel, who were received in the ante-room by Mr. Pendleton, and for a brief moment the ladies and gentlemen and other invited friends in the House greeted each other in the red room. Col. Casey then announced that everything was ready, and assigned the party to carriages. As they passed down the avenue they were greeted with cheers and waving of handkerchiefs from the assembled thousands, who, by this time, lined every avenue from end to end

At the Capitol an imposing scene was presented. After the presidential party had filed into the Senate-chamber, the gorgeous diplomatic corps, headed by Sir Edward Thornton, preceded by Secretary Evarts, entered and occupied the best seats on the right of the Vice-President All the legations in Washington were represented All appeared in court dress, except the Mexican and Chilian legations, who were in evening costume.

The Supreme Court then appeared in robes, and took front seats reserved for it.

The procession was formed, with President Hayes and President-elect Garfield at the head, and proceeded through the corridor and rotunda to the east front, where the platform was erected from which the vast assemblage would listen to the inaugural address. When the dignitaries with their families were finally arranged, silence was maintained for a few moments, that the group might be photographed. Then Mr. Garfield stepped to the front and delivered his noble inaugural address, in tones so clear and eloquent that the multitude, even in the distance, heard. Before he closed his address the clouds broke above him, and pure sunlight fell in benediction upon his head. As he concluded, Judge Waite, of the Supreme Court, presented the Bible to him on which the Presidents are sworn, and proceeded to administer the oath. At the conclusion, President Garfield reverently kissed the sacred volume, and returned it to the judge. Then, turning to his aged mother, who had wept tears of joy during the delivery of his address, he imprinted a kiss upon her cheek, and another upon that of his wife, the two persons, next to himself, most deeply interested in the transaction of that memorable hour. The President and his attendants withdrew amidst the wildest demonstrations of joy by the concourse of people.

Immediately followed the imposing military and civic procession, which was said to be more elaborate and grand than anything of the kind ever witnessed in the capital of the nation. It was three hours passing a given point, and was reviewed by President Garfield from a stand erected in front of the presidential mansion

The opening of his administration was somewhat embarrassed by both the action and non-action of a faction in Congress, the leaders of which were not inclined to harmony or justice

There was one trouble which he encountered early in his administration, and it was all the more annoying because it arose within his own party. President Garfield did not believe in a custom of the United States Senate called " Senatorial courtesy "—the custom of allowing senators to designate who should be appointed to fill certain offices in their respective States ; and, in the exercise of that manly independence for which he was ever distinguished, he resolved to ignore the custom. Therefore, instead of consulting Senator Conkling, of New York, respecting the nomination of a man to fill a certain important office in that State, he made the appointment himself, according to the requirements of the Constitution This act was construed as a mortal offence by Mr. Conkling, and those who moved at his beck At once there was war against the administration

After the lapse of several weeks, in which Senator Conkling had an opportunity to rally his forces and train them to an organized opposition, the nomination by the President was confirmed. In the meantime Mr. Conkling had sent his resignation to the Governor of New York, and his associate, Mr. Platt, did the same ; evidently thinking that the legislature, then in session, would immediately return them.

A contest in the Legislature of New York was inaugurated at once—perhaps the most bitter and acrimonious contest ever waged between party factions in a State legislature. When the members were elected, a large majority of the Republicans were the friends of Mr. Conkling ; and this fact, doubtless, caused him to feel confident that his action in opposing the administration would be promptly endorsed by his speedy return to the Senate. In this, however, he was wofully disappointed The opposition to his re-election was decided and strong in the outset, because the popular feeling sided with President Garfield.

XXV

ASSASSINATION

WHILE the contest was going on in the new York Legislature over Senator Conkling's re-election, an attempt was made upon the President's life which startled and shocked the nation. He had arranged a journey to New England, for the purpose of attending the Commencement at Williams College, Williamstown, Mass , the annual meeting of the American Institute of Instruction at St. Albans, Vt , extending his trip into Maine, where he would be the guest of Mr. Blaine, Secretary of State ; thence into New Hampshire, in response to an invitation by the Legislature of that State, then in session , returning through Boston to Washington ; hoping thereby to recruit his somewhat exhausted energies by a brief respite from official duties. On Saturday morning, July 2, he left the Executive Mansion at a few minutes past nine o'clock, in his carriage with Secretary Blaine, for the Baltimore and Potomac Railroad Depôt. At twenty minutes past nine o'clock he entered the depôt, arm in arm with Mr. Blaine, when two pistol shots were fired in quick succession, the first one sending a ball through the right coat-sleeve of the President, doing no damage, the second one driving a ball deep into his body above the third rib. The unexpected shot well-nigh paralyzed the bystanders Mr. Blaine turned to seize the assassin, but found him already in the hands of an officer. As he turned back, the President sank heavily upon the floor, and the fearful tidings

spread through the city · " *The President has been assassinated !* " The telegraphic wires took up the terrible
news and conveyed it over the country, startling every
town, village, and hamlet as they never were startled
except by the assassination of President Lincoln. By
twelve o'clock the entire country was apprised of the
appalling calamity, except in sections beyond the reach
of telegraphs and telephones. The dreadful news flashed
over the Atlantic cable, astounding and affecting Euro-
peans almost as sensibly as it did Americans. The
manifestations of unfeigned sorrow were gauged by this
remarkable fact. The South seemed to vie with the
North in profound grief over the fearful crime and
heartfelt sympathy for the illustrious sufferer.

Physicians and surgeons were speedily summoned ;
and, within an hour, he was removed to the White
House in an extremely prostrated and critical condition.

The President was still conscious while prostrate
upon the floor at the depôt, and fearing that the intelligence of his injury might over come his wife in her
feeble state of health, he dictated to Colonel Rockwell,
who was at his side, the following despatch to her at
Long Branch.

Mrs Garfield, Elberon, New Jersey :
" The President wishes me to say to you from him that he
has been seriously hurt—how seriously he cannot yet say. He
is himself, and hopes you will come to him soon. He sends
his love to you. " A F. ROCKWELL."

It should be stated that Mrs. Garfield was recovering
from a severe sickness of several weeks, and a few days
before the President accompanied her to Long Branch
to hasten her restoration. Her life was despaired of for
a time, and her husband's watchful and tender care of
her, night and day, when her life hung quivering in the
balance, in connection with official duties, made a heavy
draft upon his strength.

A correspondent of the New York *Times*, who was an eye-witness, said that when the President " was tenderly lifted from the vehicle with the pallor of death stamped upon his countenance, glancing up to the window, he saw some familiar faces, and with a smile which those who saw it will never forget, he raised his right hand and gave the military salute, which seemed to say, ' Long live the Republic ! ' "

Soon after the President was laid upon his bed in the presidential mansion, his nervous prostration passed away, and he became composed and cheerful, greeting members of his cabinet, and other intimate friends present, with a cordial pressure of the hand and words of cheer. He was so much like himself, genial, calm and hopeful, that both friends and physicians thought it was the harbinger of recovery

Sunday, July 3, was a day of anxiety and tears to the American people. The churches were filled with mourning thousands, and the burden of sermons and prayers was the great sorrow that had fallen upon the nation. July 4th was such an Independence as the country never saw. No one had a heart to engage in the festivities of the day Many well-arranged celebrations were abandoned.

But the assassin—how about him ? His name was Charles J. Guiteau, an eccentric, pettifogging lawyer, about forty years of age, of a weak, disordered mind, who had tried in vain to get an appointment to a foreign consulate. In his chagrin, poverty, and disappointment, as some suppose, reason was partially dethroned, and he committed the crime in his desperation. Others suppose that, since he sympathized with Mr. Conkling and Vice-President Arthur, in their opposition to the Garfield administration, relating to the New York appointment, he made himself believe that, President Garfield out of the way, and Mr. Arthur in his place, the appointment could readily be secured Be that as it may he coolly perpetrated the deed, and within an hour was safely lodged in the District jail.

The profound sympathy and sorrow of the people of this and other countries was manifested by telegrams from every quarter, letters of condolence, and resolutions of public bodies and organizations, conveying to the President expressions of grief and prayer for his recovery. The Queen of England, King of Spain, King of Belgium, Emperors of Russia, Japan, China, and Germany, and other foreign rulers, sent despatches full of sorrow and expressions of good-will.

But another and still more serious relapse awaited him on the twenty sixth day of August, destroying the hopes of the physicians and attending friends The bullet-wound was doing well, discharging healthy pus freely ; but an ugly abscess, occasioned by pus poisoning, appeared upon the neck, and the stomach ceased to assimilate or retain food. At four o'clock p m., on the twenty-sixth day of August, he appeared to be rapidly sinking He was unconscious, and breathed heavily, like one suffering in the last stages of apoplexy. A consultation of the doctors resulted in the decision that the last ray of hope had vanished, and a few hours more would put the seal of death upon all that was mortal of the illustrious President

On Saturday the churches of Washington consulted together, through representatives, and it was decided to observe the following day as one of fasting and prayer in behalf of the President, who still lived Telegrams were flashed over the country, inviting Christians of every name to spend Sunday, August 28, in supplication for the recovery of the President.

While the Christian men and women of the country were yet upon their knees, the President rallied from the extreme prostration of Friday and Saturday ; his stomach resumed its functions. his pulse fell, and he said in a stronger voice than he had ~~~d for a week,

" I am better ; I shall live." His strength was apparently renewed, and the change was so decided that the hopes of the nation were once more revived.

The physicians became satisfied that the malarial air of Washington was very unfavourable to the recovery of the President. From the time he was striken down the public were extremely anxious about this danger. It was not until Tuesday, the fifth day of September, however, that he was removed to Long Branch, New Jersey. Preparations were made to remove him upon his bed, with the least possible excitement and motion ; and at six o'clock in the morning of that day, he was taken from the White House to the special train in waiting, accompanied by his devoted wife and loving daughter, together with his medical attendants and other friends He was comfortably lodged in Francklyn Cottage.

The change appeared to benefit the patient at once, and he enjoyed the sea air with a keen relish On the fourth day after his arrival, Dr Hamilton said to Mrs Garfield, " I am afraid to tell you how confident I feel of your husband's recovery " The public participated in this confident hope, and there was renewed talk of a national thanksgiving

The buoyant hopes raised by the removal of the patient were dashed, however, in a few days, by the undoubted evidence of blood-poisoning, and the presence of an abscess in the right lung Many thought the last hope was gone. Others still clung to the hope which the patient's great physical vitality and uniform courage inspired. But he grew worse ; and, on the seventeenth day of September, appeared to be beyond mortal aid. The medical attendants well-nigh despaired of him, although there was no evidence of speedy dissolution. Two days later, September nineteenth, there appeared slight improvement

T   .   .   .   .   ..arfield

and the physicians retired ; and the illustrious sleeper was left alone with his watchers.

Within ten minutes after the physicians and Mrs Garfield retired, the President awoke with a groan Placing his hand upon his heart, he said to General Swaim, " Oh, Swaim ! what a terrible pain I have here ! " Dr. Bliss was summoned from an adjoining room hastily, and the moment he fastened his eye upon the sufferer he exclaimed, " My God, Swaim, he is dying ; call Mrs Garfield " From that moment he appeared to be unconscious, although he fixed his eyes upon his wife as she hurriedly entered the room, and seemed to follow her as she moved around to the other side of the bed to take his hand in hers His eyes were wide open, but dazed ; his pulse only fluttered ; he gasped and was no more. At thirty-five minutes past ten o'clock, Dr Bliss pronounced life extinct ! A sudden and terrible change from the hope inspired at ten o'clock ! The President of the United States—her favourite son, scholar, and statesman—was dead !

XXVI

INCIDENTS OF HIS MANHOOD

A FITTING close of this volume is a collection
of incidents from Garfield's public life, illus-
trative of the qualities we have traced in his early
struggles for a livelihood and education   They will
serve to establish, more fully if possible, the drift of
our effort · viz., "THE BOY IS FATHER OF THE MAN."

The thoughtful consideration that he devoted to
issues of importance, and the deep reverence for the
Scriptures that was begotten in his soul by maternal
training and the grace of God, appeared in the current
of his thoughts and acts after he had determined to
enter the army.   He went to his home at night thinking of his dear mother and dearer wife and child, as
well as the small property he should leave them if he
laid down his life on the battle-field.   Opening the
Bible which his mother gave him, to see what it would
say to him upon the subject, he read, and read, and
every passage seemed like the voice of God, saying to
him, "Go! Go!"   Far into the night he thought and
read, and read and thought, more and more satisfied
that his decision was in the path of duty

When he went into camp, to drill his regiment before
joining the army, his thoroughness and systematic way
of doing things, as well as his tact and use of carpenters' tools, came into immediate use.   He was ignorant
of military tactics, and so he sat down first to the task
of instructing himself before he undertook the instruc-

tion of his regiment   " Bringing his saw and jack-plane
again into play, he fashioned companies, officers, and
non-commissioned officers, out of maple blocks, and,
with these wooden-headed troops, thoroughly mastered
the infantry tactics in his quarters.   Then he organized
a school for the officers of his regiment, requiring
thorough recitation in the tactics, and illustrating the
manœuvres by the blocks he had prepared for his own
instruction.   This done, he instituted regimental, company, squad, skirmish, and bayonet drill, and kept his
men at these exercises from six to eight hours a day,
until it was universally admitted that no better drilled
or disciplined regiment could be found in Ohio "

His decision and force of character, so noticeable in
his early life, were illustrated by the promptness and
energy with which he met a singular disappointment on
the day his regiment left Columbus for the seat of war.
By some mistake or misunderstanding he had not
reached the depôt when the train started.   Coming up
within five minutes, he remarked to the superintendent
of the road " I was never behind time before in my life,
and I will not be now ; " and he chartered an engine,
was off in a few minutes, and overtook his regiment in
less than one hour.

Colonel Garfield's orders were, to open communication with Colonel Cranor, and form a junction with his
forces, although his command did not number half that
of the enemy.   The first indispensable thing to be done
was to find a trusty messenger, to bear despatches to
Colonel Cranor   He must be a man who would die
rather than betray his trust ; for Colonel Cranor was a
hundred miles away, and the messenger must go through
a region inhabited by disloyal people, and infested by
guerillas   He applied to Colonel Moore, of the Fourteenth Kentucky.

" Have you a man who will die rather than fail or
betray us ? "

" I think I have," the Colonel replied, after a little reflection, " John Jordan."

The man was called, a strong-looking fellow, tall and lean, with a squeaking voice, his speech the uncouth dialect of the mountains, where he was born and reared, subject to the hardest toil and privation. He knew much of nature, in whose lap he was dandled, but very little of books, except the " Course of Time " and the Bible Some officers would have thought him too simple for a spy, or expert messenger ; but Garfield read him in a minute—a rude, unlettered, trusty, Christian man.

Colonel Garfield wrote his despatch on tissue paper, rolled it into the form of a bullet, coated it with warm lead, and delivered it to Jordan. At the same time he provided him with a carbine, a brace of revolvers, and the fleetest horse in the regiment. Jordan started upon his perilous journey at night, after the moon was down He was to ride by night, and hide in the woods, or rest in loyal families, if they could be found, by day.

Before Jordan returned, another incident transpired, showing how great service Garfield's life on the canal was to him, in another direction. One day a loyal scout presented himself at his head-quarters, and, grasping Colonel Garfield's hand, exclaimed, in a jolly way :

" Jim ! "

Garfield looked at him with surprise, for a moment, but did not recognise him

" Who are you ? " he inquired.

" Yer old companion, Jim," answered the scout.

" *My* old companion ! " ejaculated Garfield.

" Yis, yer old companion ! Yer see, I was a scout in West Virginia, under Rosecrans ; and hearing of the Sandy Valley expedition, and that James A Garfield, of Ohio, had command of it, I thought as how that must be my old companion on the canal boat ; and so I mad

" Harry ! " exclaimed Garfield, shaking his hand heartily, as he recognised one of Captain Letcher's crew, whose name was Henry S. Brown, but known as " *Harry* " on the boat. The marks of a very dissipated life had obliterated the traces of his former self, so that it was not strange that Garfield did not recognise him. Brown was strongly attached to " Jim " on the canal, and now he desired, above all things, to serve him

" Colonel Garfield," at length Brown said, laying aside the familiar title by which he was known on the canal boat, and addressing him respectfully, as any loyal soldier would address his superior officer. " Colonel Garfield, I'm at yer service "

" Just the man I want for a scout," answered Garfield, heartily He had confidence in Brown for that business, and trusted him at once

On the following night, as Garfield lay in sound sleep, about midnight, Jordan came riding into camp from his dangerous trip. Alighting from his foaming steed, he rushed into his commander's quarters, and shook him until he awoke

" What ! back safe ? " exclaimed Garfield, as soon as he recognised Jordan. " Have you seen Colonel Cranor ? "

" Yes, colonel ; he can't be mor'n two days ahind o' me, nohow."

" God bless you, Jordan ! You have done us great service," said Garfield warmly

" I thank ye, Colonel," answered Jordan, his voice trembling ; " that's more pay'n I expected."

He had returned safely , but the Providence which so wonderfully guarded his way out seemed to leave him to find his own way back ; for, as he expressed it : " The Lord He cared more for the despatch nor He cared for me ; and it was nat'ral He shud ; 'cause my life only counts ꞏ ꞏ ꞏ ꞏ ꞏ ꞏ ꞏ ꞏ ꞏ ꞏ ꞏ Kent , l y."

The use of Jordan and Brown for scouts initiated Garfield into the condition of a successful " secret service." When he became chief of General Rosecrans,' staff he organized a " secret service," which Rosecrans called the " eyes of the army " ; and it was acknowledged to be the most complete and efficient scout system of the war.

We have seen that Garfield was a born leader among the companions of his youth, and that the magnetism of his personal presence inspired hearts around him with a kindred spirit. When he became a teacher, we have seen that he excelled other teachers in awakening the enthusiasm of his pupils, and leading them to pursue their studies, or a life-purpose, with singular devotion. It was equally so in the army. In the first victorious battle that he fought—that of Middle Creek—many incidents transpired to establish this fact.

We learned before that President Lincoln made Garfield brigadier-general for gallant services in this battle. The President was much depressed at the time of this victory, because of the repeated disasters to our arms in the " Department of the East." A distinguished army officer was present with him when he received the news of this victory, and Mr. Lincoln said to the officer .

" Why did Garfield, in two weeks, do what would have taken one of your regular officers two months to accomplish ? "

" Because he was not educated at West Point," replied the West Pointer, laughingly.

" No," answered Mr. Lincoln, " that was not the reason   It was because, when he was a boy, he had to work for his living."

After the battle of Middle Creek, Garfield's soldiers were exhausted, and short of rations   The roads were well-nigh impassable, because of the deep mud, and the Big Sandy was swollen to a torrent, rendering the deliv   ..f   ..r'ic. du.ñ. ³.   S. . .h'ng ·rr · i ·done.

Garfield proposed to go down the river to hurry up supplies, but the oldest boatman refused, saying, " Impossible, it can't be done ! "

Brown, the scout, had returned, and Garfield opened the subject to him

' What do you think of it, Brown ?   The boatmen say that it is sure death ; what do you say ?   You and I know something about boating."

The scout's reply was characteristic.   " It's which and t'other, Gineral Jim : starvin' or drownin'.   I'd rather drown nor starve   So, guv the word, and, dead or alive, I'll git down the river ! "

" All right, Harry, we'll go ! "   And they sprang into a small skiff, and committed their lives to the raging torrent   It was a fearful sail, but they reached the mouth of the Big Sandy in safety ; and here Garfield's experience on the canal boat served him well.   There he found a small, rickety steamer, named *Sandy Valley*, tied up at Catletsburg

" I am under the necessity of taking possession of your steamer to carry supplies to my troops," Colonel Garfield said to the captain, who was a Secessionist, and who, of course, would have preferred that his troops should starve rather than to feed them.

" This craft can't stem such a current, nohow ; it'll be the death of us," the captain replied   There was some reason for his saying this, for the water in the channel was sixty feet deep, so swollen that trees along the banks were submerged nearly to their tops.

In turning a bend in the river, the steamer swept round and grounded on a bar of quicksand.   The usual efforts were made to relieve her, but in vain.   And now that tact and sound common sense for which we have seen that Garfield was distinguished from boyhood, came to his rescue.

" Get a line to the opposite shore ! " commanded Garfield, particularly addressing the sulky captain

" A line to that shore ! " shouted the rebel captain, in reply. " It's death on any man that, 'tempts it."

" It can be done, and it *must* be done," cried Garfield ; and he leaped into the yawl, calling Brown to follow, and steered for the shore. The wild torrent swept them down the stream a short distance, but they rallied by almost superhuman strength, reached the shore, fastened the line, constructed a windlass, and, in a short time, the steamer was drawn from her bed in the mud, and was on her triumphant way up the stream From Saturday until nine o'clock Monday morning Garfield stood at the wheel, night and day , and when he reached Paintsville his troops were reduced almost to their last cracker. His experience with rough men at the " Black-salters," and on the canal, qualified him to deal with such a rebel as the captain of the *Sandy Valley*.

When the steamer drew up to the Union camp, Garfield's men were almost frantic with joy. They cheered and yelled, and seized their brave commander, and would have borne him upon their shoulders to head-quarters had he not resolutely protested against it

General Garfield's tact, sagacity, fidelity, spirit of self-sacrifice, and undaunted courage, so conspicious in his early life, are illustrated by his famous ride from General Rosecrans to General Thomas, when the army of the Cumberland was almost routed in the famous battle of Chickamauga It was necessary for General Thomas to know the disaster that had befallen Rosecrans' forces in order to meet the rebel General Longstreet victoriously Garfield proposed to undertake the fearful ride, and reached Thomas, through a hurricane of bullets. His noble horse was shot, and fell dead at Thomas's feet.

Garfield's terrible ride saved the army of the Cumberland from remediless disaster.

His life in Congress abounds in thrilling incidents of moral courage, loyalty, and defence of right. " Peace
h ·   ' ¡   .   "

President Lincoln vetoed a bill, in 1864, providing for the organization of civil governments in Arkansas and Louisiana, and appointed military governors. Many Republicans criticized him severely : among them Garfield His constituents disapproved of his course, and resolved not to renominate him.   The convention of his congressional district, the nineteenth of Ohio, met, and General Garfield was called upon for an explanation. When he went upon the platform the delegates expected to hear an apology from him ; but, instead, he boldly defended his course, and that of Wade and Davis, who criticized the President sharply in the *New York Tribune ;* and he gave the reasons for his action, adding :

" I have nothing whatever to retract, and I cannot change my honest conviction for the sake of a seat in Congress.   I have great respect for the opinions of my constituents, but greater regard for my own conscience. If I can serve you as an independent representative, acting upon my own judgment and convictions, I would be glad to do so ; but, if not, I do not want your nomination ;   I would prefer to be an independent private citizen."

It was the coolest, plainest, most fearless speech, probably, that was ever made before a nominating convention in Ohio.   Garfield withdrew from the hall as soon as he closed his speech.   No sooner had he withdrawn, than a delegate arose and said :

" Mr. President, the man who has the courage to face a convention like that deserves a nomination.   I move that General Garfield be nominated by acclamation."

The motion was carried so quickly, and by such a round of applause, that General Garfield heard it before he reached the hotel.

General Garfield prosecuted a European tour in the summer of 1868, for his health.

On the fourteenth day of April, 1865, President Lincoln was assassinated. The following morning New York city presented a scene of the most perilous excitement. Placards were pasted up in New York, Brooklyn, and Jersey City, calling upon loyal citizens to meet around Wall Street Exchange, at eleven o'clock. Thousands came, armed with revolvers and knives, ready to avenge the death of the martyred President. Fifty thousand men gathered there, their blood boiling with the fires of patriotism.

For an instant, vengeance and death upon every paper and every man opposed to Lincoln seemed to move the mighty crowd Possibly the scene of the French Revolution would have been reproduced in the streets of New York, had not a man of commanding figure, bearing a small flag in his hand, stepped forward and beckoned to the excited throng.

" Another telegram from Washington," cried hundreds of voices It was the silence of death that followed It seemed as if every listener held his breath to hear

Lifting his right arm towards heaven, in a clear, distinct, steady, ponderous, voice, that the multitude could hear, the speaker said :

" Fellow-citizens : Clouds and darkness are round about Him ! His pavilion is dark waters and thick clouds of the skies ! Justice and judgment are the habitation of His throne ! Mercy and truth shall go before His face ! Fellow-citizens : God reigns, and the Government at Washington still lives ! "

The speaker was GENERAL GARFIELD.

Printed in the USA
CPSIA information can be obtained
at www.ICGtesting.com
LVHW022116290923
759527LV00005B/466